They Called Me Crazy

A FORMER INMATE'S JOURNEY TO SPIRITUAL FREEDOM

Gheorghe Ignat

TRILOGY CHRISTIAN PUBLISHERS

TUSTIN, CA

Trilogy Christian Publishers
A Wholly Owned Subsidiary of Trinity Broadcasting Network
2442 Michelle Drive
Tustin, CA 92780

They Called Me Crazy

Manufactured in the United States of America

10 9 8 7 6 5 4 3 2 1

Library of Congress Cataloging-in-Publication Data is available.

ISBN: 978-1-68556-196-3

E-ISBN: 978-1-68556-197-0

Endorsements

"When I met Gheorghe in HMP Huntercombe, I was very struck by his great love for Jesus and passion for sharing the Gospel with others. I remember him addressing the men in chapel with eloquence, authority, and an earnest desire that not one of them would miss the message of salvation. With his bright face and powerful frame, he was known as 'Big George,' but his strength and size were matched by a gentle, caring nature and serious desire to understand spiritual things.

A natural leader, Gheorghe put his faith into action by employing ex-prisoners even while he, himself, was still inside, something he had been led by God to do. Since he has been released and reunited with the family he loves so much, he has continued with bold, creative initiatives to minister to those in need, despite all the obstacles and challenges that have come his way. Truly he is a transformed man.

George shared his feelings and experiences with great emotional honesty then, as he does here. I recommend his story to you."

- Susan Cuthbert Prisons pastor for St. Aldates Church, Oxford, and Anglican Chaplain (this is the person the author calls S in the chapter "God Sends Me an Angel")

"The life of Gheorghe Ignat demonstrates that without Christ you can be imprisoned even when free and with Christ you can have freedom even when Imprisoned. This is a journey of suffering, surrender, perseverance and faith that will inspire and instruct you in living a life for God. It's the redemptive story of God using the disqualified to accomplish the impossible for his people!"

- Gregg Dedrick, Co-Founder of Iron Bell Ministries and Former President of KFC

"When Gheorghe gave me his book, "They Called Me Crazy," I couldn't put it down. I, literally, could not stop reading, fascinated by this unusual and unexpected story that is relentlessly human and surprisingly, dare I say, non-human all at once. Told with winsome vulnerability, this book takes us into the heart of a man living in a world most of us will never experience, revealing a deeper world that all of us do, indeed, experience, whether or not we realize it. It also happens to be told by one of the strongest, kindest, godliest, and most lovable human beings I have ever been privileged enough to call "friend."

- Leticia Ramirez Hashem Co-Founder of Infused Impact, Inc.

"

A transformed person can be a tremendous influence on those who shape the ideas and cultures of the next generation. Gheorghe Ignat's life is proof that the Gospel has the power to transform individuals, families, communities and nations. This book is an inspiration for believers to achieve great things through God's transforming power that will outlast their lives and make a lasting impact for His glory."

- Dr. Benjamin Levi MOSES, Executive Director Global Leadership Geneva-Bern, Switzerland.

"They Called Me Crazy" is written by one of the strongest men on the planet. In humility, Gheorghe opens his heart with us and reveals that supernatural strength is not found in the center of a ring, but in the center of God's will for our lives. God's grace shines brightly through his story and fills the reader with great hope for all that is possible through the goodness of God. Are you feeling pinned down? Gheorghe shares his story to help you overcome the pressures of this world and find victory in Jesus."

- Rev. Dr. Brian Mowrey, lead pastor of Walnut Hill Community Church and author of *On The Other Side Of Yes*

"Radically Saved" was a popular contemporary Christian song in the 1980's that was one of my favorites. This book, *They Call Me Crazy*, written by Gheorghe Ignat brings those lyrics powerfully back to mind. "The world thinks I'm crazy... I am just radically saved!" Is a line from the song. I was captivated and inspired as Gheorghe masterfully and transparently conveyed his story of the redemptive power of Jesus Christ in his life.

His story of living in darkness to being transfigured into a new life truly exemplifies 2 Corinthians 5:17; "Therefore, if anyone is in Christ, he is a new creation; old things have passed away; behold, all things have become new." His book is an example of not only encountering the miraculous saving power of Christ, but also communicates a passionate fire of conviction to share it with others, love the unlovable, honor those in authority, and forgive as Jesus did. From those who have yet to meet Jesus, to the new believer, and to those seasoned Saints, this book will ignite a greater blaze to radically live for Jesus and the advancement of His Kingdom.

- Don Sturiano, Sr. Lead Pastor of Kingdom Life Christian Church, Bradenton, Florida and author of *Shattering the Cloud of a Powerless Gospel*

"When I first met Gheorghe in Huntercombe prison, I thought I was dealing with a religious fanatic or a crook, a guy who was trying to use religion for certain purposes. I treated him like that at first, then I started studying him. Things went way different then I first, thought. It was almost unbelievable to me what I was going to witness there, things that I had never seen before.

I have seen hate at the highest, and I have seen Gheorghe fighting for his life, Man... this story may seem out of this world, in fact I believe it is. But what you are going to read, really happened, I was there."

\- This statement comes from M, the Huntercombe prison mate of Gheorghe written of in the book.

Dedication

To God, who is the most trustworthy friend I ever had, who put together all the pieces for this book to become reality. To my sweet wife, Adriana, who is not only the most beautiful woman on earth but a woman with the most beautiful heart in the world.

To my Mom and Dad, my sister, and my little brother, thank you for all the unconditional love you showed me in all these years.

To all people who made this book possible, good or bad: you are quite a few, and you have done more than I have ever expected. Thank you.

They Called Me Crazy

A Former Inmate's Journey to Spiritual Freedom

Gheorghe Ignat

Contents

Foreword

What you are going to read is the extraordinary life story of a man dear to my soul, a man I have known for a lifetime. I was with this man for better or for worse. I sat next to him when it was the hardest; I was there, and I was happy with him when it was best.

I have witnessed the extraordinary transformation that God has made in his life, such a dramatic, such a visible change, with such a powerful impact, that only God can do it.

You will find below the story of a broken, persecuted, incomprehensible man, but at the same time the story of a victor, the story of a champion who surrendered his life in the hands of God, who let himself be shaped and used by the Divinity, and the results are clear. His life is so different, and I don't know how I could describe it in words.

The events set out in this book might make you wonder in some places if such a thing could have happened; I want to assure you that everything written in this book is true!

I invite you to open your heart to Gheorghe's life story and to what God wants to tell you through what he has written.

—Adriana Ignat

Preface

I struggled mightily in deciding whether or not I should write this book. One part of me did not want to write down personal struggles and weaknesses. They do not cast me in a good light, as a natural man would wish to be cast.

Yet, the other part of me wanted, at whatever price, to write about my problems, my struggles, and my weaknesses in order to offer some help to those who are where I was. I recognize that the first part is simply my pride, the part of me that is concerned with my reputation, while the second is the better side, the part that wishes to help another regardless of what the sacrifice may be.

Please note that in order to protect the identity of some persons, some names—of both people and places—have been changed. Otherwise, I have attempted to describe, as accurately as possible, my experiences and struggles both as a prisoner in Great Britain and as an ex-convict in Romania after my liberation. I do, however, understand that all that is written is *my point of view* and is therefore likely to be biased.

I recognize that I did wrong to society, but I am equally well aware that I am a changed man. Nothing is left of the man I once was; I was changed from the root. We live in a world where any change for the better is viewed with skepticism, and I have therefore had some negative reactions from those whose trust I tried to win.

You will read in this book about the struggles that I went through because of a society unwilling to offer a second chance to those who broke its laws, whether or not those men have changed. The attempt to rehabilitate, when a man is already battling with his old habits and his previous mentality, is made twice as difficult when society refuses to allow him another chance; the things written in this book come from the heart of a man who knows. In my desperate struggle to become a better person, I encountered roadblocks, obstacles, and traps, often placed by those from whom I was expecting support.

As a man who was a law-breaker, I can say that I would never want to live in a world where men who are as I was are allowed to walk the streets unchecked. In fact, I do not believe that anyone would want to live in world devoid of authorities that protect people from evil. The question is whether these people are there to protect us all the time or if some of them are abusing their power.

This book is about a part of my traumatizing experiences. Some may say that I deserved them, while others will think it unjust. Regardless of the reader's response, I have chosen to always oppose abuse, whether that comes from someone in authority or from another source. It does not matter what a man's name is, how much money he has, what title he possesses, or how dangerous he is. Every person is equal before the law and before God. Every man has the right to dignity, to liberty, and to a second chance.

I have tried to find a reason for abuse. I have attempted to understand what motivates men to abuse their power, but I have failed to find a reasonable explanation. Abuse can never be justified. There is but a small step from the position of the abuser to the position of the victim and vice versa. I kidnapped people; I emptied thousands of bank accounts; I inspired fear in the hearts of many good people. I was the abuser.

I then came to the place where I shook with fear—for no reason—for nights on end on the cold floor of a prison. I came to the place where I was mocked and subjected to crude jokes by the prison guards, police, and others. In a very short time, the tables were turned, and the abuser became the victim. Therefore, abusers beware! Things can change rapidly!

Now, as I write these lines, I am fortunate to be with my family again. I am blessed with a wonderful, supportive wife, and we are happily raising our four boys. I hope with all my heart that this book can be an encouragement both to those who have broken the law as well as to those that enforce the law. I would like to encourage those that wronged society by saying that a second chance exists, despite the obstacles. I would like to encourage those that enforce the law to accord that second chance and to never abuse their power. If we do so, we will all live in a better world.

—Gheorghe Ignat, 2021

Introduction

Becoming a man in the Romania of the 1990s was not always easy. I remember a bit, just a few years, of communism, and I spent my adolescent years in Romania after the fall of the Iron Curtain. I will tell you a bit of how this transition from communism to capitalism was viewed by a child, an adolescent, and a young man.

I was born and raised in Suceava, at the foot of the Carpathians, just a few kilometers from the border of the USSR. My mother, a cook, and my father, a trucker, raised me and my siblings, a younger sister and brother.

My parents were unusually good folks—hard-working, honest, and of modest means. They educated me well, sacrificing what they could to ensure we kids had a good start, for which I am profoundly grateful.

My father was gone nearly every week from Monday to Friday, hauling materials for the electrical company for which he worked. Under communism, it was a very good job, giving my father access to goods that were out of reach for the majority of the populace in our region. We could have such exotic treats as oranges and Pepsi at Christmas time, which Dad—thanks to his job—could procure on the black market.

My mother worked as a cook in the cafeteria of a big high school in Suceava. Though the rations that the government permitted its citizens to buy were very small, we had no lack since we could go visit Mom at work and get at least one square meal a day. While we did have some difficult times, in general, we never lacked for food.

My earlier years were spent in a beautiful village called Todirești, my father's birthplace. I was cared for during the day by a kind, elderly lady named Maria who was tremendously patient with me, a muscular kid who loved to wander the hills and forests surrounding the village. I was an active youngster, though often a bit mischievous.

When I was seven years old, my parents moved us to the city so I could go to school. As I was a country boy, it was difficult to adjust to city life, but I managed with time to adapt.

At twelve years old, I went to a gym where they taught Greco-Roman wrestling. I was a big kid for my age, standing at one point eight meters (five feet eleven inches) and weighing 100 kilograms (220 lbs). I was often bullied by the older kids and began practicing Greco-Roman wrestling in order to defend myself, having no older siblings to do it for me.

I caught the attention of a trainer by the name of Gherasim Valerică, who saw potential in me. After meeting me for the first time and taking my measurements, he told me, "Keep fighting, and I'll turn you into a champion." Roughly a year and eight months after he uttered those words, I won my first Romanian national title in Greco-Roman wrestling.

I went on to win a total of ten national titles and a number of international titles and medals. At fourteen, I was selected to join the national team, and at only sixteen, I was asked to join the Romanian Olympic team. I considered it an honor to be a part of the team and represent my country on the international stage.

At eighteen, I was a well-known wrestler in my native Romania. I held the Greco-Roman heavyweight title for a number of years and dreamed, like many athletes, of winning an Olympic medal. I had all the necessary ingredients to reach that goal, but one bad decision derailed my career and destroyed my dreams.

I must say that a career in sports was not the most lucrative employment in Romania at the time. As a professional athlete at the top of his game, I was paid only fifty dollars a month. Of course, to remain at the top, an athlete had to eat well, and social pressure drove him to dress well, so fifty dollars did not go very far.

Frustrated, I saw that I and my fellow athletes who worked hard and sacrificed much made very little money, while there were other people, some of whom I began to make acquaintances with, that made fabulous sums. They drove the best cars, lived in the largest houses, were members of high society, and had children that were simply rolling in money. "Will I ever get to the point where I can afford a nice car and a big house?" I wondered. It was a legitimate question for a young athlete that had been in professional sports for several years but saw no reasonable chance of a better life ahead. I looked at the athletes that were at the end of their careers; while they had been the best of the best, making top money in the sports world, most of them were struggling to just survive, still fighting the poverty that had dogged them all their lives. It was a disheartening picture.

I remember seeing a man that had been one of the best athletes of the 1980s working at a car wash to make enough money to support his family. While there is nothing necessarily wrong with that, a worker at a car wash in the 1990s did not have the working conditions of those that do the same job today. This man who had won at least one European championship was dirty from head to foot with one shoe badly torn and soaked to the skin while the temperature was barely above freezing. It was the picture of a retired athlete, and it was many such a man who ended his life alone and penniless in the pitiless years after communism fell. Looking at that man, knowing that that was all my country could promise men like me, my heart filled with an intense feeling of frustration. Even while my brain screamed a vehement denial, a thought flashed through my mind: "I will have the same fate." I promised myself that I would never end up like that, that I would make a better life for myself and my family, even if it meant doing the impossible.

Romania after 1990 taught me that the most important thing was to survive. Professional athletes that practiced contact sports such as wrestling, boxing, and judo often had two choices when it came to a career other than sports. One was to become a police officer, while the other was to get into the dark world of organized crime. The underworld was always looking to recruit contact sports veterans; such men had been trained from little up to push an advantage, to stand their ground and never give up, making them very loyal.

The first ones to offer me a "job" were men of great wealth with a standard of living of which I could only dream. I did not hesitate to accept the proposal of some prosperous Bucharest businessmen (or so I thought) to work for them. I was told I would make good money and live well, all while being able to continue my athletic career. It seemed like a golden opportunity, so I left for Bucharest, turning a deaf ear to the protests of my parents and my trainer.

My decision was to take me further from my dreams; though it did bring money, it doomed my athletic future. These "businessmen" were, in fact, some of the leaders of organized crime rings in post-communist Bucharest, but my inexperience and lack of money led me to join them. Like many other decisions that I made over the years, it was a foolish, foolish move, and I learned the hard way that we cannot go back and undo foolish decisions. We can only be wiser moving forward.

I began living a double life: on the one hand, I was a well-known sports young man known to many people, while on the other hand, I was a developing gangster, a criminal, known only to myself and a select few. I continued my sports activities, trying hard to stay at the top of my game, but such things are difficult while running around with the wrong crowd.

My life began to change. I dressed in expensive clothing and drove a car that only a short time before I could not have dreamed of owning. I made fabulous sums of money. I was still a sports personality that dreamed of winning medals in the Olympics, but my choices had already taken me down the wrong road.

I continued my path to "success," defined in this case as a lot of fast money, but the success I had dreamed of growing up was an ever more distant possibility. The problem with money is not only "easy come, easy go," but easy money also brings a lot of problems with it.

Besides the sports I already practiced, I began to get into MMA (mixed martial arts), at which I did very well, winning six fights without a single loss. When I began hoping to fight in UFC, the pinnacle of MMA, I tried to get out of my life of crime and focus again on sports, but it was too late. My poor decisions were going to kill my dreams again.

I had everything I needed for a successful career in sports, whether Greco-Roman wrestling or MMA, except for one thing: patience. The life of a gangster offered me moments of satisfaction here and now, but those times were short and fleeting, far too much so to warrant the price I had to pay for them, even from an earthly point of view. That "happiness," so easily won, ended up costing me my dreams, my career, my liberty, and nearly my life.

I did make a few wise choices as well; the best, without question, was to accept Jesus Christ as my Lord and Saviour. I had come to an end of myself; my decisions had made a complete wreck of my life, and Jesus was the only one that was willing to come to my aid. Fascinated by His power and love, I began a new life with Him and, with Him, formed new dreams about which you will read in this book.

Who is the author of this book? He is a man who made mistakes that almost destroyed his life, a man who started all over again, a man whose life has been completely rehabilitated, a man whose family has been rebuilt, and a man who now is fighting to help others who are in the same darkness as he once was. This man started up the path of true success only through the unconditional support that Jesus Christ is ready to give to all those that completely trust Him.

This is the true story of what came next.

Part 1

Botosani Penitentiary and Suceava Prison, Romania

Long-Awaited Liberty

As the muggy month of August 2017 was dragging toward its end, I finally heard it one day from the end of the corridor of section five of the Botosani Penitentiary: "Ignat, you're free!"

It was the guard on duty who had received the call instructing me to prepare to be released. The long-anticipated moment had finally arrived, and my heart shouted a prayer: "Lord, thank You! Thank You that, though I was sentenced to four years in prison, You worked it out for me to be released after only two and a half years behind bars." I had become a Christian a few years before ending up in prison for credit card fraud I had committed long before turning to God.

Before I left, I gathered with my brothers in Christ—eight guys, all that were left of the twenty-four that had accepted Jesus Christ as their Lord and Savior since I had been incarcerated—in the room known as the "Sports Club." For the last two and a half years, this hall had served as the meeting place of the "church behind bars." Together with my comrades, I prayed and thanked the Lord for the time that we had spent together in the Botosani prison and for each detainee that had received

Jesus Christ as his personal Lord and Savior in the time that I had been imprisoned there. We also thanked the Lord for each prisoner that, through our work, had heard the good news of the gift of God—salvation through His Son. After our meeting, we hugged each other and promised that we would pray for each other.

There were six of us inmates that were waiting for the doors to be opened, releasing us into the world and freedom. Our friends and colleagues from the prison gathered to wish us well. Their own desire for liberty could be clearly seen on their faces; how they wished it was their turn to be set free! How many times I had been there, watching with mad longing as my former cellmates had gone to their freedom! But each time, I had said to myself, "Drop it, man. Your day is coming..."

Now, it being my turn to walk out of the prison a free man, I looked into the eyes of those being left behind and said, "Buck up, guys! The day is coming when you all are going home!"

At those words, several cheers went up, then the door swung open, and we entered the prison courtyard. From there, we were led to an office building where they were to take our fingerprints and return our IDs and the money in our accounts. On the way to that building, we met the guard named R. He had never liked me, largely because he didn't like evangelical Christians, but now he came up to me, grasped my hand, and said, "You were a model prisoner! I want to thank you that you have never caused any trouble in all these years!"

"You don't have to thank me," I replied, "but the Lor..."

"I know, I know, 'the Lord.' Hmmm, maybe He *can* change people? I don't know exactly what to say, but—I wish you well and stay out of trouble."

"Thank you. All the best."

My feelings were indescribable. My thoughts floated to my little boy, Philip: when I left, he was so small; now he was three years old. I thought of the happiness I would bring to my wife, Adriana, and our other two boys, David and Levi. I thought of my parents and my siblings. Still, in the middle of all the joy, I did have, somehow, a twinge of regret. I had had some wonderful times with the Lord in that prison; there were times of great happiness shared with others—people I had never met before my incarceration. Now I was leaving those guys that, in my time here, had become my close friends, my brothers in Christ. Just before they opened the gate that led out of the penitentiary and to freedom, three men entered the room where we were, one of them carrying some documents in his hand. They all looked at me for a moment, then called me aside.

"Mister Ignat, we regret to inform you that we have some unpleasant news for you. We want you to guarantee us that you will react reasonably and that you will not cause any trouble."

"I promise you there will be no problems. What are you talking about?"

"We regret to inform you that we are here to rearrest you."

I couldn't believe my ears. "*What* are you doing? You are...?"

"We are rearresting you. We have a European Union arrest warrant under your name from the authorities in Great Britain through Interpol."

I smiled at them, even though all my dreams were crumbling before my eyes. I knew what it was all about; they had an arrest warrant for a crime I had committed in London over ten years before while I was living there. My thoughts raced to a promise I had made to God, also ten years ago; it was a promise that I had not kept. That broken promise was closely connected to what was now transpiring.

One of the guards seemed to know me. "George, please be calm. We don't want any problems; we are just doing our job."

"Don't worry; I'm as calm as I can make myself right now, but let's get out of here."

They could see the frustration that was threatening to explode inside of me.

The Lord's Response

I was handcuffed and placed into a police van. I was carsick for much of the ensuing trip; I had not been on the road much of late. Besides, it was unbearably warm in the van and extremely stuffy—not a breath of moving air could be felt. After about an hour, I arrived in custody in my native town, Suceava.

I was greeted by the prison guards. Some of their faces looked vaguely familiar since this was not my first time at the Suceava prison. Some of the guards were quite young, their uncertainty indicating their nervousness and inexperience. One of those who recognized me cheerfully welcomed me to my cell: "Welcome back, Mister Ignat!"

He closed the door behind me, grinning sarcastically. They all knew that I had been released and rearrested the same day.

It had been a hard day; when I was alone in my cell, I immediately fell to my knees. To start a prison sentence all over from the beginning was too much. I knew I couldn't do it on my own strength, so I poured out my heart to God. I prayed, knowing that He was no stranger to my situation; He knew every detail. Even so, worry gnawed on me over what lay ahead in England and how I should respond to these latest charges, charges much more serious than those that had incarcerated me in Romania. I was accused of breaking and entering, kidnapping, blackmail, and assault (grievous bodily harm). I had no answers for the questions that plagued me, so I turned to the only source of answers I had—the Lord.

So I asked God what I should do, and His answer came quickly; it was short and to the point. "George, if you tell the truth, I will be with you, and you will see Me working in a powerful way."

His words gave me hope, but they also gave me a responsibility. I took the good advice that the Lord had given and purposed in my heart and mind to do exactly as He had said.

In my cell, I got to know Dănuț, a young shepherd. He was here because one evening, when he was drunk, he covered his face with a mask and robbed a priest. He had taken about $170, none of which he had been able to spend before his arrest. Now, because of one thoughtless moment, he would have to spend the next years of his life in prison. I met a number of people who lost a good part of their lives because of many foolish and hasty decisions. I was one of them. I was already serving my third year in prison and was now facing new charges, more trials, and more years in prison.

One night while I was in my cell, one of the guards suddenly opened the door. He was one of the service guards.

"Mr. Ignat, you can come to the library for a few minutes; I want to talk to you."

I didn't know what this was about. It was quite late, but I got out of bed, put on my shoes, and went with him.

Once in the library, this guard offered me a chair, and I sat down at the table there. I was quite surprised, and I think it could be seen on my face.

"Mr. Ignat, I bothered you because I wanted to ask you something. Are you kind enough to give me your autograph?"

"Okay, so that's what this is about. Sure, guard, do you have a pen and a sheet of paper?"

"Of course, I have a pen, but instead of a sheet of paper, I allowed myself to print some of your photos on Facebook. I have them with me, and I would like you to write on these photos. Is it okay?"

"Sure, let's get started."

As I was there in that cellar, I had a strange feeling, signing autographs on photos of me during sports competitions, with a guard standing next to me; it was the first time I had experienced this. After signing several of those photos, the guard asked me.

"And these two for my boss, please."

I smiled. "Sure, no problem."

"Mr. Ignat, no matter what some or others say, you remain one of my favorite athletes. Can I ask you if you will fight again after you are released from prison?"

I looked at him. He looked like a good man, so I smiled and told him, "I will fight again but never in a cage or in the ring. Now I have other battles to win, spiritual fights; that is now the cage and the ring where I fight."

He smiled, held out his hand, and greeted me, although he didn't seem to understand what I meant by the spiritual fights, and, unfortunately, I didn't have much time to explain. He turned the key in the cell door, and I took off my slippers and climbed into bed. Danut was already asleep, so I prayed and fell asleep.

At home, my wife, Adriana, was waiting for me; she was and is a tremendous help and a steadfast partner, way beyond what I can express. My three boys were also waiting for me: David, who was ten years old; Levi, who was six; and Philip, who was now nearly four. My parents were also looking forward to my return, two extraordinary people who had raised me well and given me a good, sound education but had suffered a lot on account of the stupid things I had done in my youth.

In Suceava, after my arrest, my family visited me twice. They were able to bring me fries and fried eggs, food that I had not tasted since before my incarceration. I also had the chance to eat my favorite cheese and raisin cake—something else I had not eaten in years—which my mother made especially for me. I thanked the Lord for time I could spend in Suceava.

I had also been visited by my brother in Christ and my business partner, Puiu. One year before being sent to prison, I opened up a small packaging production line with him. He was one of the few people to stay next to me and my family in the years I spent in prison.

To London After Ten Years

On a Friday morning, nine days after I had been rearrested, I was taken by special transport under police escort to Otopeni airport in Bucharest. Once there, I was taken to the basement level of the airport and escorted into one of two large cells, which were supervised by several Romanian guards. The other cell was occupied by another Romanian, awaiting transport to Poland for trial. After a half-hour of confinement, four British Interpol officers arrived to escort me to Great Britain. After telling me who they represented and what they were about to do, the one that seemed to be the leader stepped to my side, took my arm, and introduced himself.

"I am Peter."

"I am George," I responded.

"Okay, George," he warned, "you have two options: you have an easy option, in which you make no trouble. The other option..."

"I choose the option that will make everyone happy. You will have no problems with me, I can promise it. As a matter a fact, I am looking forward to resolving my problems in England."

Upon being assured that the giant ex-prize-fighter whom they were to escort was not inclined to be cantankerous, they breathed a sigh of relief, as if a great deal of weight had been removed from their shoulders.

"Perfect! Then let's get these documents signed."

In less than an hour, the four officers escorted me to the airplane. We walked down long corridors that felt like tunnels until, arriving at the end, I was thrust into a patrol vehicle that took me to my destination. We were to arrive at the aircraft before the other passengers, boarding by the back door. I took my seat on the left side of the plane in the very last row. The two seats in front of me were vacant, while the seat to the right, between me and the corridor, was occupied by one of the officers, the other three seating themselves in strategic places in the immediate vicinity.

The flight was a nightmare; there was major turbulence. It was not pleasant at all, and I had always disliked air travel. However, the present situation presented an opportunity to speak with the officer beside me. I told him some of my background and how the Lord had changed my life, giving me meaning and a purpose. The flight being somewhat bumpy at times, I told him that our life is like a vapor or gust a wind that is there one second and gone the next, and that each person needs Jesus Christ in order to be saved. The officer, though seeming to be a fine man, did not share my views and spoke freely of what he believed. I thought we had a constructive conversation. At one point, he winked at the book he was reading and suggested I write one about my life.

"I will! I really want to! The Lord has worked powerfully in my life, and I think it could be an encouragement to many others."

At any rate, I had had the idea of writing an autobiography, expressing the wonderful way in which God had transformed my life, but at that moment, I had not the foggiest notion of what I still had to go through and what I would actually end up writing. But I had learned that when we trust Jesus Christ, He leads every step of the way and works in every situation with our eternal well-being in view.

Arriving in London Heathrow on the 9th of September, 2017, I was immediately delivered to another special escort. The officers took me to the airport police station, where I was searched, my charges were read, and my fingerprints and photograph were taken. After that, they put all my belongings in a transparent plastic bag and prepared to send me to my cell empty-handed. Before I left the room, I turned toward the officer and respectfully asked him for my Bible, telling him that, for me, it was one of my most essential belongings. He began by repeating my rights, saying that they did not include having my Bible in my cell. At that moment, a higher-ranking officer, hearing our discussion, approached and, dropping a hand on his colleague's shoulder, assured me that it was quite okay to have my Bible with me in my cell. I do not know everyone's feelings about this book, but I believe the Bible is the living Word of God, without which it would have been difficult to pass victorious through so many difficulties. Many times this book took the place of my family, my friends, and even my lawyer. God had spoken to me through the Bible too often to leave it behind.

I was immensely thankful that that officer understood how important it was to me and allowed me to keep it with me.

I also had in my Bible several pictures from home of my children and of Adriana, my wife. I looked at those pictures until late into the night, after which I read my Bible and prayed. I was sure that, despite the serious charges I was facing, I would soon be returning home to my loved ones.

The following morning I was taken to the Magistrate's Court before a judge. My charges were read once again, and I was informed that, in light of the serious charges I was facing, I was to be tried in the Crown Court.

After a tiring day, I was pushed into a vehicle and taken to the Wandsworth maximum security facility. On the way to the prison, we passed through the center of London, and through the steamed-up windows, I recognized, with a sting, many locales and streets that I knew well since I had spent a number of happy years living in that city. I had missed London. Now, after ten years, I was back, not on a visit, but on trial for felonies that I had committed while London was my home.

Part 2

Wandsworth Prison, United Kingdom

Wandsworth Prison

Arriving at the famous Wandsworth Prison, I was searched again, and everything I had brought with me from Romania was taken. A young Pole named Karim, with an Algerian father and a Polish mother, and who had grown up and studied in Poland, had ridden with me in the prisoner transport vehicle, or "meat wagon," from the Magistrate's Court. On the way, we had become friends, so when I was assigned my cell, I asked if they could put the two of us together, which they did. Around 10 p.m., they took us to section E, where all newly incarcerated prisoners were kept, gave us some food, and locked us in our cell. I no longer remember my cell number, but I know it was two floors above the ground level.

I was so tired that, once we were in our cell, I exchanged only a few words with Karim before I fell asleep. Around 2:00 a.m., I heard some loud clattering and some thumps and sprang from the bed as if touched with a branding iron. I had no idea what was happening. Then I heard more noise and yelling getting louder and louder. After a few minutes had allowed me to wake up completely, I understood what was taking place.

Several prisoners in the cell next to ours had started beating the thick, metal door of the cell with their steel chairs, making a vociferous racket. In addition, when someone did such a thing, others in surrounding cells usually joined in, yelling and beating the walls and doors with anything available. All this madness this created gave me the impression we were in a psych ward.

The hullabaloo lasted for about two hours, so I didn't fall asleep again until after 4:00 a.m. I found it difficult to understand what was happening. I had come from a Romanian prison, where, it is said, prisoners are more ill-behaved, but in the nearly three years that I had been incarcerated there, I had never seen anything like this.

It could be said that in Romania, prisoners show a sort of respect for each other. For example, if one of us wished to sleep in the afternoon, all the other detainees made sure that he could by speaking in whispers. This was not done in fear but out of mutual respect. I realized that such respect was non-existent in British prisons, and I would have to learn how to deal with the environment. I knew that lack of good sleep would affect me and that the following day I would be good for nothing. Still, I expected that what had happened was out of the ordinary and that, in general, nights would be quiet, allowing me to sleep.

The next day they opened up our cell since each day we had one hour to get out of rooms, call our families, and take a shower. I left the cell and hurried toward the showers, but I did not get there. Suddenly a deafening alarm went off, and an army of guards rushed in to put us back in our cells.

When I saw what was happening, I asked one of the guards, "Why are you locking us in our cells again? We had barely been left out, and I didn't have time for a shower. I didn't even get to call home."

He replied that it was not his fault and explained, "One of your colleagues, another prisoner, punched a guard in the face. When something like that happens, all inmates must immediately be returned to their cells. It's a matter of procedure."

"Well," I inquired, "when will I be able to shower?"

"After twenty-four hours!" he replied. "But of course, this is only true if all is well. If not, it'll be forty-eight hours."

Now I began to understand how things worked around here.

Back in our tiny room, things were as close to normal as could be expected. I opened my Bible, a bilingual Romanian-English edition, and began to read in English so Karim could understand. He, a Catholic, was glad to listen to the Bible being read. He was very upset that he had been arrested just as he was returning from vacation with his wife and one-year-old daughter. Though he was now living in England, he had been sentenced by the Polish courts to nine years in prison. Poland had then contacted the British authorities, by whom he had now been arrested for extradition to his homeland, where he was to serve his sentence.

It made him very happy whenever I told him that God would take care of his wife and daughter. He would often say, "I can take care of myself, but what about them?"

He was always seeking assurance that, if he prayed for them, God would hear him and look after his wife and daughter in ways that surpassed his expectations. These words always gave him the courage to keep going. We began praying and reading the Bible together every day, one chapter in the morning and one in the evening.

I stayed in Section E for about two weeks. The conditions left much to be desired. In our small cell, there were two bunk beds, a small table, a sink, and a toilet that was only thirty centimeters from the head of the bed. The toilet gave us considerable trouble because there was nothing around it that gave us a shred of privacy. When I first arrived, I did not use the toilet for nearly three days. I could not bring myself to sit on the toilet with someone else only a few centimeters away. It felt impossible. I tried all kinds of ways of sitting, but nothing worked. Finally, I asked Karim to sit facing the door whenever I needed to go because I just found it so dreadfully awkward.

The nights continued being just as noisy as the first. Beatings were the order of the day, so noise and commotion were the norm.

"The newly-arrested are brought to this wing, Mr. Ignat," said a guard when I asked him to explain what was going on. "It is a bit difficult for them to adjust, and that is why they react that way. I think it will be better in the future."

Several days later, I met an inmate from Lithuania, a good guy that worked in Section E, helping prisoners to adjust to life behind bars. In conversation with him, I discovered that the penitentiary had a gym, but the new inmates, those from Section E, were not permitted to use it. He promised me that he would help me get moved to section B as soon as possible. From that section, access to the gym was much more easily obtained.

A few days after my conversation with the Lithuanian, a guard called my name. "Pack your bags! You are moving to B wing."

How happy that made me! I knew that it was due to my Lithuanian friend's action. I thanked God and moved to B wing along with Karim. The second morning I was surprised to be called to go to the gym.

The Big Fight

The first day in the gym, I worked out very little, spending my time getting to know others and doing just a few exercises for each group of muscles. I knew that if I were too aggressive, I would be terribly sore, so I took it easy. The guard at the gym promised to take me out the next day, but he failed to keep his word. I subsequently found out that I was allowed to go to the gym only three times a week.

At the beginning of the following week, I went to the gym for the second time. I went in and began my workout regimen. Everything was normal for the first thirty minutes until a white prisoner got into a heated argument with a black prisoner. In that moment, the gymnasium of the Wandsworth prison became a war scene, with roughly twenty white guys trying to beat up on thirty black guys.

Seeing what was happening, I quickly looked around, trying to locate a piece of equipment behind which I could take shelter and stay out of the fight. Just then, a white guy, a short man, threw a dumbbell, hitting a massive black man on the head. The man that was hit collapsed like a ton of rocks and lay on the floor, motionless. This told me that this fight was serious, and I would be wise to get out of there as quickly as possible. As

I was putting my plan into action, I saw something that made me change my mind and rush back toward the fight.

The chief guard on duty was a small woman and she, rather than taking shelter as her colleagues had done, rushed between the two sides, trying to stop the fight. She yelled at one side and then the other, but with no visible effect. Her behavior, the courageous response of a petite woman, was a lesson in bravery to everyone present.

Seeing her in the middle of the fight, I thought to myself that this lady is not mentally sound, and she doesn't realize what might happen to her. Therefore, without really weighing the possible consequences, I pressed forward toward the fight. Getting to her, I grabbed her by the shoulders with both hands, lifted her off the ground, and carried her out. It seemed to me that she was in great danger, right in the middle of the ruffians with the air full of flying objects; I felt she ran a high risk of waking up with a dumbbell or weight plate in her head.

After I set the guard down a few meters from the battle, I turned back toward the fight, my focus on the giant black man that was still immobile on the floor. I grabbed his legs and began to pull him away from the melee. At that moment, several whistles were heard, and a large group of guards stormed the room, stopping the festivities and herding us back to our cells.

Arriving at my cell, I sat on the bed and began recounting to Karim what had transpired. While I was speaking, he interrupted me.

"My dear friend, let me tell you something: you have three children and a beautiful wife at home, waiting for you to come safely back to them. What you did today was courageous but also stupid, putting yourself in harm's way like that. That group of black and white prisoners is fighting for supremacy; they deal in drugs, phones, and alcohol. They do business with each other, and when things do not go according to plan, they settle their disputes with fights, as you observed. You would be wise to stay out of their altercations in the future. You must arrive at home alive and uninjured, so, from my point of view, you would be wise to mind strictly your own business, pay no attention to anyone else, and look after yourself. It wouldn't hurt to talk to the leaders of the two gangs to make sure you didn't put a bull's-eye on your own back and ensure that they have nothing against you."

Karim's words made me start thinking, and I began asking myself a hundred questions.

Perhaps Karim is right! Why did I get involved? Why did I risk taking one to the head? Why don't I mind my own business? But after all, there was a man's well-being, perhaps even his life, at stake. My impulse was to help. Maybe my intervention saved a life...

Even with Karim's words ringing in my ears, I was at peace, knowing that I had done the right thing.

The next day, surprise! At seven o'clock in the morning, the head guard of the gym, the petite lady, wakes me up. I walked out of the cell, and she immediately told me to go back and get my workout equipment. I stared at her and finally said, "But today is not gym day for me."

"Ordinarily, no, but I decided that you can go," she responded.

"Fine. Thanks a lot!"

"No, George, I thank you," she said quietly. "Now hurry."

I was surprised by the lady's attitude, and I asked myself why she thanked me, but I did not think about it much. Happy that I could go to the gym again, I descended to the ground floor where I waited a few minutes, after which I, along with the other prisoners, went to the gym. I worked out comfortably for about two hours. Around nine o'clock, I had to return to my cell since another group of prisoners was coming for their exercise, but I had not yet completed my workout regimen. I, therefore, approached the guard that was on duty, asking if I could stay a bit longer, until ten o'clock. His response shocked me.

"You can stay until lunchtime, after which you should go and eat. After lunch, you can come back to the gym. Starting today, you will be the full-time gym orderly."

I couldn't believe my ears! "Me? Gym orderly?"

To get this job, one had to be incarcerated in that prison for at least six months and, in all that time, have an irreproachable record. I had been there only one week!

In my heart, I praised the Lord Jesus, yet my bewilderment showed on my face, and the guard responded.

"Yes! That will be your responsibility. Don't look at me; the decision was handed down from my superiors. You will work with us here in the gym."

At lunch, while eating with Karim in my cell, I told him the miracle. He began to smile.

"It seems to me that your actions yesterday turned out for your good. To work in the gym is the dream of every inmate. There you have freedom to move around, and you can work out as much as you want! Good job!"

"I don't get any credit, Karim. This is just the goodness of the Lord. I don't know why all this is happening, but I cannot but thank God for it!"

The War Begins

Things were going well for me, and I thanked God daily for everything. I had the opportunity to work out every day, which made me think that perhaps, after my release, I could get into professional sports again. At the gym, I worked out with prisoners from many different countries whose sentences varied widely. Some were there for petty theft, while others were incarcerated for some of the most serious of crimes: armed robbery, drug trafficking, murder, kidnapping, or even terrorism. Some were awaiting trial, while others were nearing the end of their sentences.

For the majority of the inmates, the gym was their favorite place to be since it allowed them freedom to move around and burn accumulated energy. Prison politics, as it relates to gyms, is much different in England than it is in Romania. In Britain, prisoners are encouraged to lift weights and get involved in sports. In Romania, on the other hand, inmates exercise very little since there is little effort on the part of the government to give them the opportunity to do so. The mentality is that: if the inmates become fit and muscular, it will encourage them to get into fights and possibly even beat up the guards. This is a false hypothesis; the truth is that if the inmates can go to the gym and burn their pent-up energy there, they are much less likely to have the energy or the inclination to get into brawls.

One evening, after coming back from the gym, while watching a documentary on television, I learned of a man that had been wrongfully convicted and spent many years behind bars. I was shocked that the authorities would make such a terrible mistake.

I thought to myself, *How is it possible to steal a man's right to a normal life? How tragic it was for him and his family! His kids are now grown, and his wife has moved on with her life.*

In my opinion, this man's life had been destroyed, but I was amazed that, even though he had spent so many years incarcerated unjustly, when they asked him about it, he could smile. His expression was that of a victor, not of a man destroyed by a situation beyond his control. That man's story made a deep impression on me. At that time, I had no idea what kind of a psychological impact it would have on me.

One morning after my workout, when I was changing in the gym's locker room, I became acquainted with an inmate from Greece. I had a burning desire to tell every man with whom I came in contact about Jesus Christ. This aspiration had been growing in my heart for several years, and I wanted to tell as many as possible, in any circumstances, how God had changed my life through His Son.

Striking up a conversation with the Greek prisoner, I asked him, "Why are you here?"

"For trafficking drugs," he replied. "I was sentenced to fourteen years."

I mentioned that I would soon stand trial, and I told him about my crimes, then added: "I want to tell the truth in court. God clearly told me to do so."

"I would say that you should not tell the truth," he told me. "If ten years have passed since your misdeeds, you would be better off pleading not guilty."

At the end of the conversation, I shook his hand, smiled, and thanked him for his advice. I knew what the Lord had told me. I knew that He is sovereign and could never be wrong, so I knew what I had to do.

After taking my leave from him, I went up to my cell. Upon my arrival, Karim spoke to me: "Lucky you, you're in the gym all day. I am dying of boredom, but you, after just a few days of confinement, become the gym orderly."

"Karim," I countered, "I don't know how you see these things, but I see them as blessings directly from heaven."

"Just so you know, George," my cellmate went on seriously, "I have been asking myself some honest questions concerning what you have been telling me about God. I have even started praying for my wife and daughter. I feel that everything will be fine."

I smiled and silently praised the Lord. Even so, while speaking with Karim, a thought struck me that troubled me deeply. My thoughts flew to the Greek I had spoken to in the locker room. Suddenly, fear seized me; I feared that he might want to do me harm, and somehow, he would accuse me of his own misdeeds. Terrified, I stood up and began pacing my cell. I said to myself, "What a stupid thought! What is wrong with me? How can I even think of something like that?"

I calmed down for a few moments, during which time I resumed the conversation with Karim. I didn't know—I couldn't even imagine—what was going to happen.

I walked around my cell for a bit, and the same thought struck me again. I began to get worried and to feel guilty for even talking to the man. I thought, *Why did I even enter into conversation with him? Why did I tell him my name? Why did I ask him about his life? What will happen now? Will I be unjustly convicted of his crimes on top of my own?*

Immediately my condition worsened, and I began to believe these stupid thoughts. Karim looked at me and asked, "Hey, bro, you feel okay? You look as if you've seen death. What's up with you?"

Hearing what Karim said, I went and looked in the mirror. It was true. My face looked different. I was as red as a crayfish, and the veins on my temple stood out. I was becoming extremely tense, and my head began to throb.

I looked around the cell, not understanding what was happening to me. This was the first time I had ever felt such panic. The feeling was indescribable. I did not know what to do; then it came to me: *the Bible, the Word.*

I turned and strode to the window, thinking I needed oxygen. I opened it and inhaled deeply; it helped not at all. The feeling remained unchanged; I felt an immense amount of pressure in my head. I turned to the place where I kept my Bible and grabbed it. Being convinced that the Bible is the Word of God, that everything in it is 100 percent true, and knowing that the Lord had spoken to me many times in a very personal way through the verses I read, I opened it at random. It fell open to the book of 2 Samuel, and my eyes fell on the verse in which David was addressing Mephibosheth: "Do not fear, for I will surely show you kindness..." (2 Samuel 9:7, NIV) I will never be able to describe in words the peace and calm that took over my heart upon reading that verse.

I read several more verses and relaxed completely. After reading, I sat and talked with Karim for a while before we lay down on our beds. Having found such peace, it was difficult for me to imagine what had happened a few hours before. I put all my mental capacity into finding a logical solution for why it had happened, but in vain. It was a strange feeling.

"Forget it, George," I told myself. "It was all in your head; it's over now."

Evening came, and I slept. In the morning, like normal, I went to the gym at seven o'clock. As I was leaving, I grabbed a change of clothes, as well as some cereal with milk and a banana, so I would have something to eat after my workout. When the guard opened my cell door, I hurried off to the gym.

Upon arrival, I greeted my colleagues and the guards on duty. It was just another day in prison, another day to work out, another opportunity to tell those I was with about my relationship with Jesus Christ. Everything went well until, without any warning, I was seized with the same sense of overpowering terror like the day before; I turned pale, my heart began beating like a drum, and I became completely tense. Seeing the Greek I was talking to the day before worsened my condition even more; something unprecedented and extraordinarily serious was happening to me, and I didn't know what it was.

I started walking around and praying with all my heart; after that, my panic subsided.

Days followed, one after another, and I did not have another panic attack. I continued reading my Bible, sometimes alone, sometimes with Karim. We prayed together frequently. I spent a lot of time in prayer in my cell, but I also prayed in my spirit while at the gym. Through the avenue of prayer, I tried to keep a close relationship with God. I knew from experience that this was the best way to resolve any problem.

What had happened to me a few days before was something unusual. I felt weak, defenseless, helpless. Not a day passed without me wondering what had been wrong and why I had had such thoughts. When a person goes through such an experience, he cannot help but ask questions. I was looking for a purely logical explanation, which did not exist; unfortunately, I did not know that at the time.

The Problem with the Watch

I had the pleasure of having my brother, Nicu, who lived in England, visit me during my time at Wandsworth. I was always overjoyed to see him, and he always made me feel as if everything would be alright, even though the charges I faced were extremely serious and my two accomplices had been sentenced to eight and ten years, respectively. Nicu's visits always made me feel good. Brothers in the faith also visited me, both Brits and Romanians. I was visited by some friends that I had not seen since I left England, ten years previous. All of those visits did me a lot of good.

I often wore a watch that had served me well, but the battery had died, so it was of no further use to me. One day during a visit, Nicu mentioned that the watch he was wearing was a good one, an atomic timepiece very similar to mine, and it wouldn't hurt for us to trade. Even though I knew it was not allowed, I took my watch off, and Nicu did the same.

But, as we were trading, a guard, an older man, walked over to our table and said, "Hey, big guy! You know what I think?"

"No, I don't," I responded, concealing the watch in the palm of my hand.

"Well, I don't think you really want to give your brother the watch that you are hiding in your hand, and I don't think you want to take the one hidden in his hand. Right? Or perhaps I'm wrong."

Surprised, I looked at him and began asking how he knew about the watch. But, looking him in the eye, I knew that I was speaking to a guard with a lot of experience and the wisdom borne of years. This man had worked with tens of thousands of young guys like me.

"Well, you know, I..."

"You're a good guy! I was told how you came to the aid of my colleague in the gym. I don't want to rat on you. From the time you came here until this moment, you have done nothing worthy of punishment, but the minute you make that trade with your brother, I will be forced to make some problems, such as cutting out your visits for the next two months, plus other annoyances."

"Thank you so much for your advice!" I replied. "You are a good man. You are right that I was going to exchange watches with my brother because mine has a dead battery. But now, I will not do so. I didn't realize that it was that serious. God bless you!"

He grinned at me and left. From that day forward, we were friends. We always greeted each other, and I told him repeatedly that he had the eyes of a hawk.

One day some time later, he came to me and asked to see my watch. I showed it to him, he looked at it closely, and several days later, he brought me a battery for it. How happy he made me!

Attacked Again

The days passed. My trial kept getting postponed for various reasons, but that did not bother me. I trusted God and knew that if I stayed close to Him, everything would be fine. Romans 8:28a (NIV) often came to mind: "...all things work together for good to those that love God." I knew that I loved God. Therefore, I knew that whatever happened would be for my good.

One week, I was on my way to the visiting area—the parlor—I met my Lithuanian colleague, the one that had facilitated my transfer from E wing to the much more comfortable B wing. We greeted each other with a hug.

"Hey, George," he said, "I heard you're working at the gym and doing well. How do you like Wandsworth?"

"I'm great," I replied. "Praise the Lord, I really am doing wonderfully. At the gym all day..."

"I believe you're doing great," was the rejoinder. "Who wouldn't want a job like you've got!"

We bade each other farewell and entered the visiting area, where my brother, Nicu, was waiting for me. There were three men waiting to see my Lithuanian friend; judging by their blond hair, I guessed them to be either Brits or Lithuanians. They took their seats about two tables down from us. After a moment, my Lithuanian acquaintance said something, and his three companions turned and looked at me. I looked at them, smiled, and resumed my discussion with my brother.

After a few seconds, like a bolt of lightning, I felt that same intense pressure that I had felt some time before, and hundreds of bad thoughts, like a flood, came tumbling into my mind.

These thoughts completely changed me. Instantly I was smothering in panic, in that same paralyzing fear. I looked at all the other tables, first right, then left. I couldn't concentrate on what my brother was saying; I didn't even hear him.

"Hey, George, what's wrong? What's with you, man? Look, take this tissue. Wipe your forehead; you started sweating all of a sudden. What happened? Are you okay? You look terrified. Tell me what bit you."

I looked at Nicu, but I couldn't hear him; he seemed to be talking to the walls. He was right; I was terrified. At that moment, I could think of nothing other than that I would be wrongfully convicted of the crimes committed by other people, I would have no way of establishing my innocence, and I would stay in prison for many years, separated from Adriana and my kids. I could not tell my brother what came over me. At first, I wanted to, but I was ashamed to open my mouth. *How can I tell him the idiotic thoughts that are going through my head? What will he think of me?*

I forced an artificial smile and tried to act normally.

"I'm fine, Nicu. I'm fine."

"You don't look fine," he retorted. "What's eating you? Have you been having any problems here? Tell me so I can talk to your lawyer and get you moved to another prison."

Just then, I snapped out of it somewhat. I knew I was in an embarrassing situation.

"No, Nicu, I'm having no trouble. Have you ever known me as man incapable of solving his own problems?" I laughed.

"Good," he said. "I know you were always a strong guy and could take care of yourself in the worst of conditions. I have a lot of confidence in you, but if something ever happens and you're in trouble, or someone is making problems, please tell me..."

"Sure, of course. Don't worry; nothing will happen."

Even though I vehemently denied that anything was wrong, deep inside, I felt something crying for help. I didn't know what was happening with me and from where this condition was coming—this crushing pressure and these bizarre thoughts. However, my thoughts always led me to that TV report about the man who was wrongfully convicted. How could these crazy ideas trick me into believing them? I was beginning to realize that this state of mind was changing me, even altering the way I looked and acted. Something was not right, but I had no idea what. "Na, what can I do?" I would ask myself in the times when I could think clearly.

Several minutes after Nicu and I had parted and I arrived in my cell, I was feeling more or less okay. Then the attack started again. The same thoughts from before came roaring back. I felt the same restlessness and intense pressure, so strong that it felt as if my head would split. I paced around the cell for a few moments, then sat on the bed, then got up and went to the window, then to the door. The cell was very small, and I needed more room to walk around. The narrow cell seemed to make my restlessness worse. In the grip of that attack, I felt that there was no resolution until my thoughts again, in a momentary lull, went to the Bible.

Like a drowning man, I grasped my Bible and began reading verse after verse, chapter after chapter, and slowly, I began to relax. I read for more than an hour uninterrupted. Finally, toward evening, sheer weariness overcame me. I laid my Bible down and dropped to my knees in prayer, after which I went to bed, full of peace.

The Brothers from Nigeria

At Wandsworth, I got to know a group of Nigerian Christians. In addition to the Sunday morning service, I decided to go to one of the meetings that these brothers were having. I found it very difficult to get used to their style of worship since it was very different from the model that I had been used to heretofore. I grew up in an Orthodox Christian environment, where only the priest spoke in church. Later, when I wanted to know more about Jesus, I began attending an Evangelical church where again, at least in Romania, the mode of worship emphasized reverence for God.

At this meeting in the prison, however, the African and Jamaican brothers sang and danced, moving all over the room. I was shocked, feeling unable to join in worship with them and preferring to pray as I knew how. After the meeting was over and I arrived back at my cell, I prayed and asked the Lord if I should continue going to their meetings or not. These brothers seemed sincere, and they loved the Word, but I was not used to the way they jumped all over the room when they sang. The Lord, in His goodness and love, spoke to me very simply and said that He loved them as much as He loved me and that the difference between us was only the culture from which we came. I thus received answers to questions that I had had for some time, namely, how to relate to those that worship the same God as I do but in a different way.

Many times, as Christians, we are tempted to judge by appearance and to take the place of God, deciding what is good and what is bad, what is appropriate and what is not. I want to continue worshiping in the way that the Lord has shown me, but I have learned that the world is a vast place with billions of people and thousands of ways of worship. I believe that the exact mode is of little consequence. The Lord wants a sincere heart; that is the most important part.

I continued attending these brothers' services. I rejoiced with them, even if my method of doing so was different than theirs. I couldn't bring myself to clap and dance as they did; they understood that and accepted me as I was. The mutual acceptance made it a joy to worship together.

A Friend in Prison

Some time had passed since the last spiritual attack, and I was feeling better. But one day at the gym, everything started again, and in an instant, out of the blue, all the pressure and panic engulfed me again. I couldn't believe what was happening to me. Immediately my face changed color; even my way of speaking changed. Of course, those around me began noticing that something was wrong and wanted to help.

One of the colleagues I was working out with, a Brit from southern London, pulled me to the side one day and asked, "George, what is happening with you? You are terribly unpredictable. One moment you're fine, smiling, and sociable; the next, you're shut up inside yourself, want to speak to no one, and go to your room alone. What is happening?"

Standing before the man, I did not know how to respond. How could I open up to this person I barely knew? In my heart smoldered the desire to talk to someone about these problems, but at the same time, I was overwhelmed and completely embarrassed. How could a man of my physique, an athlete who all his life practiced some of the roughest of sports, a man who had lived a demanding life, tell a relative stranger about the battles in his mind and the paralyzing fear that he faced?

"Hey, George! George, listen to me! If you have some problems at home, maybe your family is struggling or something, tell us. Maybe we can help."

Suddenly, I thought of a way out. In an effort to escape, I said, "Well, Lee, if you must know, my mother is not feeling well, it was true. That is the deal, but I think she'll be recovering shortly."

"It's good, bro, don't worry about anything. But you're a Christian, aren't you? You should be trusting in God."

That man taught me a lesson because it was true, I was constantly talking about God to everyone, but when faced with one of my attacks, I felt helpless.

The attacks varied widely. At times I was fine for days on end; other times, I felt as if I carried a boulder on my head. I was confused and did not know which way to turn.

At one point, I didn't want to go to the gym anymore. For some reason, I was not feeling safe there. I wanted to avoid the gym; I would have to give up my job as a gym orderly, but that would not have done me good either, since physical exercise seemed to help when I was in turmoil inside. Even so, I finally could take it no longer, and I excused myself on the grounds that I didn't feel well. I stayed in my room for ten days straight, not even leaving it for food.

At that time, I was staying with an Albanian. He noticed that I did not want to leave the cell and asked, "Why are you never leaving the room? Why don't you go to your job in the gym? You will lose your post if you keep acting this way."

I didn't know how to respond. I felt as if I was sinking into a black hole, into the unknown, in something completely new and impossible to understand. All I could say was, "Lord, help me!"

It seemed that whatever I did, any attempt to return to normal was doomed to failure. I was caught in a trap, and I had not the slightest idea how to get out.

In Search of a Solution

I started looking for an explanation on my own for the problems that I was facing. I borrowed a smartphone from a Romanian prisoner, even though I knew smartphones were not allowed in prison. I tried to respect that guideline as much as possible, but, considering the inner turmoil I was dealing with, I felt it necessary to use the internet to look for some information. I asked my colleague for the use of his phone, and for several nights in a row, I read everything I could find about groundless fear, panic, paranoia, etc.

I hunted desperately for an explanation for my inner conflict, but I still felt unprepared to discuss it with someone else; I found it all too embarrassing. Something inside just simply would not allow me to talk to someone about what I was going through, but that unwillingness to speak did me no good.

I thought no one would understand, and they would laugh at me. I made the decision that, regardless of what happened to me, I could never allow anyone to laugh at me and my problems. I considered myself a big, strong guy, and I was determined not to be so easily conquered by this previously unfamiliar conflict. I was determined to fight.

At that time, I had no way of knowing that this conflict was only going to intensify; it was only going to get more and more real, making my condition more and more critical.

After I had stayed in my room for ten days, I went down to the gym. There, the guys that I worked with and trained with, as well as the chief guard, could see that I did not feel well. They did not know exactly what was eating me, but it was evident that they did everything they could to help and support me. They treated me ever so well. I am not exaggerating when I say that I felt those people were somehow with me in the fight. They often spoke with me and offered words of encouragement, especially the chief officer of the gym; this little woman had an extraordinarily large heart. While I was going through that difficult battle, their support meant the world. I desperately needed the message that they so warmly conveyed—the message that simply said that I was accepted. They were people inclined to help, very different from some of the people that I would meet later on.

The days and weeks passed. At times my struggles were more difficult; other times, they were easier. I waited impatiently for my lawyer to give me an idea of when my trial would be held. Finally, I received word. I was so happy to finally know the date of the trial, praying that everything would soon be over and I would know how long I would have to serve. I felt that when I knew that, my mental battles would subside, and I could move on with my life.

My Millionaire Cellmate

A week before my trial, I was pretty optimistic about how it would go. What would happen in the courtroom worried me not at all. I entrusted the entire problem to God and rested on the promise that He had made to me while still in Romania. With that not resting on my mind, I could think of nothing else but the invisible foe that had appeared out of nowhere and was trying to break my spirit. That was the biggest conflict that I faced.

My Albanian cellmate moved into another cell with one of his countrymen, leaving me alone. That actually felt good, so for several days, I refused to let anyone else into my cell. Again, I started isolating myself. I did not want to have contact with anyone, but I also knew that I could not continue that way indefinitely. One evening around ten o'clock, a guard opened my cell door, and a man about fifty years of age entered. When I saw him, I greeted him, invited him to sit down, served him some tea, and then we began talking. I discovered he was a British businessman who had been convicted in a major corruption case. We spoke long into the night. He was extremely depressed because after his trial had dragged on for nine long years, he had just been imprisoned and on his son's fourteenth birthday. I encouraged him as much as I could; then, I told him that God is the one that can help him. Though he was in the dumps, he did listen, although I felt he was only there physically, judging from his vacant stare.

I spent a lot of time with this man. He was an intelligent man that, in his prime, had over ten thousand employees. I asked him all kinds of questions on how to run a business, and I wrote down in my small notebook a number of things that I learned from him. He taught me a lot of useful things about the business world. I wanted to learn all that I could because, though I was in prison, I had a business at home that, by the goodness of God, was flourishing.

I had gone into partnership with another Christian, and we had opened a plant to make packaging for fast-food restaurants. When I was arrested, the business had only a single employee, a single customer, and a single machine. In the three and a half years I had been incarcerated, the business had grown to where it now employed thirty-five people; it had acquired a lot more machinery and was servicing some of the largest restaurant chains in Eastern Europe.

Knowing that sooner or later, depending on my sentence, I would get back home, where I would have to get involved in the business again, I was interested in all that my businessman cellmate could tell me, constantly asking him different questions on how to keep a business running smoothly.

It was the fifth day after the arrival of R (as I will call him). I was nearly back to normal since it had been several days since my last attack, and I was feeling well enough to go to the gym again. I had been reading the Bible constantly, as well as other Christian books that had been a great help to me. I was, in fact, searching for a book that dealt specifically with the problem I was facing, but I had not come across anything yet. Therefore, I believed that what was happening to me was probably something extremely rare and that there probably were no books written on the subject. It was difficult to come to grips with the fact that I could neither understand nor explain my condition.

That evening, which was two days before my scheduled trial, I was sitting and talking with R. Suddenly, he grabbed a piece of paper and a pen and began asking me all kinds of questions about my life and family, my athletic career, etc. After I had answered several questions, I asked him why he wanted to know all these things.

"George, your life is amazing," he replied. "I mean, look at all that you've done up until now! Being a professional athlete, then getting involved in a lot of troubles, after which, as you say, God changed your life. I want to write about you to my family and friends so they know that I am a cellmate of a champion prize-fighter, and they don't have to worry about me."

I was looking at this man; I liked him as a person, a very intelligent man, a man who had a lot of money, who knew a lot of influential people, who had it all except freedom. I thought then in my mind, *What joy could someone have, even if he had all the money in the world, if he does not have the freedom to enjoy his life and his beautiful family?* More important than enjoying life is what Jesus says in the Gospels: "For what is a man profited, if he shall gain the whole world, and lose his own soul? Or what shall a man give in exchange for his soul?" (Matthew 16:26, KJV) Our soul is all the more important than this life we live in this body, yet most people refuse to believe this truth; they refuse the One who could give them eternal life. Since I met God, the values that guide my life changed enormously, it is not my merit but God's; no one could have changed my mind so profoundly but Him alone.

That day passed somewhat normally. Evening came, and I knew that the following morning I was to be taken to court for my trial. Even though I hoped I could return to Wandsworth, I knew that it was very possible that I would end up incarcerated elsewhere, so I hugged R and wished him well, after which we turned in.

The Truth Will Make You Free

I slept barely three hours when a guard swung open the cell door and called, "Mister Ignat, please get up! You must go to your trial."

I had been preparing the evening before. I had put all my belongings into two nylon bags; I had to take all my things since, as I said before, in England, when someone goes to their trial, they often do not return to the same prison except by sheer chance. Rather, upon leaving the courthouse, the prisoner is placed in the first available vehicle and taken to the prison that happens to be the destination of that particular van.

I spent about two hours at the reception of Wandsworth, where they searched me multiple times and prepared my documents. Then I boarded a prisoner transport vehicle for the trip to the courthouse.

There were numerous other inmates in the same vehicle. Two of them were quite unhappy with their situation and expressed their displeasure by swearing at the guards who were accompanying us. The noise they made did not bother me, since I was already accustomed to such racket, so I prayed the entire way to the courthouse. I asked the Lord for wisdom as well as strength to do what He had shown me that I must do. I was full of peace and rest.

Upon arrival, I was taken to a cell in the basement of the courthouse. Roughly thirty very small rooms were there for the purpose of housing the inmates for several hours while awaiting their turn in the courtroom. Beside these cells were an additional ten or so rooms specially designed for meetings between the defendants and their lawyers. In one of these rooms, I was destined to fight one of the fiercest battles I had yet faced: the battle for the truth.

"Good morning!" a voice greeted me. "I am attorney F. I was paid by your brother to represent you. I believe we have seen each other on a teleconference call."

"Good morning!" I replied. "I am George. I'm pleased to meet you!"

"Okay, George! Here is how your case looks: from my point of view, it's very simple. Over ten years have passed since these events. Looking at your case, I saw that there is no video footage, and there were no witnesses that saw you directly. Even the victim does not know exactly who you are. I do not know if you are guilty or not, nor do I care. I am here to look after your interests and to ensure that you get out of this situation in the best possible way."

I was happy to hear my lawyer himself say that things could be easily resolved, but at the moment, I did not know what to think. I was waiting with some impatience for him to tell me his plan and how things should be done.

"Good!" I responded. "What is to be done? How do you plan to go about it?"

"After analyzing the evidence in your file, I think the best option is for you to plead not guilty. I believe there is over a 90 percent chance that you will be acquitted. Judging from my nearly thirty years of experience in this field, I think you have an excellent chance of walking out a free man. The only chance you have to get out of this situation with a favorable verdict is to plead not guilty."

He was right. Everything logical said that I had a very good chance of being freed immediately if I pled not guilty. The data all said that the authorities had a very small chance, almost zero, of convicting me. This attorney was among the most highly educated and experienced lawyers in London. He had been recommended to me by several of my relatives who were living in England; they were intelligent people who knew the difference between a windbag and a good, skilled lawyer.

This defense strategy seemed well-planned and nearly foolproof, but, as I was listening to the lawyer speak, I remembered what God had told me while still in Romania: "George, if you tell the truth, I will be with you." As I remembered those words, I determined not to consider any other possibility, and in my mind, I clearly heard the following words: "The truth will make you free, George. Not lies."

"Mister F, I would love to plead not guilty, but I would like to tell you what I have decided. I want you to know that I believe in God, have a personal relationship with Him, and speak with Him directly. I asked him about this trial, and He told me that if I want Him to intervene, I must tell the truth. To speak straight, sir, I am guilty and am not innocent. Therefore, I wish to plead guilty."

The lawyer's expression changed, and he looked at me strangely, saying, "George, perhaps you do not understand the situation clearly. You had two accomplices, one of whom got eight years, the other—ten. Besides, your circumstances are even worse because four years ago, the punishments for these kinds of crimes doubled. From my point of view, if you are unfortunate and get a more severe judge, you risk getting over ten years in prison. For these charges, you could get fifteen years, and I don't think you want fifteen years behind bars."

"I know and understand perfectly what is at stake, but God told me..."

"I understand," he interrupted. "I am a Christian as well, but we are talking about a criminal trial, with which I am well-acquainted. The bottom line is this: we are talking about your life! You have three kids that are waiting for your return. Consider well what you want to do! I would hate to see you get a harsh sentence, but I can do nothing more than advise you. Consider well!"

"I have contemplated it, and my decision is to plead guilty, regardless of what may happen. God wants me to tell the truth; of that, I am convinced. At this point, it is more important for me to tell the truth than to be freed on a lie."

The lawyer rolled his eyes and slapped his forehead. He was visibly irritated with my determination to plead guilty because I believed it to be God's will. He had tremendous experience in penal law, and, from the viewpoint of human logic, he was perfectly correct in what he said. I am certain that he wished to help me and wanted my good, and that is exactly what made him upset.

"George, your brother paid me to take your case. I was not taught how to lose. The majority of my cases I have won. I will speak with your brother now..."

He left the room for several minutes, leaving me alone. During this time, he called my brother, who was on his way to the courthouse, and told him that he had encountered a problem as he was preparing my defense. The man told my brother that I seemed to have some serious mental problems because I said that I had spoken to God, and He told me what to say at the trial. My brother, knowing in large part what my attorney was talking about, told him that the chances of convincing me to do otherwise were very small and asked him to do all that he could in the situation as it was. I was determined to plead guilty, so he just had to work with what he had.

"Okay, George," he said upon returning to the room. "I understand that you refuse to consider anything other than a guilty plea. It is your choice and whatever happens, remember that it was your decision. Having said that, I would like to ask something of you."

He pulled a piece of white paper from his briefcase and asked me to write a declaration of responsibility, in that I declared that I had decided how I would plead and that, regardless of the results of the trial and the sentence I received, I would not sue him for moral damages. I wrote what he asked me to and signed my name. One of his colleagues also signed as a witness, and then he signed it.

"I want you to know," I said, "that regardless of what happens and what sentence I get, I will never sue you."

"Believe me," he grunted, "I have seen other brave guys like you that refused to listen but who, after getting a large sentence, demanded damages to the tune of hundreds of thousands of pounds."

I thought the man was wise to take some security measures and agreed with his actions.

"In half an hour," he continued, "we will enter the courtroom. It is possible that you will be sentenced today. The judge that is on the bench today is not the best, but neither is he the worst. I just hope you won't get more than ten."

I left the room and returned to my cell, and thirty minutes later, I was taken to the courtroom. There, I saw my family. I saw the anxiety written on their faces, so I tried to convey the message that everything would be fine and that they should not worry. The trial began with me sitting behind a large glass window. Just before I was asked how I would respond to the charges brought against me, my lawyer came to the front of the glass, looked at me, and told me to give myself a chance and plead not guilty. In the man's eyes, I could see that he really cared and genuinely wanted to do what was in my best interest, but he could not understand my moral obligations or see things as I saw them.

"To the first charge, Mister Ignat," intoned the judge, "how do you plead?"

"Guilty."

"The second?"

"Guilty. Guilty. Guilty." I replied to each of the charges that the judge read.

The prosecuting attorney rubbed his hands gleefully to each guilty plea; it meant a lot less work for him. My lawyer was quite right when he said that they would have had an exceedingly difficult time proving my guilt with the evidence they had. It would have been nearly impossible. Now that I had admitted my guilt, conviction was certain. In my mind, as well as that of my lawyer and those I loved, the only question that remained was, "How many years?"

Eventually, the sentencing was postponed because my lawyer asked for some clarification regarding the transfer procedures from Romania to the United Kingdom. Some of those details were not very clear, and he thought that we might gain something if we waited until all aspects of my transfer were clarified.

The date of my sentencing, as well as the name of the presiding judge, was soon to be determined. My lawyer would relay all that information to me.

The sentences that the judges handed down could vary widely. For example, for an infraction that carried a sentence of five to twenty years, a lenient judge may give only five, while his colleague would give twenty. Which judge was on the bench on the day of one's sentencing—some being extremely harsh while others tended to be more kind—played an extremely important role. The man behind the judge's desk, the one holding the gavel, would decide how much time I must still spend behind bars.

At this moment, I was very happy; I had an extraordinary feeling of gratitude; I thanked God with all my heart that He gave me the strength to overcome all obstacles and to plead as He told me. I was living one of the most beautiful moments of life when you knew that you had fulfilled what God had asked of you.

Part 3

Wormwood Prison, United Kingdom

Wormwood Scrubs—Fighting at the Next Level

Immediately following the trial, I spoke with my lawyer for several minutes in the basement of the courthouse before being hustled into another van and taken to another famous penitentiary: Wormwood Scrubs. I was to stay for several months, which isn't necessarily long, but it was a very intense time. I did not feel well while there, being lost in a labyrinth of negative thoughts; my condition deteriorated to a state of affairs I had never experienced before, and from which I considered it impossible to ever recover.

Looking back, I believe that considering my condition, it would have been much better to have returned to Wandsworth, where I had friends and was already familiar with both the inmates and the staff. That is the way it seems to me, but who knows? God was, still is, and I pray that He will continue to be in control of my life; He must know why I had to go to Scrubs.

I arrived at Scrubs during the night, and they put me in a cell with a Nigerian with whom I spoke much in the following days. He was a Christian; he prayed, but—in my mind—he had a problem. When I told him that we had to admit what we had done and accept the punishment, thus showing that we are true Christians, he did not agree.

"You have no idea how it works here, do you?" he challenged, grinning.

I shrugged.

"Let me tell you!" he continued. "Here, if you stole a mosquito, they will say you stole a stallion. You have to be shrewd and never admit anything."

I told him that I faced some serious charges and God had told me that I was to tell the truth, which I had done since; more than anything, even more than liberty, I wanted to do God's will.

"Hey," he rejoined, "that doesn't mean you're a Christian, just a fanatic. How can you do something that will be harmful to yourself simply because you think God asked it of you? That is nothing short of religious fanaticism!"

"But why," I countered, "would God ask something of me that would do me harm? I must still disagree with you. I know that if I listen to God, it will be for my good, not for my hurt."

"Listen, bro," he said quietly, with a snap in his voice, "at the end of the day, it's your call. If you think you must acknowledge some things you did ten years ago and get convicted, do what you want. From my point of view, only a fool would do such a thing."

After this discussion, we went to bed; he moved to the top bunk so I could have the bottom one. That was a sign of respect, in which he showed me that I was welcome. Though I laid down in bed, sleep evaded me since I kept thinking of the man's words.

What should I do, Lord? I thought. *Did I bungle things? Did I mistake your voice and admit my guilt out of a twisted desire to prove that I am a Christian?*

The answer came to my mind in a soft whisper: "You did well! Look not to the right hand, nor to the left."

I thanked God for His response and went to sleep.

After several days, my Nigerian friend left and was replaced by another inmate who smoked weed from morning until evening. He, too, claimed to be a Christian and to believe in God.

"How can you smoke drugs all day?" I asked him. "Is that something inherently Christian?"

"God made weed to grow on the earth," was his rejoinder. "These drugs are actually divine medication, put here by almighty providence for men to smoke."

The next day, I respectfully asked my new cellmate to look for another room to which he could move. He looked at me and said that he was a peaceful man and didn't want a scene. I didn't want a scene either, which was precisely why I pleaded with him to look for another cell. The truth was that the previous night I had not been able to breathe very well because of the amount of smoke in the air.

Soon after we spoke, he went to the showers, and when he returned, he told me that he had met his cousin, who had told him that he had room in his cell. Quite happy, he packed his bags and, calling a guard, moved to his cousin's room. After he left, I aired out the cell, making it liveable again.

My panic attacks had subsided. Several good days had passed since the last attack; I was feeling well and thanking God for it. Every Sunday, we had the opportunity to go to church, which I always took advantage of. In addition, I began going to a Bible study every Wednesday.

All in all, things were going well at Scrubs, though they didn't serve much food. Still, once a week, I could buy what I needed to complete my diet. I had to stay in my cell twenty-three hours a day, but that was no problem, as it gave me an opportunity to read. At any given time, I had three or four books that I was reading, spending two or three hours with one before putting it down and reading another for an hour or two, and so on until night came and I slept.

I focused on the lives of great missionaries and men of God, such as Charles Spurgeon, Hudson Taylor, Richard Wurmbrand, and Billy Graham. I studied closely the lives of men who had been devoted servants of God because, in my heart, I longed to become an evangelist. I had often thought that once freed, I would take mission trips and preach the Gospel. I made plans and prayed that when I had my liberty, God would open the necessary doors for me in order to serve Him.

An Irresistible Offer

Scrubs was a large penitentiary with inmates from all over the world. Every day, numerous fights broke out, and not infrequently, a prisoner was stabbed. Every few days, the news would circulate that someone had been killed. In this context, I was one day called to the office of the overseer of that section of the prison.

"How's it going, big guy?" he greeted me. "How do you like it here?"

"What should I say? I'm fine, thank God. Trying to take care of myself and waiting for my trial to see what kind of sentence I get."

"Okay! I would like to offer you a job, but we should probably wait until after your sentencing to see how many years you'll get," he said, looking at my file on his computer to see the charges I was facing. "If you get between ten and twenty years, I'll keep you here. I'll give you a good job and a comfortable cell. That is, of course, if you are willing to help me. Have you seen the broad-shouldered guys whose cell doors are open all the time and that go to the gym every day? Well, they help me keep order, and in return, I help them by making their stay here as pleasant as possible."

Indeed, the guards were stretched too thin when it came to keeping the place quiet and secure. The brawny guys of which he had spoken were always together, four or five in a group, and when a fight or an altercation would break out in the section, they would run to the scene and put an end to the confrontation. Of course, most of the brawls were resolved using brute force. In fact, most of the bouts ended with a large amount of blood on the floor or walls of the prison. These guys could use violence without needing to answer for it since they were supported by the boss of that section of the prison. Seeing that I was a bigger guy and that I would be a fit for his "team," the chief of the guards did not hesitate to propose our collaboration.

My response was spontaneous and immediate. "I am very sorry, but I do not think that one of your teams is the best place for me. With all due respect, please permit me to refuse. I do not believe I will receive a sentence of between ten and twenty years, anyway."

He looked again at his computer screen and said, "Yes, that is probably true. If you get a sentence of over twenty years, I will not be able to use you very well. You will be moved to another prison."

"In fact," I hurried to reply, "I would like to tell you that I won't even get ten years. There is no way I'll get twenty. You are stretching things."

I did not like what he said; his words made me think, but I believed he was only trying to scare me.

"I don't want to ruin your day," he returned, "but, judging from the charges in your folder, do not expect a short sentence because you simply won't get it. You must be realistic."

As I opened my mouth to tell him that I am a Christian and believe in God, another guard entered the office.

"Good, Mister Ignat," he stated, "that will be all. Please consider my proposal, but before that, we will have to see how many years you get at your sentencing. We do not have long to wait."

I returned to my cell and thought about his proposal. It was tempting because of all the benefits I would receive, but I could not accept the proposition under any circumstances. I was a child of God, and I could not take part in what those inmates were doing, even if it meant missing out on the chief guard's good graces.

Time dragged. I got to go to the gym once a week if I was paying attention when they called. Most of the time, I just stayed in my room, reading, meditating, and waiting for my sentencing, full of faith.

This case had begun ten years before when the other two men with whom I had collaborated in committing the crimes had been caught. As a general rule, I should have been expecting a sentence roughly the same as they had received, between eight and ten years. But since that time, the situation had changed since, as my lawyer had pointed out, in 2014, the punishments for my crimes had increased, nearly doubling. He had told me clearly that if I get a disagreeable judge, I was likely to get more than ten years, perhaps fourteen or fifteen years.

The most optimistic scenario had me getting sentenced to about ten years. I figured that if I did get ten, I would ask to be transferred to Romania to serve my sentence and, upon arrival there, ask the courts to deduct the four years I had already served for my other crimes. In that case, I thought I would be out before Christmas of 2023. That was the most optimistic scenario. I was mentally prepared for it and knew what I had to do at the courthouse, so everything seemed to be in order.

A Surprised Colleague

One afternoon, after one of my cellmates had been moved to another cell, a guard opened my door and steered a young man, roughly twenty-two years of age, into my room.

I looked at the new arrival, at which point the guard commented, "I have brought you one of your own, a Romanian. I hope you get along well."

I was quite happy and began talking with the young man. I discovered that Mirel had been born and raised in the same area I had come from: northern Romania, or, more precisely, the county of Suceava. I was shocked that he came from a family of practicing Christians, his father being a church leader. I was extremely curious to find out why he ended up in prison, so it was not long until I asked him what he had done.

He told me that he had had a good childhood in a home of true Christians, but after he turned eighteen, he moved to London with one of his older brothers. His brother found a job in construction and, with time, started a family; at the present time, he already had two children. On the other hand, soon after he arrived in London, Mirel had started hanging out with some young people that were using drugs. Eventually, he started going with them when they broke into houses at night in the upper-class neighborhoods of London, stealing valuables that they could easily sell at low prices to obtain money for drugs, gambling, and visiting prostitutes.

I asked him if he had read the Bible recently, and he told me that he had not read it since he left home. His regret for his actions was evident on his face. He was sorry for the pain and shame that caused for his parents and older siblings. He lamented over the time he was wasting in prison, especially since his trial was approaching and he was expecting a heavy sentence.

"Do you believe in God, Mirel?" I asked.

"Sure, I do, bro," he responded. "How can I not believe in God?"

"Okay then, would you like to read some verses from the Bible and pray together?" I inquired, pulling my Bible from the cabinet.

"Don't tell me you're a Christian!" he gasped, shocked.

"Oh yes, I am! And I try every day to put into practice what the Bible teaches."

"Man, you surprise me!" he exclaimed. "I can't believe it! You can tell me you're an athlete; I can see that from the next postal code. Tell me you're a gangster, and I'll believe you, particularly since all the Romanians here in prison say you've kidnapped people. But to tell me you're a practicing Christian, that's too much! It is too hard to believe. In the first place, a true Christian has no business in prison."

"Here's the thing, Mirel," I replied. "I was not always a Christian. Okay, I claimed to be, but only in name. I occasionally went to church, perhaps at Christmas or Easter, but I did not even come close to living as the Bible teaches that a Christian should. Ten years have passed since I committed the crimes with which I am charged; I have now come to answer for them. When I committed the crimes, I did not know the living and true God, but since that time, I have come to know God personally, and I know what Christianity actually entails and what it truly means to be a Christian. Now, I try to conform my life to the teaching of the Bible."

"Aha!" was the response. "Now I understand. So, you repented. You left your old life, but the sins of your past still brought you to prison."

"Exactly! That is precisely what happened."

Mirel began to smile, and from that moment, we were friends. He went on to tell me how the group he hung with had led him down the wrong road. Then he told me that he wanted to change, but he didn't have the strength. I told him that, unlike people, God loves each man so much that, through His Son, Jesus Christ, He is ready to forgive all that admit their misdeeds, ask forgiveness, and are willing to start a new life.

"Do you think God will forgive me for disregarding my parents' advice?" he asked. "I put them through so much grief. In fact, it is because I did not listen to my parents that I am here and will now very likely get a ten-year sentence."

"God is ready to forgive you and to do something more for you besides," I said earnestly. "You know what that is?"

"What?"

"He is ready to intervene at your trial so you will receive a lesser sentence. He is ready to show you how much He loves you. Do you believe that?"

"I don't know what to say," he stammered.

"Okay, look, let's sing a song of praise to the Lord Jesus. I have a songbook here..."

"Wow!" he interjected. "You have a songbook here in prison? Let me look through it a bit. I grew up with these kinds of books."

As he began paging through the book, tears appeared in his eyes. At one point, he stopped flipping pages and asked, "Do you know the song 'Only Grace'?"

"Of course, I know it. Let's sing it, but before we start, I must tell you that I'm not much of a singer; I don't have a very good voice."

"No problem!" replied Mirel, grinning. "I'm not a great singer myself, but what does it matter if we're off-key? Do you think we'll make the guards mad, and they'll kick us out of prison?"

"Not a chance," I replied, laughing.

We began singing, putting our whole heart into it without caring whether it sounded good or not. Our voices resonated through the halls of the prison. There was a momentary lull in the noise from other cells as other prisoners stopped to listen, not knowing what was happening, but soon their noise started again. Two of them even swore at us, one in English and the other in Albanian. One inmate from the next cell over immediately turned his music all the way up. All of this bothered us not one bit; we were enormously happy, singing to the Lord Jesus with all our hearts. We were radiating joy.

For the past several weeks, my spirit seemed to be strengthened, and I was having a good time. The attacks nearly stopped altogether, and that feeling of paralyzing terror and awful panic slowly began to become nothing more than a memory. However, there was something inside of me that kept me from letting down my guard but warned me to watch, pray, and be prepared because there was a possibility that I would again be hit by that panic I had experienced earlier.

I was struggling to keep my inner peace, so I decided not to speak to many of the other inmates and not to inquire too much about them and their situation. Satan was again attacking on the level of the mind, making me think that anyone among the inmates might devise schemes against me that would keep me confined, far from family, friends, and liberty. These battles were strictly in my head because, in reality, those ideas were unfounded. They were only lies with which the enemy was bombarding my mind.

I was awaiting my sentencing with some impatience since I knew that my charges were serious and the punishments severe. I believed the promises of God and hoped that He would help me and work on my behalf.

The Terrible Judge

The long-anticipated call finally came, but when I had spoken to my lawyer and was told the date for the sentencing, I returned to my room in a somber state of mind. Besides telling me the exact date and time, he had given me some information that worried me.

"Of all the twenty-four judges that work in that court," he told me, "the one you got is the harshest one of the lot."

"But who chose the judge?" I asked him.

"Well, he was chosen randomly by a computer," was the response.

"What can be done to avoid sentencing by this particular judge?" was my next question.

"Nothing!" my lawyer replied. "We can do no more than hope we catch him in a good mood, in which case perhaps he will be more lenient than normal."

Arriving back in my cell, the first thing I did was to drop to my knees. I asked God how He would help me now, seeing He had given me the judge with the worst reputation in the district. It would have been much easier to look forward to the sentencing, knowing that I had a judge renowned for his kindness. But with what I had heard, it was difficult to believe that everything would be okay.

Still, I found hope in the promise the Lord had given me before leaving Romania, that if I told the truth, He would be with me. I had done my part and told the truth at my trial; now, I wondered how God would intervene to make everything turn out well. I had no idea what would happen, particularly after getting a court date when a judge known for his severity was on the bench. Even so, I believed with all my heart that God knew everything and could do anything.

I began inquiring among my fellow inmates of the judge named Curtis. I asked everyone, right and left, until one afternoon when I was out in the corridor, an older prisoner approached me.

"I hear you will be sentenced by Judge Curtis, from Kingstone Court," he said. "Is that true?"

"It is," I replied. "Why do you ask? Do you know him?"

He smiled humorlessly. "I was sentenced by that judge too. I had committed a minor infraction: since winter was coming and I was homeless, I broke into a vehicle and stole something. I figured petty theft like that wouldn't land me more than three or four months, just enough to let the coldest weather pass, and in the spring, I would be free again."

"And what happened?"

"I was sentenced by Curtis..." Again the mirthless smile.

"And?"

"This is the *second* winter I am spending behind bars, after expecting to be here only one! For small-time stealing, he gave me three and half years! Ridiculous! And there are other inmates that were sentenced by him too. Ask anyone, and they will tell you that man always gives terribly long sentences, usually close to the maximum. Besides, he's a racist, and seeing that you are a foreigner, I don't think you got the best judge."

He turned and walked away, lurching a little. After taking a few steps, he again turned toward me and said, "He's a bad one, a very bad one! Beware!"

I did not reply, nor did I ask anyone else about this judge. In fact, knowing all that information did me no good. I went back to my room and waited for Mirel, who had been gone to his trial. He had been quite nervous, and I was wondering how he fared. We had been praying a lot the previous week, and I hoped that God would do a miracle at his trial so he would see how much the Lord loves him.

Around ten o'clock that evening, the normal time when inmates returned from their trial, the cell door opened, and Mirel entered. He looked at me, smiled widely, hugged me, then said, "Praise God! I'm going home soon! The judge dropped most of my charges, and I got a rather short sentence, the best I could have hoped for. God is good!"

"I'm awfully happy for you!" I exclaimed. "You know, I expected nothing else. God is always good!"

After talking for a while, we went to bed. The following day we had a wonderful time talking to God by singing and praying. Now Mirel's sentencing was passed, and mine was coming up, so we began praying earnestly for my situation.

Brother Puiu

With my trial approaching, there was one person I often called and on whose prayers I very much depended; his name was Brother Puiu. God used him very much to strengthen me spiritually. Even so, this man was more than just a brother in the faith; he was my business associate in the company that we had started before I was incarcerated.

Although I had been in prison for three years already, Puiu ran the business, and God blessed the work of our hands; I say our hands because I had remained co-owner, even though I was behind bars.

Though I thanked God every day for the business, I also thanked Him every day for Puiu. He, being a true disciple of Jesus, chose to stay close to our family even in the difficulties through which we were passing, and he ran the business that we had started, always being transparent about everything he did and why he did it. By way of the business, Adriana and the children had a steady source of income every month; while not being large, it was enough to pay the bills.

From a financial standpoint, God had worked powerfully, and I could relax. It is so important to a prisoner to know that, while he is incarcerated, his dear ones at home have everything they need for survival. God used brother Puiu, as well as other brothers, to ensure that Adriana and the children had everything they needed for day-to-day life.

One day, Puiu called me and asked me for prayer. He told me that one of the machines at our factory was not working and no mechanic seemed to be able to repair it. That evening, I got on my knees and prayed. I was not surprised when talking with Puiu the following day, he told me that the machine that made our cardboard cartons had started working again. That occurrence did not shock me because I had seen Him intervene in my life so many times. I remembered something that happened about two years before when I was in the Botoșani prison in Romania. Puiu had come to visit me, as he did every few days, and we, as we often did, talked about God's love and prayed together, which always did a lot for me. We also talked about our growing business, which was causing a lot of headaches for Puiu, since it was growing so fast that it was difficult for him to stay on top of things, especially since he was alone in making decisions. He told me how much he wished I was at home so that the work and stress would be divided between us, making it easier for him.

After that visit, I returned to my room and laid down on my bed, feeling sad because of what Puiu had told me.

"Lord," I began to pray, "if I would be at home, I could contribute to the business as well, but as it is, it rests all on Puiu's shoulders, and it's a heavy load. Together, we could do so much more."

God, in His faithfulness, responded very quickly, saying, "What could you do, George, more or better than I have done? If you had been there, could you help more than I do?"

I was ashamed. "Lord," I said, "have mercy. Please continue leading both our lives and our business. Thank you!"

After that, I always tried to consult God before making any major decision. From that day forward, when Puiu told me that something wasn't working or that a machine was on the blink, I dropped to my knees, full of faith, knowing before I started that God would resolve the problem.

My trial was drawing closer. This was not the first time I had asked Puiu to support me in prayer; from my first day in prison, we had been praying for each other constantly. Now I needed prayer more than ever, not necessarily for a favorable ruling, since I had already been praying for that and knowing that—since I had done my part—the Lord would do His, but that God would give me victory in the terrible battles that assailed me from time to time.

I called all the faithful brothers that I knew could support me in prayer. I often called the church of which I was a member in Suceava, knowing that the brothers there prayed for me a lot. Though I did not know why those attacks came or what caused them, I believed with all my heart that God could change the way things were. I knew that, regardless of the problem, God is the solution.

Brother Puiu was one of the few people that stayed close to me; I knew I could always depend on him. When you put your life into the hand of God, He will make sure that, even in difficult circumstances, you have other people giving you the loving support that you need.

The Day of the Sentencing

On the morning of the day I was to be sentenced, I was awakened a little after four o'clock by a guard. That is standard procedure in order to ensure that the inmate will not be late. I was quite familiar with the routine; in the previous five or six years, I had been to many court hearings.

After coming down to the prison's reception area, I was locked into a cell with other inmates who had a court date that day. Most of them were worried, while others joked and laughed freely. Not knowing a single one of them, I leaned against a wall and began praying silently. It was the big day, the day I was expecting to receive my sentence. I had been awaiting this day for some time and was anxious to see what God was going to do.

One by one, we filed out of the prison doors and were loaded into prisoner transport vehicles, after which each van left for the courthouse. At one point, the van in which I was riding stopped beside a cell window for a few moments. As I looked out the window of the van and into the cell, I saw, on one of the walls, the name "JESUS" written in large, capital letters. Seeing the name of Jesus on that wall made me happy and invigorated my spirit since it served as confirmation that He would be with me. In a few minutes, however, the van was on its way to the courthouse.

I turned toward a window so I could see beautiful London going by. We were passing through some areas that I remembered, and I was happy to see again, after so many years, the splendid city in which I had once lived.

Everything seemed fine. The next moment, everything changed. I had been feeling well, but, without warning, I was again savagely attacked by the enemy. My frame of mind was instantly transformed. I began sweating, and my hands became clammy; my heart began beating wildly. I was seized by that crazed feeling of panic, but at that moment, I knew that, in order to be victorious, I had to take action. Resting my elbows on my knees and dropping my face in my hands, I closed my eyes and began to pray fervently.

The devil, coward that he is, always attacked when I least expected it. All sorts of thoughts came flooding into my mind, bringing with them that incredible pressure. I can never fully explain that feeling because it is difficult for one who has never experienced it to understand such a state of mind.

This particular time, the evil one assaulted me with the following thoughts, *I made the worst mistake of my life, pleading guilty to all charges. The lengthy sentence I will get will be my own fault because I was stubborn and insisted on telling the truth.*

The enemy was trying to convince me that the advice that I had received from God in prayer— that I should admit guilt— was a terrible suggestion that would cost me many years of my life. He told me that I would lose my children and my wife, that by the time I arrived at home, my elderly parents would be gone as well, and that even God would have completely forgotten about me.

Normally, a born-again Christian with a personal relationship with God should chase such thoughts from his mind, but for me, I had a problem. The paralyzing fear overwhelmed my mind with such brutal force to the extent that I no longer had any idea how to cope with it.

In addition, the enemy used real events or people to bring numberless lies and to build a kind of false reality within the mind and then used that false reality to bring down his victim. For example, the fact that I had told the truth and that I would be facing a harsh judge, were real events, but the devil used these truths to make me believe his lies, such as the idea that I would receive a long sentence or that God had forgotten me.

In this kind of moment, logic helped a lot. I should not receive a longer sentence than had my two companions. However, though logical thoughts would help for a short time, they did not remain long. When the enemy attacks, logic can lose power if the mind under attack believes the deceptive thoughts sown by the enemy.

In my athletic career, I was a participant in several hundred matches in sports such as Greco-Roman wrestling, sambo, and mixed martial arts (MMA). It was not easy, but with training and intense preparation, I managed to win the majority of those contests. In a good fight, the opponents face each other, they look at each other's eyes, and they both know the rules of the fight. But I had been thrown into a fight that was taking place in the dark, with an opponent I knew nothing about and with rules that were unknown to me. In this fight, I was taking sudden and unexpected blows. I was at a terrible disadvantage with this opponent, knowing neither his name nor what he looked like nor what he wanted. I was, however, to find out later who this adversary was and what he was after.

I continued praying until we arrived at the courthouse, where I was taken to another cell. Once there, I immediately fell to my knees and continued praying. I desperately wanted to be peaceful and relaxed as I faced the judge, and I knew that the only way to get that peace was to implore the Lord for it. But the fight only seemed to get worse and worse.

A guard opened the door and called me; my lawyer had arrived and wanted to talk. I left the cell and walked toward the special room where defendants met their lawyers. I greeted my attorney and sat down at the table. I had before me not just a lawyer but a man that genuinely wanted to help me; I had felt it the first time I spoke to him.

"George," he greeted me, "today we will find out what your penalty will be. I'm going to tell you straight, hiding nothing. I will tell you exactly how things stand."

"I am all ears," I replied.

"As I told you on the phone," he continued, "you will be sentenced by a judge that is known for the long sentences that he hands down. I spoke to your family about it, and I tried to prepare them psychologically as best I could. George, if you get a harsh sentence—over ten years—today, don't worry; we will appeal and win the next round."

"Mister F, I understand that this judge is a harsh man, but he does not have to be my judge. Please try to postpone the sentencing, at least a little bit, in the hope that I can be sentenced by another man."

"George," he responded, shaking his head, "believe me, I tried that. It is impossible. We have no good reason to postpone. I am sorry, but you were the "lucky one." The bottom line is that you assumed some risks when you pleaded guilty. But who knows? Perhaps God will intervene, as you say."

After this discussion, I was again taken to the cell. I had another thirty minutes until I was to appear in the courtroom, so I knelt in prayer again. "Lord, I pray for this judge. They say he's a man with a heart of stone, a very, very hard man, but you, Lord, made this man too. You can change his heart. Only you can soften a heart. Please do that today!"

I stood up and waited for the guard to take me to the courtroom.

Several moments later, I found myself in the courtroom, in a small enclosure made of very thick glass, containing several chairs. Before me stretched a large room full of people. On my left, in one of the first rows, were my loved ones: my mother, father, wife, brother, and some friends. Near them, also on my left but closer to me, was the prosecuting attorney with an open laptop. On the right, in the same row as the prosecutor, was my attorney, also with an open laptop. On the other side of the room, in front of me, at a big table up on a platform, was the judge, a serious-looking man with glasses. As soon as I entered the defendant's box, he looked me directly in the eye.

I could read sadness and worry in my loved ones' bearing. Later I discovered that my lawyer had told them that, in his opinion, I would receive a long sentence of more than ten years that day, and he wanted them to know it beforehand in order to be emotionally prepared. I knew I had two options: to worry, focusing on the demonic attack and the critical situation with which I was confronted, or to focus on and believe the promises that God had made to me some time before.

From the box, I looked intently at my brother, Nicu. He had tears in his eyes. He was expecting the worst. He looked at me, and though I still felt fearful, I tried to put on a brave face, smiling and winking at him. I tried to convey the message that everything would be alright. I had mentally chosen the second option, to put my hope in God, though I must admit that the sense of panic still lay just below the surface. I succeeded in communicating my thoughts to my brother, for his expression changed, lighting up somewhat.

"Mister Ignat, please rise to your feet," I heard from the speakers in the glass box in which I sat.

I stood, and immediately the judge began speaking. "You are Gheorghe Ignat, born on the date of ..., in the city of ..., Romania?"

"I am."

"We understand that you admitted guilt at your trial. In this case, we can finish the proceedings rather quickly. Today you will be sentenced, Mister Ignat."

I nodded and resumed my seat when my lawyer gave the sign to do so.

"Sir," continued the judge, now addressing the prosecutor, "please bring to our attention the charges and the way in which the criminal activity transpired."

"Certainly, Your Honor," replied the prosecuting attorney.

A number of years had passed since I had committed these crimes, so some details, even some important ones, I had forgotten. Now this man was reading them to the whole world while a lady translated into Romanian so everyone present, such as my mother and my wife, could understand everything. I wanted to sink through the floor from shame. The deeds about which he was reading were terrible: kidnapping, two counts of false imprisonment, and other similar crimes. I was ashamed of my past, but all these things were a part of who I had been, so I had to own up to them.

The prosecutor spoke for long minutes on end, detailing exactly what had occurred. He did so in an effort to show that I was a dangerous man, deserving a lengthy sentence. Only after about ten minutes of reading, he was interrupted by the judge.

"Sir, please pause for a moment. It appears as if we have some technical problems. I cannot see Mister Ignat's entire file. Essentially, several pages of the file seem to be missing, and I cannot follow the discussion on my computer. Does the system appear to be working on your laptop?"

"Yes, Your Honor," affirmed the prosecuting attorney, "everything seems to be in order."

"And on yours?" inquired the judge, addressing my lawyer.

"And on mine as well, Your Honor," was the reply.

"In that case, we shall have to take a short break to check what happened to my computer," declared the judge.

Everyone agreed to his proposition. The judge picked up the telephone that was at his elbow and called someone, probably an IT specialist of the court; after speaking about two minutes, he hung up, picked up the laptop, and left the courtroom, telling us the break would be extended. I was puzzled, not knowing what was going on. I looked at my lawyer, but he only shrugged and signaled for me to remain seated and to see what would happen. I trusted God and knew that He was working, but I did not know exactly what He was up to.

The judge returned about thirty minutes later, visibly happy; he even smiled as he took his seat.

He connected his laptop to the cable and pushed a button, after which he picked up his microphone and said, "Mister Prosecutor, we may resume. The problem has been resolved. Please start at the beginning of the charges."

The prosecuting attorney again began reading the charges. The entire courtroom was all eyes and ears.

I looked upward and asked God, "Lord, what is Your plan?"

I received no answer at the moment. The proceedings continued. Even so, I felt at peace.

After another ten minutes in which only the prosecutor was heard, the judge again stopped him. The entire courtroom was stunned. It was as silent as a funeral. Everyone wanted to hear what the judge would say.

"Mister Prosecutor, please cease reading."

The judge again called a recess, during which time we all stared at each other in silence. He was pushing buttons on his laptop, and no one knew what he was doing or why he had called another break.

After a moment, he looked up at the courtroom and announced, "I am very sorry, but I no longer have access to the file. I believe there are some problems with the network. A half-hour ago, I could see some of Mister Ignat's file, but now the entire folder has vanished from my screen. I can see nothing at all."

At that moment, my lawyer, who was sitting facing the judge with his back toward me, turned and looked at me strangely. He looked shocked by the incident. He told me later that he had looked at me, thinking that perhaps I had done something to the network. He knew that Romanians are skilled hackers and thought that perhaps I had orchestrated a hack. I laughed loud and long when he told me what he had been thinking.

The judge wanted the proceedings to continue even if he could not see my folder. He said that he had had enough time that morning to look over the information in my file.

However, the prosecuting attorney disputed that, saying, "Mister Ignat has a right to a fair trial, Your Honor, in which you have access to his file. There are many details contained in it that may influence your decision. Therefore, we asked that the sentencing be postponed until the network problems are resolved."

I could not believe my ears. The *prosecuting attorney* was coming to my defense? The prosecutor is the one that accuses you, trying to get you locked up whatever the price, or at least, that was what I learned from my experiences in Romania. But, after this occurrence, I realized there is a great difference between how the justice system in England works as opposed to that of Romania.

In Romania, the defense attorney entered by the same door as the spectators, while the prosecutor and the judge used a separate door, sometimes joking and laughing with each other as they entered the courtroom. The prosecutor then took his seat on the same level as the judge, while the defense attorney's seat was on the level of the spectators. In England, on the other hand, both the prosecution and the defense entered by the same door and sat on the same level. When I discovered that, I felt better about my opportunity to a fair trial.

My lawyer then stood, supporting the prosecutor's request. Therefore, the judge had no recourse but to reschedule the sentencing. My lawyer sensed a great opportunity to not only postpone the trial but, more importantly, to get a more favorable judge to hear my case. After consulting his calendar, the judge gave several dates in the following days in which he would be available to hear my case. My lawyer immediately refused those days on the grounds that he had other obligations.

The judge did not give up and made me the following offer: "Mister Ignat, seeing that your attorney is busy on the dates when I can be here, I will give you the chance to be defended by a lawyer that the Court will provide. You must only say the word."

I couldn't believe my ears. Here was our chance to ask for a date when I could be sentenced by someone else, but this man really wanted to have the opportunity to sentence me. He even offered me the possibility of changing lawyers just so he could be the one to give sentence. I don't know why he was so persistent, but when I turned down his offer, he was obliged to hand my case off to one of his colleagues, who would preside over my sentencing in about three weeks.

In fact, the moment the judge's computer, for no apparent reason, had stopped functioning properly, my lawyer had seen the opportunity to reschedule in order to obtain a judge with a better reputation. That morning, I had prayed that God would soften the heart of this judge who was known for the harsh sentences that he handed down. Besides, I believed with all my heart that the Lord would do as He had promised and that I would see His hand in the proceedings, but I had not known how.

"I am sorry," the judge went on, "but I will have to pass your case to a colleague of mine; your sentencing is to be held on January 9. And now, sir guard, please take the prisoner to his cell. The court is adjourned."

I breathed a sigh of relief, knowing that I would get another judge. It was one battle won. Immediately, a guard, a mountain of a man that stood nearly a head taller than I, came and handcuffed me. It had been he that brought me from my cell to the courtroom, so it was also his duty to escort me back.

I left the courtroom handcuffed and chained to the guard. While we walked the long hall that led to the stairway that would take us downstairs, I thought about what had just happened. I knew that God, in His goodness, had worked a miracle in making my file vanish from the judge's computer, making way for me to be judged by another man. But there remained several question marks in my mind. I wondered if the network had a history of crashing, making such things happen from time to time. I realized that, if I wanted to know, there was no one better to ask than the guard who was escorting me.

"Excuse me, sir, may I ask you a question?"

"Certainly!" he replied pleasantly. "Go right ahead."

"Today, you were with me in the courtroom, and you saw all that happened," I continued. "I would like to ask you about the network here in the courthouse: how many times per week or per month does the network here have problems? How many times does the judge's laptop act up? Once a week? Twice a week? About how often? I am curious to know what the chances were that the network would crash during my sentencing."

The guard stopped and turned toward me. "Sir," he said, "in the six years that I have worked here, I have never seen the network crash until today. It was the first time I have witnessed anything of the sort."

I was surprised. I knew that it hadn't been pure luck, but the guard's response confirmed that it was completely the hand of God at work. I could do nothing but praise the Lord.

Soon I was taken to the prisoner transport vehicle for the ride back to Scrubs. Looking through the windows on the way back to prison, I marveled at what had happened. I thought of the way the day had started: I was in panic and struggling to block the lies that the devil was putting in my mind. But what a day! What a wonderful day! What victory I had had! I felt as if I was floating in air. When one sees with his own eyes God fulfilling His promises, it leaves him with a feeling that is difficult to describe with mere words. But even so, the battles that I faced inside were far from over.

Back at the prison, I again began normal activities. Mirel was much more relaxed now that his trial was passed. Now he tried to encourage me. We prayed and sang together every day, and I read a lot. At the encouragement of brother Tony Anthony on one of his visits, I began to write.

There were still three weeks until my next court appearance, but before my next court date on January 9, Christmas and New

Year, the winter holidays, had to pass. I was incarcerated on the top floor of the prison and could see all the buildings in the vicinity and the people preparing for the holidays. London was all abuzz. From my vantage point, every day, I could see parents walking with their children. At those moments, I would miss my own children indescribably.

I could not bear to think of my own kids as I watched the children in the vicinity run and play. How I longed to arrive at home and be with them. In fact, one thought that the evil one brought to my mind in those times of panic was that I would never see my children again. It was not at all easy, but in the period between my two court appearances, I began to understand that these thoughts were only lies brought by the evil one, so the attacks began having less and less effect on me. I fought each lie that came to my mind with the miracle that God had done in the courtroom. Therefore, for a time, the enemy no longer had the strength to get me down.

The Final Sentence

The three weeks finally passed. I was again in the basement of the courthouse, waiting impatiently for my lawyer. A guard opened the door, saying that he had arrived. I came out of the cell, very much wanting to hear what he had to say.

"Hello..."

"Hi, George," he said. "Today is the big day! Are you ready?"

"I am! I have prayed a lot for this day. It will go well; mark my words."

"We hope. You have another judge. This one is a senior judge with the highest possible grade that a judge from Crown Court can have. He is known for his propriety; just as the other judge was known for his harsh sentences, this one is known for his justice. He handles everything very correctly."

"Praise the Lord!" I exclaimed. "I know he is exactly the man that the Lord chose for my case."

"With that being said," my lawyer continued, "Let us not get ahead of ourselves. Your two accomplices got eight and ten years, respectively, so you should be expecting a similar sentence."

"I am glad to hear that you changed your opinion and lowered your estimate," I replied. "That is the amount of time that I am expecting."

"My expectations changed with the judge," he explained. "Under the other judge, you had every chance of getting more than ten years, but with this one, I think it will be less than ten. I see things as they are; I am a realist. You had some incredible luck at your last court appearance. Really unbelievable luck!"

"I would replace 'luck' with 'the hand of God,'" I replied. "That is what I think happened."

"Every man sees things differently," he shrugged. "What is certain is that you escaped a man that could have ruined you."

"Praise the Lord!" I exclaimed again.

"Fine," he interjected. "Now that I've said my piece, let's go up to the courtroom."

In less than ten minutes, I was again in the courtroom in the same enclosure in which I had been three weeks before. Everything was the same except that this time there was a different man on the bench, a senior judge. Even the clothes he wore were different. He was an older man with a kind disposition. He looked at me and asked my name and, having identified me, began the proceedings, asking the prosecutor to say his piece.

When the prosecutor was finished, it was my lawyer's turn. When he had finished, the judge began to speak. No one was expecting the words that came from his mouth.

"Ladies and gentlemen, it is time to come to a decision for Mister Ignat. I have looked over his file very carefully and would like to point out a few things. It appears that I have before me two persons, one who has done some unfortunate things in

2007, and another one that has come to pay for the deeds committed by the first. I have before me two persons, but with the same name: Mister Ignat. The man that stands before me today is a different man than the one from 2007, of whom the file speaks. The person here today is a changed man. I would prefer to sentence the Mister Ignat that is before us today rather than the one spoken of in the documents.

"In addition, I would like to point out that one of the letters I received relating to this case was noteworthy for its sincerity. I refer to a letter written by your wife, by Mrs. Ignat."

The judge then turned toward the area where my family was seated—to Adriana.

"Mrs. Ignat, I would like to thank you that, together with your children, you made the effort to travel from Romania to England to support your husband. This shows the unity of your family."

Adriana nodded, shocked by the judge's words. His comments surprised everyone in the courtroom. The letter to which he referred was nothing more than a few lines written by my wife addressed to the judge at the suggestion of my lawyer. There were numerous people and organizations that had written letters of recommendation to the judge that had arrived at his desk by way of my attorney. Among these were the church where I was a member, a sports club to which I had belonged, and two federations that specified that I was a part of the Romanian national team. In all, there were over thirty letters of recommendation in my file, but the judge was impressed by the sincerity expressed in my wife's writing. I had no idea what Adriana had written, but I was eager to find out. I later discovered that in those few lines, Adriana had not asked the judge for clemency; rather, she had simply presented her viewpoint. She candidly told the judge what was on her heart; she said that I am now a good husband and father and that she was tired of all that she and the children had to suffer because of the foolish things I had done when I was younger. She was sick of walking through prison halls—both in Romania and the UK—for so many years with children in her arms. She wrote that, from her point of view, I was no longer a menace to society but rather could be an asset. The judge appreciated the sincerity that bled from Adriana's words.

After the judge had made these comments, a deathly hush fell over the courtroom; everyone was waiting with bated breath for the judge's next words.

After making his decision, the judge looked at me and said, "Mr. Ignat, after meticulously studying your case, I have decided to sentence you to five years in prison, with credit for time already served. You may serve your sentence here in Great Britain, or if you wish, you can be transferred to a prison in Romania."

There was a moment of silence, after which a hum was heard in the courtroom as everyone began whispering to each other. Everyone present was amazed, I most of all. I was shocked nearly out of my senses. That was the absolute minimum I could be given, and with my colleagues having received twice that, I could hardly believe my ears. My family was in ecstasy. I looked at my mother; she had tears in her eyes. I knew that she had prayed for me so much and had suffered tremendously because of my wild ways. Now she was happy, knowing that she would soon see me at home with my wife and kids. Adriana, my brother, Nicu, my father—all of them were euphoric, but in several minutes the judge asked for silence.

In England, a judge has the liberty to reduce a sentence by thirty-three percent, at his discretion, based on the defendant's behavior during the trial.

"Mister Ignat, that is not all! Because you told the truth, I will further reduce, by thirty-three percent, your sentence of five years, which comes to three years and four months, or forty months. In England, you must serve only half of your sentence before being eligible for parole, so that comes to twenty months. I will now adjourn the court. Sir guard, please take Mister Ignat to his cell. Thank you all!"

The guard rose and handcuffed me. I said good-bye to my family, who was as dumbfounded as I was. I did not know if I was living in reality or not. I couldn't believe it; it was impossible! I was expecting something in the eight to ten-year range; my lawyer had told me that it was quite possible I would get even more than that, but the judge had cut thirty-three percent off of five years. Needing to serve half of that, I had twenty months, of which I had already served five, leaving me with only fifteen months of prison time remaining! Could this be real?

I often searched the Bible for a text that could describe how I felt then. I found Psalm 126, which says,

When the Lord brought back the captivity of Zion,
We were like those who dream.
Then our mouth was filled with laughter,

And our tongue with singing.
Then they said among the nations,
"The Lord has done great things for them."
The Lord has done great things for us,
And we are glad.
Psalm 126:1–3 (NKJV)

This was exactly the way I felt.

Arriving in the courtroom basement, I stood for a moment, trying to grasp what had happened. Everything had happened so fast; I did not know where to start. After several seconds, the judge's words reverberated through my mind: "...because you told the truth...because you told the truth...." Instantly, I remembered the words of God when I was arrested in Suceava: "George, if you will tell the truth, I will be with you, and you will see My hand at work." I burst into tears. This was it! God had kept His word! I dropped to my knees to thank Him.

After a short wait, I was taken to a van for transport back to prison. I sang to God the entire trip, not because He needed my song, nor because I am a good singer, but because He had been so good to me, I could not help but sing.

At the gate at Scrubs, after getting out of the van, I was taken to the guard that verified the documents of those coming from their hearings.

He called me aside and asked, "What happened at the court? Did someone make a mistake?"

"I don't think so. Why do you ask?"

"Because I see here a sentence of three years and four months for crimes that should carry a much longer sentence, over ten years."

"I know," I grinned. "God was very good to me! There is no mistake."

The guard shook his head in amazement, asked me to sign at several places, and sent me for my physical, which is mandatory for all inmates who receive a sentence longer than three years.

At the medical office, the doctor inquired, "How do you feel with the sentence you just received?"

"I'm great!" I replied.

"Here, take this pill," he instructed. "It will help calm you down."

I took the pill in my hand and threw it away as soon as I left his office. Arriving at my room, I found Mirel who was eagerly waiting to find out how long my sentence would be. When I told him, he was astounded and then praised the Lord with me.

More Good News

The goodness of God toward me did not end on the day of the sentencing. Several days later, I went to the gym of Scrubs prison, where I exercised with two colleagues. The gym was a place where every prisoner would have loved to work. I did not yet hope to get a job there, but I went every week for my workout, and sometimes twice if the guard was feeling kind.

I was working out when I heard the guard call my name, and I went to see what he wanted. He informed me that an agent from the Home Office had come to Scrubs to speak especially to me. I told my buddies that I would be back shortly and left for the office. Upon entering, I met a man that was dressed differently than any of the prison guards.

"Hello, Mr. Ignat!" he greeted me.

"Hello!"

"I am Agent B from immigration and have come to discuss your situation."

"That's fine," I replied, a bit uncertainly.

"You have committed some rather serious crimes in Great Britain," he went on.

"I know," I winced. "They were shameful actions."

"Yes," he replied, "but in spite of the seriousness of your deeds, you got a pretty easy sentence, I would say. Anyway, that isn't my problem."

"Yes, I did," I responded with a smile.

I saw on the agent's face that he was a bit annoyed at my easy sentence, but he resumed. "I want to be as brief as possible. You will be released in several months. You have fifteen months more to serve, I believe."

"Yes, sir!"

"We cannot release you on British soil because of the seriousness of your crimes," he went on. "Therefore, we will have to deport you to your home country, to Romania."

"But you know, sir," I asserted, "I am no longer a threat to anyone. I have repented."

"You did what?"

"I have become a Christian. God has changed my life. I am a different man, one whose life is guided by the teachings of my Savior, Jesus Christ."

"I see," he replied, "but immigration really doesn't care about religion. I look only at what is in your file."

"I understand," I returned.

"I must tell you that you can challenge our decision in court. You may ask a judge to reverse our decision to deport you and to stay in Great Britain, but you would have a very small chance of winning your case. In addition, another court case would mean time and money for both of us, so we have an offer that we hope you are willing to accept."

"And that is...?"

"Well," he continued, "if you will sign a document saying that you agree to be deported, and in the same document you promise not to set foot in British territory for a period of ten years, we are willing to cut an additional nine months off of the fifteen that you have left to serve. This means that, in only six months from now, we would send you to Romania, a free man."

I tried not to act stunned or to look happier than necessary.

"Who is saying this? What document do I have to sign?"

"The one I have in my hand."

I reached out, took the document from the agent, and began reading. Indeed, the institution called the Home Office did have the authority to cut nine months off the final sentence of any inmate that was willing to sign the agreement. I smiled.

The agent also smiled. "Come on, Mister Ignat, at the end of the day, you have nothing holding you here in England. Your children and your family are all in Romania, and nine months is a fair amount of time to have cut from a sentence. What do you say?"

Before the agent could say any more, I signed that document and another two that needed my signature. The first thought that came to my mind was that I must thank God. His goodness was so great, and it seemed that His miracles on my behalf were unending.

Although it seemed that liberty was just around the corner, some of my greatest struggles had not yet begun. I believe that God allows the worst struggles only to those soldiers of His whom He wants to strengthen and perfect.

Now that I was to be released much earlier than anticipated, there remained only two things to do. The first was to concentrate on spreading the Gospel so much the more and faster among my fellow inmates, and the second was to try to land a job at the prison gym.

The head of the section where I was incarcerated was none too fond of me since I had refused to cooperate with him and his "peace-keeping" crews. Now that I had been sentenced, I expected him to approach me again with his offer, as he had promised, and indeed, so he did. I, of course, refused the position politely, but, in speaking with him, I made the mistake of commenting that I would like a job at the gym. I said I made a mistake because afterward, I saw how he did everything in his power to keep me from getting any such job.

One day, in the hall, I met one of the inmates that controlled what happened in the prison. He was a large specimen, originally from Greece, imprisoned for money laundering. He was a gangster in every sense of the word, from a well-known family of mobsters in Great Britain.

"Good morning, big guy!" he greeted me.

"Good morning!"

"Where are you hurrying off to?" he inquired.

"To a Bible study," I replied. "I must be there in ten minutes."

"A Bible study, you say. Interesting! An MMA fighter turned kidnapper lands in prison then starts frequenting Bible studies. Very interesting!"

I looked at the huge man, wondering what he wanted with me. I didn't think he wanted a row, but I did have to be ready to defend myself. When I was first imprisoned, I had asked God to keep me from any situation in which I would have to defend myself. I knew I was to turn the other cheek as many times as someone wanted to hit me. Still, I had prayed, saying, "God, keep me out of those sorts of situations. I don't know if I am strong enough to turn the other cheek every time."

I must say that although there had been situations in which a fist had been held in my face or when I had been cursed, God had not allowed more than I could bear. In all my time in the prisons of both Romania and England, I never had to lift a finger in my own defense.

"Yes," I replied, "I study Scripture with some guys and the prison chaplain. We'd be happy to have you come too."

He grinned. "I watched some of your fights yesterday. I read about you on the internet, and you seem to be a good guy. I saw you have a family; you have kids. Tell me, how can I be of assistance to you?"

"Uh, what do you mean?" I stammered.

"Tell me how I can help you. Would you like some KFC? McDonald's?"

It was my turn to smile. I understood that he had all kinds of connections and could probably get anything he wanted into the prison.

"I would love to go to the gym more often," I replied. "I've been here several months and go once a week. You think it would be hard to get me a job at the gym?"

"I don't know what to say," he replied thoughtfully. "I'll see if I can put in a good word for you at the right places."

He gripped my hand and wished me well, and then, we each started on our own ways. After a few steps, he called after me.

"Hey, big guy!"

"Yes, what is it?"

"Pray for me too when you get to the chapel," he requested.

"Absolutely!"

"We'll be in contact!" And he was off.

I had heard rumors that outside the prison, this guy controlled millions of pounds sterling, and inside the prison, he seemed to be some sort of administrator. No more than forty-eight hours passed from the moment I told him that I would like a job at the gym until my first day of work, in spite of some of the obstacles caused by the head of the section, who wanted me to remain nothing more than an ordinary inmate.

After nearly three months in which I sat in my cell for twenty-three hours a day, I could finally go to work. I had a schedule that allowed me to be in the gym for eight hours a day.

Horror at Scrubs

I was doing well. I worked at the gym and was beginning to work out regularly. With time, I moved to another, more peaceful section of the prison. There, beatings and stabbings did not occur daily, but, at most, twice a week. I met and spoke with Romanians from all sections of the prison. Time was passing rapidly.

I had nearly forgotten about the attacks. The last one had taken place more than a month before, on the morning of my sentencing, when the judge's computer malfunctioned. I had been fine since then, but still, there lingered a sort of expectation in the back of my mind. When one has once experienced those kinds of attacks, his guard is never fully let down since he never knows when it may happen again. So it happened with me.

That which I feared finally came upon me again. I was again attacked with those horrible thoughts after an inmate told me in great detail how he had been wrongly convicted and incarcerated for a crime committed by his cousin. If I had known what was coming, I would not have listened, not for a minute, to his tale; but after the guard had locked me in my cell, I was hit, out of nowhere, with the thought that I, too, would wrongly be convicted of something, just like that other inmate had been. *Oh, no, not again!* my mind screamed.

A moment later, I was nearly swept off my feet with that familiar sense of petrifying fear. And so began again a fierce battle in the mind. The story I just heard was similar to the documentary I had watched several months before about the man wrongly convicted, and the effect on me was the same.

Several terrible days passed. I could not recover from that state of panic. The only thing that could occupy my mind was the possibility that one day soon, I would be wrongfully charged with who-knows-what and rot in prison for many years.

Just as several months before, the enemy had attacked me with the certainty that I would receive a long sentence at my trial; now that the sentencing was passed, he began attacking me with other things that took my peace.

My mind was being attacked repeatedly, and each time when there was a lull in the battle, I could see that the thoughts in my mind were nothing more than lies from the devil. Even so, every time the attack was renewed, I was certain that this time, my fears would be realized.

About four days after I had again begun wrestling with these lies, my parents and brother came to visit. My mother took one look at me and told me that I had dark circles under my eyes. She asked if something had happened to me and whether I was sleeping at night, to which I smiled and said that I was fine, that I was sleeping and eating well. But that was not at all the case.

They would have suffered too much, knowing what I was going through. While my mother took my word for it, my brother, having seen me in this condition at Wandsworth, knew that something was definitely wrong.

For several nights in a row, I could barely sleep. I woke up nearly every hour, shaking with fear. When I would think of the man that had been imprisoned unjustly, I would break into a cold sweat. Plagued with such thoughts, I lost my appetite and soon developed a stinging sensation on the right side of my abdomen. I thought it must be my liver. With little rest, poor nutrition, and the stress and exhaustion of fighting my battles of the mind, my body was showing the effects.

One day I decided to call a dear brother from London and tell him that I had lost the peace in my heart. Hearing that, he told me that something was wrong and that I might be doing something to allow the devil to make those attacks. It began a pattern. When I would tell a brother, a Christian, about my condition, I nearly always received the same response: "Somewhere, there is a problem of hidden sin. You must investigate, find out what it is, and stop sinning." But that was not the case. I sought God with all my heart, trying to find out why I had upset Him. But, looking back, I understand that sin need not be present in order for the devil to attack the mind. From the moment one gives his life to the Lord, he is a danger to the devil by what he says and does. Therefore, the devil will do everything in his power to bring him down. Peace and joy are fruits of the Holy Spirit, so I kept wondering, *What is wrong with me? Why have I lost these fruits of the Spirit?*

While I was suffering from this situation, I was visited by an evangelist, who had, himself, spent some time in prison. I told him that I was not feeling well, but I was too ashamed to tell him all the thoughts that were coming to my mind, so I only told him snippets of my experiences. We prayed together, and he encouraged me with some verses from the Bible. As he was leaving, he told me that the secret to victory over these assaults lies in the power of prayer. He winked and smiled, communicating to me that he, too, had faced these sorts of battles at one time.

While this brother's visit had helped me a lot, I was also helped by the Greek that had put in a good word for me in order to get the job at the gym. He took time to talk to me, even though he had no idea of what I was going through. He probably saw that I needed some encouragement, so whenever I went to the gym, he would make it a point to spend some time talking. Later, I found out that he had spoken to the other guys at the gym to take care of me and, if the need arose, to help me. Though his attitude surprised me, I thanked the Lord for this Greek. In this fight against an unknown and unseen adversary, the only thing I knew was that God is the only One that can give me light and the strength to fight.

I soon asked to be transferred from Scrubs. Though everything was going well, the attacks, as they often do to men that face them, left me feeling unsafe and vulnerable, and I insisted on being transferred. I thought perhaps I would feel safe in another prison. I didn't know that, by my move, the devil was preparing an even bigger trap.

After several days, I found out that I was to be moved to HM Prison Huntercombe. I heard that this place was in a forest, a quiet spot. Being surrounded by green trees and silence, with a gym with a flexible schedule, I figured it was exactly what I needed.

Part 4

Huntercombe Prison, United Kingdom

Your Name is...Idiot?

Arriving at Huntercombe, I was taken to reception, where I and my belongings were searched. There I met a guard who seemed to take an instant dislike to me.

Immediately upon seeing me, he said, "Hello, and welcome to Huntercombe!"

"Thank you!" I replied.

"I looked through your documents and saw your name starts with the letter "i," he continued.

"Yes, that's correct. My name is Ignat."

"Oh, I thought it was 'Idiot' since that starts with 'i.'" He and his colleagues burst out laughing.

As I was seeing them making fun of me, my knee-jerk reaction was to respond in kind, but, being a Christian, I simply let it go, smiled, and, taking my belongings, started toward my cell.

I was passing through a difficult time—my mental battles still plaguing me—and, having arrived here, I only wanted peace and rest. I felt that the war was wearing me down, and I was finding nothing with which to defend myself.

I was put in a cell with a pickpocket, a Romanian from Botoșani. Huntercombe was a prison especially for immigrants, so I met many Romanians there, along with a lot of people from all over the world. After having been caught, my cellmate spent some time in prison and now was soon to be deported and sent to a prison in Romania. I started talking to him about God; that always seemed to give me the strength to go forward. As I said before, the attacks were driving a wedge between me and God. When under attack, I could think of nothing but the pressure in my head and negative thoughts with which I was bombarded, so I learned that when I could concentrate, I had to use every minute to tell other inmates about God, the Bible, Jesus, and the new life that faith in Him would bring.

I remember one day in particular when I was pacing the halls of the prison, fighting my battle. Suddenly, as I was trying to pray, I began feeling better. In fact, I felt elation, an extraordinary freedom, as if a great deal of weight had been lifted from my shoulders. I cannot describe the sense of liberation when, in the intensity of those feelings, the heat of the attack suddenly faded. Even so, I knew that the new feeling would not last long, so I went directly to a Polish comrade to whom I owed an explanation.

Several days before, I had been talking with this particular man about the Bible when suddenly, in the middle of the discussion, I was seized by panic. Instantly, I was in no state to continue the discussion, so I fled, leaving the discussion hanging. Now, feeling better and seeing him out walking the halls as well, I went directly to him and started the discussion again. I spoke about Jesus' sacrifice on the cross through which all men can be saved. I told him that God loved us so much that He sent His own Son to die. It was one of the most uplifting moments of my life. Having experienced the emotional back and forth, it was not surprising when a few minutes later, fear gripped me once again, I was again clutched in the talons of that familiar sense of panic, and I had nothing left in my mind but those terrifying thoughts.

The next day, an older guard came to me and asked what sport I had practiced before my incarceration. When I had told him, he said I should get in contact with the guards at the gym and see if they didn't have a job for me there. He gave me the name of the guard in charge and wished me luck.

One of my friends from that section of the prison was a trainer in the prison gym, and I asked him to put in a good word for me. He spoke with the head guard, who then called me to the gym one evening, where we spent some time talking. I asked if he could give me a job at the gym, and he said that he would see what could be done and would let me know. After about three days, another guard at the gym told me that I could work there part-time; the other part of the day, I would take a hygiene course, which was necessary in order to get a full-time job there.

I accepted the offer and began my work. After only several days, Huntercombe prison seemed like heaven on earth. For the first time in weeks, I slept well at night. I felt much better and began to hope that everything would return to normal. All the guards, as well as my fellow inmates, were good guys. It seemed I had found a place where I could grow stronger, both physically and psychologically, until my release.

Preaching in the Prison Church

The first Sunday at Huntercombe, I went to the Pentecostal church service and stayed for the Anglican service, which was immediately following. I enjoyed them both, but I particularly liked the Pentecostal pastor, a black man originally from Jamaica who had an extraordinary zeal for preaching the Word of God.

About a week later, I met him again in the halls of the prison and exchanged a few words. At the end of our dialogue, as he was leaving, he asked me if I would like to give a short message at church the following Sunday. I accepted and prepared for the assignment.

Sunday came, and the pastor announced that one of the inmates would speak, after which he invited me to the front, and I spoke for about fifteen minutes. Those few minutes were full of the grace of God, as I had an extraordinary anointing of the Holy Spirit. I shared some of my testimony, as well as speaking from the Word of God. I asked my fellow inmates to forgive each other—or anyone that wrongs them—and all that were present were challenged.

The guard that had met me when I came to Huntercombe, the one that called me "Idiot," was there that day, and after I spoke, he came to me. He cordially grasped my hand, saying, "Congratulations! You speak like a true preacher. I was impressed with your courage in sharing some of your weaknesses. That kind of thing, especially in a place such as this, puts you in a bad light and can make you look weak. I see that that does not bother you."

"I believe that if you love people, you won't think about whether what you say puts you in a bad light or not," I responded. "The only thing that matters is that your message reaches the hearts of the hearers. Jesus Christ gave up all the glory that came with being God's Son in order to be slapped, spit on, made fun of, and, ultimately, to be crucified. He suffered Calvary out of love for me, for you, and for the whole world."

"Hmm." He pursed his lips. "I am no Christian, but I did like what I heard today."

"Thank you for the encouragement," I said as he left.

I was so happy, seeing God's hand at work! This man that had run me down several weeks before, calling me "idiot," now shook my hand with respect. Who, outside of God, can change men in such a manner?

The pastor and his wife shook my hand, saying that they as well had been encouraged. I could do nothing but give praise to God!

Each day, I went to my cleaning class in the morning and to the gym in the afternoon. My job was to clean the gym, and after I had finished, I could do all the exercise that I wanted. What more could I wish for?

After all I had gone through in the last months, with court cases and battles of the mind, I was now entering a time of renewal and rejuvenation. With only five more months to serve, I thought it wise to exercise hard so that I would be in top physical shape when I arrived at home; and being now in good shape psychologically, I began to see life in a new light. I began making plans for how I would serve God after my release, as well as plans for my family and my athletic career. Everything was going well, and I thanked God for it, but I had no idea what lay ahead.

Thrust on a Team of Stoics

One afternoon, one of the gym guards, whom I will call B, stopped me. "Hey, I saw and read about you on the internet. Congratulations on your athletic record!"

"Thank you!" I returned. "I think I could have gotten an even better record if I had chosen my friends more wisely."

"Don't worry about it, George! We all make mistakes; some get caught, some not."

He winked at me. I was surprised by that remark, though I had heard it many years before in Romania, from the mouth of a law enforcement officer.

"So it is!" I replied. "But I did want to thank you for accepting my application to work here in the gym. It means a lot to me because I would like to get involved in sports again, and training while I'm here sure helps."

"Don't mention it," he responded. "We are here to help. Come into my office for a moment please, so we can talk. I have a proposal to make."

I entered the office of the guards responsible for the gym, where I found two more guards and about four inmates. I had seen the inmates there often; they seemed to hang out in that office.

"This is George, from Romania. He was a professional athlete and will now be our colleague for a few months," began B.

I very briefly got to know the others that were present before turning my attention back to B as he continued speaking.

"Brothers, we are guards, and you are inmates, but that need not put a barrier between us. We should act together as comrades. And now I would like to receive George into our program."

I looked from one to another. This guard kept mentioning a "program" but failed to explain what he was talking about.

I was curious. "Please excuse me, Mister B. What program are you talking about?"

"George, in short, we have a program in which we teach the inmates some positive attitudes, inspired by ancient philosophies. These philosophies have much to teach us, such as how to be better people, more understanding individuals, and so on. Through it, we can teach the inmates to be better, wiser, and more productive members of society, but this can happen only if they come in contact with the teachings of the stoics, which we promote. Otherwise, they will have a difficult time returning to society as good people."

"I understand!" I exclaimed. "That seems as if it could be a real help to the inmates. I promote Christian values because God has changed my life!"

"Exactly!" he replied. "Christian values are very similar to those of the stoics. You see, we already have something in common. Stoic values have changed the lives of these four inmates that you see here. They can attest to it, can't you, Rick?"

"Yes, sir, stoicism has changed my life," replied a black inmate, though the expression on his face caused me to doubt his words.

"See, George, Rick was a violent, arrogant man, but since he came to Huntercombe and learned the stoic philosophy, he is a different man. The effect on people is really extraordinary!"

"Wow!" I exclaimed again. "I am really surprised! If this teaching can change lives, then praise the Lord!"

"Yes, they should be grateful to the head guard here," continued B. "He is the most highly educated among us in this philosophy. He started the program here and initiated us in stoicism."

"I understand," I said. "But what is it that you want me to do."

When I asked the question, Mister B looked at his two colleagues, then turned to me and said, "George, we want you to work with us. We need people that will go throughout the prison and talk to the inmates, introducing them to the stoic way of life. But we cannot send just anyone. You are charismatic and well-built, commanding respect. You are a perfect fit for being a disciple of the head guard."

"I don't know what to say, Mister B," I stammered. "Let me think about it and come back to you with a response. I don't think I am very well suited for this job."

I said what I did because there was something inside of me that was not at peace; warning bells were going off in my head.

"Ehh, forget the modesty," he replied. "You are a perfect fit. You know how to talk to people; I heard what happened last Sunday at church. You spoke very well. So, welcome to the team. At the beginning, Rick will be your guide. For the first few days, you will go with him from one section to another, meeting different groups of inmates. In a few weeks, you will be a bona fide stoic."

Though I had not given the guard a response one way or another, I was thrust onto the team of stoics.

Arriving back at my cell, I laid down in bed and thought about the guard's proposition. It had taken me completely by surprise. I decided I would try it since, according to the guard, stoicism and Christianity had a lot in common.

What do I have to lose by helping them? I thought. I reasoned that I had nothing to lose and quite a bit to gain. In the first place, I figured that, in addition to stoic teaching, I could tell those with whom I spoke what the Bible says about being a better person, such as loving your neighbor. Furthermore, working with them, I would have much more freedom to move throughout the entire prison.

And so it was settled. Things had been going well: I felt good, slept well at night, and spoke with my wife and kids daily. From all points of view, I was in good shape. In fact, I had nearly succeeded in teaching my cellmate, the pickpocket from Botoșani, the Lord's prayer. Though illiterate, he did have a good memory, so we repeated the prayer about ten times every evening.

A Christian Colleage

There were a number of Romanians in the section in which I was incarcerated, some imprisoned for petty crimes such as theft or other misdemeanors, and others for more serious crimes such as bank robbery or burglary of jewelry stores. All had sentences to serve relative to their crimes.

One day I tried to befriend a young man whom I found interesting because, among other things, I had seen a number of icons of the Orthodox church and some prayer books in his room. Seeing these things, I naturally wanted to talk with him.

In speaking with him, the fact that he was very religious was confirmed. He showed me his collection of icons and other things of an ecclesiastical nature that he had brought and told me how difficult it was to get them into the prison since some of the guards wanted to confiscate them. His tale surprised me, and I told him that we had much to discuss when we had the time. I asked if he would want to pray together, to which he replied that he would consider it.

Encouraged by the thought that this young man had a heart turned toward God, I was impatient to visit him again. Some time later, I did just that.

When I arrived at his cell, he was sitting on his bed watching a soccer game. Beside him on the bed, I saw several DVDs with explicit sexual content. As soon as he saw me looking at them, he picked up two of them and handed them to me.

"Thank you," I responded, "but I am not interested in that kind of thing."

"What?" he responded. "Every inmate is interested in that kind of thing. Come on, don't be bashful. Just have them back to me by tomorrow afternoon so I can return them to the one that lent them to me."

"Let me tell you the facts," I said. "I had a terrible problem with pornography when I was young. I was caught in that trap and spent a lot of time watching that trash. After I was born again, I still fought strong temptations to get back into that stuff. It was only after much weeping before God and earnest prayer that I was freed from that sin."

"Sin?" My friend seemed honestly surprised. "What do you mean by being 'freed from sin'? And why would you want to be freed from something that is so pleasant? I don't know exactly how to put it, but I think it helps me. I've been locked up for a number of years, and it's been a refuge for me."

"Look," I said, "you say that you are a true Christian, and I am not necessarily questioning that, but let's see what the Bible says about this sin."

"Sure!"

"Okay," I continued, "the Bible tells us to put to death what is earthly in us, such as sexual immorality, impurity, passion, evil desire, and covetousness, and elsewhere, the Lord Jesus says that whoever looks at a woman in lust has already committed adultery in his heart. Furthermore, the Bible tells us that the works of the flesh are evident, which are sexual immorality, impurity, sensuality, and so on, and it said earlier in the same passage that those that practice such things will not inherit the kingdom of God."

My comrade looked at me, surprised and somewhat ashamed. "Okay, fine, but we are in prison. Maybe in the time that we spend here, such things are permitted, but when I get out, I won't do it anymore."

"Sin is sweet," I replied, "because if it were not sweet, no one would do it. But behind the sweetness that sin offers is a lot of poison. Pornography and sexual appetite can negatively affect a man's life. God put in us a desire for intimate relationships, but that should only be between a man and his wife. If you don't have a wife, you should get married. These are not my words but God's. The Bible, the Word of God, tells us that such things are an abomination before God. Bro, how do you think that the saints represented by your icons look at that kind of thing? Doesn't it seem like two different worlds?"

I left him to watch his soccer game; *Visibly irritated by our discussion,* I thought. I went to the phone and called Brother Puiu; *My spirit needed strengthening,* I thought, so I wanted to talk to someone about the things of God.

About fifteen minutes later, as I was talking on the phone, who should I see but that same young man. He was on his way to another Romanian's cell with those DVDs in his hand. He stopped, looked at me for several seconds, then continued on his way to return them to their owner without having watched them.

Even before I confirmed it with him, I knew that was what he was doing. Furthermore, two days before my release and deportation to Romania, this young man whose sentence was not yet up came to me, embraced me, and told me that since the day he returned those DVDs, he never watched another dirty movie. In addition, he had given up on intermediaries and had begun a personal, direct relationship with Jesus Christ. I was overjoyed by his victory, but even more by the fact that he had, slowly but surely, started a personal relationship with Jesus.

This young man's testimony is mine as well and can be yours. Pornography is a terrible disease, one from which you cannot recover on your own. If you get out of that sin by your own power, you will manage to avoid it for a while, but you will certainly fall into it again.

My friend understood that the power to overcome these kinds of sin comes only from God. Even if the temptation follows you for a long while, on your knees before Jesus, you will overcome.

Stoicism versus Christianity

The time finally came when I finished my hygiene course and could work at the gym full-time, for which I was very thankful. Immediately afterward, Guard B invited me into the office of the boss of the gym guards, the senior guard. I greeted the latter; I was quite happy to meet him since both the guards and the inmates spoke highly of him.

"George," began B, "I have called you here because tomorrow you start working in the gym full-time."

"Yes," continued the senior guard, "we want to ensure that you understand the program here, that your conduct will be exemplary, and that you will be an understanding person. In short, that you will be a stoic."

"Yes," I replied, "I understand the expectations, and I don't believe you will have any problems with me. I am just an inmate that wants to pay for his misdeeds against society and get home to his family. I want nothing more than to be a Christian and leave a good witness. Everything will be fine, just as it was when I worked in the gyms at Scrubs and Wandsworth."

"We have read what our colleagues from the other prisons have written in your file," was the rejoinder. "They had nothing but good things to say about you. For that we are glad, but there is another thing we would like to discuss. We would like you to support the classes that we offer, those teaching stoicism, and to become a part of our team."

"Sure!" I replied. "When can we start?"

"This week, you will go with Rick to Section Patterson. Friday afternoon, you will meet a group of inmates there. I want you to invite more inmates to come."

"I see no problem with that," I said. "Thank you for your belief in me."

I left the office quite satisfied. Life in prison is what you make it. If you cultivate a good relationship with the guards, you have a lot to gain. If your conduct is displeasing—if you are violent or act foolishly in other ways—you only make it hard for yourself. I was happy to know this man, the senior guard, who seemed to be a good guy, always with his head up and a somewhat proud bearing. He was a promoter of stoic philosophy. He did not talk with just anyone and had an attitude of superiority.

The week passed quickly, and Friday arrived. A half-hour before the class was to begin, I went to several Romanian inmates and invited them to participate. Two responded positively, but one of them stopped me.

"You are not inviting me to the stoicism class, are you," he asked.

"Oh, yes, I am!" I responded. "Come for a half-hour and see what it's about. I don't think there's anything wrong with it."

"I have seen," he replied seriously, "that you like to talk to others about God. I see that that subject excites you, and you talk passionately about it. So I ask you: what does this teaching have in common with the Bible?"

I was shocked.

"Well," I stammered, "I don't know exactly. I haven't seen yet what the classes consist of, but I understand that they teach you how to be a good person, to take care of yourself..."

"You had better study this teaching a bit more closely," he warned. "I took half of the course, but when I realized that they wanted to shove things down my throat that I had no interest in, I quit. They don't even have a license to teach the course; what they are doing is illegal. They teach it as they wish... But I had better be quiet; I don't want to make problems for myself."

"Hey," I responded, "no one will force anything down your throat. People will just talk to you; if you want to listen, fine, and if not, that's fine too. And at the end, if you want to quit, you can."

"I quit, but that cost me. They put me in solitary confinement for fifteen days."

"What?"

"Look," he went on quietly, "Most of those that are taking these classes had a problem here in prison. For example, I got into an argument with a guard and was sentenced to thirty days in solitary confinement. After only a few days, a guard came to me and said that I could cut my sentence in half by taking these classes. Of course, I happily agreed to it, but, as I told you, after a short time, I was not comfortable with what they were teaching. When I told them that I did not agree with what they were saying, they warned me that I had better keep coming, at least for a few days, to get my sentence reduced. That made me quit on the spot; that's the kind of person I am."

"You are telling me," I replied incredulously, "that they have come up with this course that is not even approved and are using it to reduce some of the inmates' punishments? I can hardly believe that!"

"Believe it or not, that is exactly what they are doing!"

"I am going to participate," I decided. "I cannot form an opinion until I see with my own eyes what it's about."

"Then I wish you luck."

That discussion caused me to pay careful attention to what was said at the class. I had noticed nothing out of order with the course until then.

Rick came to the section, and we had the first meeting. He told me to listen to him and not get too involved in the discussion. It went well because, at the beginning, it was an open discussion about life. Rick then presented stoicism, from where it came, historical figures, and more of its history. I left the meeting with a much greater understanding of its historical roots, and after a short analysis, decided it would be to my advantage to continue going.

The following Monday, I arrived at the gym to work, where Guard B met me with a smile.

"Good morning, George! How was the course on Friday? I hope you enjoyed it."

"Yes, it was good," I replied. "Rick is an informative type. He gave us a lot of information. It was interesting."

"I heard it was good," he replied. "I'm also told you brought two more Romanians with you. Great job! Keep it up! You have great potential!"

"Sir," I inquired, "could you give me a manual on stoicism, one like I saw that Rick has?"

"Of course! Come with me!"

"I followed him to the office, where he opened a cabinet full of manuals on stoicism. He gave me one and instructed me to take care to return it as soon as I had finished reading it.

The days followed in quick succession, and another Friday arrived. Rick again came and had a discussion with the inmates in Section Patterson. Things did not go as well this time; twice, I was forced to stop Rick and contradict him because he began saying things that were contrary to Christian teaching. Rick gave me a long look, but he said nothing.

After the meeting, he came to me and said, "George, I see you're an intelligent person. You want your time at Huntercombe to go well? Be humble and listen to those that run the place. I will tell no one what happened, but you do yourself no favors by interrupting and contradicting what we are teaching because it will negate our efforts."

"I don't want to upset anyone," I replied, "but I am a Christian, and what you presented is opposed to the teachings of my Saviour, Jesus Christ. There are some limits for Christians who care about what the Bible says."

"Hey, I never said that what we are teaching these people is perfect," he countered. "I am a Muslim, and many of the things they teach disagree with the Koran. Still, we have to be smart and do what they tell us to make our lives a little easier here.

And another thing, George: don't forget that we are foreigners in this country—foreigners and inmates. We can't say or do too much."

"Thank you, Rick," I replied. "I will think about how to act, moving forward."

"Whatever you decide," he warned, "choose wisely."

Now I had to make a decision. For me, being wise meant choosing what God led me to choose and doing what He wanted me to do. I began to pray for His wisdom to make a wise decision. It is more important to be pleasing to God than to men—that was the bottom line.

I began calling some Christian friends, both in Romania and England, asking them what they know about stoicism and if it is okay for a Christian to be promoting its ideals. I received both affirmative and dissenting answers, and some of them told me that I had to pray and listen to my own conscience.

My conscience led me to explore the subject further, so I found some books in the prison library about Marcus Aurelius. Knowing that this Roman emperor was a key figure in historical stoicism, I wanted to take the book and read it, but I could not do so since I did not have a library card. In the end, I asked one of my colleagues to borrow it using his card.

Arriving in my cell, I began reading. I discovered, to my incredulity, that this emperor was one of the greatest persecutors of Christians, having killed more of them than Nero and other infamous emperors! Furthermore, I discovered that he did not believe in the existence of a Creator God but believed that each man is himself a god. I was perplexed, not knowing what to do or how to extricate myself from the situation. A wrong attitude could make me lose the job that meant so much to me. The gym was my place of refuge since physical exercise helped me to relax.

I had to make a decision again: to continue being a part of the teaching program or go directly to the guards and tell them that I quit.

What is a Stoic View of God?

Life in prison went on normally. I tried to be cautious, avoiding people that could influence me negatively, hoping that I could avoid further attacks by being withdrawn. I did my job, then my exercises, returning to my section in the evening where I sat and talked to some of my colleagues, especially Romanians.

Another week passed, after which Rick again came for another meeting. Again, several of us gathered, and Rick told us more things regarding the stoic philosophy, and again, I had several objections to what he said. This time, Rick did not stay to speak with me. Immediately after the time allocated for the meeting, he got up, shook hands with everyone, and left, visibly irritated.

The following day, in the gym, it so happened that I noticed Rick in the office of the senior guard. About a half-hour later, I was summoned by that guard to that same office. I went in and sat down, then waited while he seemed to be doing something on his computer.

"George," he finally addressed me, "I hear that you often have comments when Rick is teaching the class on stoicism. Is there something you would like to tell or ask me?"

"I am not the kind to comment when another is speaking," I responded, "but I am trying to understand exactly what this philosophy is. What specifically are you teaching us?"

"Ask me exactly what you want to know, and I am ready to tell you."

"Thank you for the opportunity," I began. "I would like to know what a stoic believes about God. What is the stoic's attitude toward a God that asks for our worship and respect, and, if you really believe in Him, whom you will love?"

"Good question," he responded, "and my answer is simple: whether or not God exists, we do not know. If He does exist, we don't know whether He is male or female."

I was sickened. I was struck with a sickening feeling of intense grief. The man observed that something had happened and asked me if I was okay. I replied in the affirmative, and he continued.

"As Marcus Aurelius said, we must live a good life. If God or gods do exist, whoever or however many there may be, we will be received in heaven based on our good works done in stoicism. If we are not received in heaven, it means it is controlled by an illegitimate God unworthy of our respect, much less our service. If no God does exist, then you have lived the best of all possible lives, that of a stoic."

I looked at the man, unable to believe what had just come out of his mouth. I had never before heard anyone speak about God with such disrespect. Having finished speaking, he lifted his eyes from his computer screen, turned toward me, and smiled.

"Are you happy with my answer?" he inquired.

"Yes, I mean, no," I stuttered. "I guess you took me by surprise. But be aware that someone that models his life on that kind of teaching stands a good chance of missing heaven and eternal life."

"Be more explicit," he requested.

"With that kind of an attitude about God, there is a real chance that we will miss our souls' salvation."

"Whether or not such a thing exists," he smiled, "we don't know. No one has ever yet returned to tell us what lies on the other side of death. All that we are told are just fairy tales."

"Oh, but Someone did return!" I exclaimed. "Jesus did! He came back and told us exactly what will happen after death!"

"George," he said, smiling and turning his chair back, facing his computer once more, "do you have anything more to say? If not, you may return to your work, and don't forget: you and Rick are a team. Say nothing against what he says. Okay?"

"Okay..."

"Another thing, George," he continued. "I see you often going about with your head down. You have got to keep your head up. You are a massive man, one that inspires respect. You must be proud of your physique and not look down all the time."

"I will think about it," I replied. "Thank you for the advice."

I was horrified by the man's response. Before arriving in this prison, I knew nothing of stoicism, of Epictetus, Marcus Aurelius, and the rest. Now that I had found out a bit about them, I wanted to hear nothing more or to have anything to do with this teaching. I realized, in my discussion with the guard, that Rick had complained that I did not agree with him and many times; instead of supporting him, contradicted him in front of the other inmates.

That evening, after I had returned to my cell, I laid in bed thinking about my discussion with the head guard. I wondered if I should open another discussion with him about God, Jesus Christ, and eternal life. I figured it would be a pointless endeavor. He was a proud man and would not take advice from me, an inmate, and a foreigner besides.

Still, this man and the team he had formed were teaching inmates that God did not exist. That excluded the possibilities of heaven and hell. In short, they were sending those inmates that believed their teaching to eternal death!

But the situation was delicate. I lived here in prison, and many of my rights and privileges as an inmate depended on these people. At the end of the day, it was they who decided when I would be freed. There are cases of an inmate's liberation being delayed two or three months from unknown causes. I did not want to cross them. I had to keep in mind my emotional and mental state. I thought of all these things, but a verse from the Bible came to mind, "Whoever is ashamed of Me and My words in this adulterous and sinful generation..." (Mark 8:38a, NKJV)

I knew then what I must do. I must speak for the truth, even if it brought me problems.

In addition, I knew I also had to take action against these stoicism classes, but I did not know where to go or to whom to speak. The guards' supervisors would not listen since they had allowed the course to be taught. I remembered what my colleague had said about how they taught the course illegally, without a license. That would have been enough to stop it, but how could I make it happen?

Someone will ask me why I did not just shut up and mind my own business. I can explain that by saying that there is a feeling of unrest in the heart of every Christian who believes the Bible to be the Word of God when he sees that those around him are being led into error, endangering their eternal future. It is my personal thought that a true Christian cannot remain silent in such instances.

A Guard in Danger

I continued going to the gym, often playing table tennis with other inmates, especially Romanians. It was a good opportunity to tell them about how God had changed my life. Many of them spoke of how they planned to return to life of crime and how they would "hit the mother lode" and get rich after they were freed. When I spoke of my previous life when I thought like them, they listened with interest, but when I spoke of how God had changed my outlook as a child of His, their interest quickly waned.

Their attitude reminded me that only God can change a person and that my best efforts, without His power, were useless. Therefore, I often prayed, *Lord, while I am here, help me to be of assistance to the people here and to advance Your work.*

One afternoon, standing in line at the cafeteria waiting for my food, two of my fellow inmates got into an argument that quickly escalated to blows. A crowd quickly gathered to watch, but I stepped aside, waiting for the guards to intervene. To my surprise, a somewhat older female guard appeared and tried to separate the two. One of them grabbed her by the hair and pulled hard. Seeing what was happening, I stepped in and grabbed the offending inmate under his arms, and—he being a rather skinny individual—lifted him off the ground, carrying him about three meters and shoving him into a corner. I then planted myself in front of him, blocking his way out.

Shortly, more guards showed up and quickly resolved the situation, but the inmate that I had neutralized began screaming at me, threatening me with death, and howling that I had no idea who I had tangled with. At the moment, all his threats went in one ear and out the other, but later, the enemy used those threats to attack me again. Even so, I did not regret that I had gotten involved; on the contrary, I was happy I could be of assistance.

A Romanian Pastor... Are You Kidding?

One afternoon, the prison warden came to our section. He spoke to some of the guards, then sat down and spoke to two or three of the inmates at a time.

I saw an opportunity, so I asked him, "Is there any possibility that you could get in contact with a Romanian pastor who could come into the prison and preach for us?"

"The prison already has an English pastor," was the reply.

"I know, I was at one of his services," I admitted. "But I am Romanian, and there are a number of us in here."

He looked hard at me. "You should talk to the chaplain. He takes care of all that stuff."

Without much further thought, I hunted up the chaplain. It was easy to see that he did his job for the paycheck and nothing more. I got the same response from him.

"The prison has an English pastor."

"I am a Romanian," I replied, "and I would like to have access to a pastor that speaks my language."

He grinned and, without saying much, turned and left, leaving me staring after him. On my way back to my cell, I ran into M, a Romanian with whom I would develop a close friendship.

"Hi, George," he greeted me. "What did you want with the chaplain?"

"As you know, I'm an evangelical Christian," I replied, "and I asked him to contact a Romanian pastor that could preach for us here in Huntercombe."

"You asked for a Romanian pastor? Are you kidding? That was pointless."

"Why?"

"You must understand that, in their eyes, you are only an inmate, an unlucky immigrant, that committed crimes on their soil," he explained.

"I don't think so, M," I replied. "Besides, there are so many immigrants in England. It is known for being multicultural.

"I've been here four years," he told me, "And believe me, you are only a number. You and your rights mean nothing."

I returned to my cell thinking about my discussion with the chaplain and with M. I was in the middle of the excellent book *The Preacher and the Presidents*, the incredibly inspiring story of Billy Graham. In thinking about the book, I saw that God had done great things in this world, touching the hearts of those in leadership positions. Therefore, I reasoned, he can work things out to get one of His servants into Huntercombe to shepherd the people there, even if they are only inmates.

Every day, I was sickened to see groups of fifteen to twenty inmates going to those poisonous stoicism classes. Any philosophy that teaches the inexistence of God is detrimental to those who embrace it.

Throughout the prison, quotes of famous people, be they Hindu, Buddhist, Muslim, etc., were posted on the walls. But the one most prominently displayed was a quote from Marcus Aurelius, posted on a huge banner right at the entrance to the gym. In it, Marcus Aurelius gives his view on God's existence, or, better stated, His inexistence. It was the same words that the senior guard of the gym had told me. "Live a good life. If there is God and He is just, then He will not care how devout you have been but will welcome you based on the virtues you have lived by. If there is God, but He is unjust, then you should not want to worship Him. If there is no God, then you will be gone but will have lived a noble life."

To make matters worse, I had not seen a single Bible verse posted anywhere in the entire prison. Whenever I tried to convince myself that it was none of my business, something inside of me seemed to rise up and force me to action, even though the chances of my accomplishing anything—me being just an inmate—were almost non-existent. Still, I felt compelled to speak, to say that what they were teaching and posting on the walls was not okay, that it was depriving inmates of an opportunity to experience eternal life through faith in the sacrifice of the Lord Jesus.

Sinister Discoveries

I was trying to adapt to the idea that the stoic promoters wanted me on their team. I kept asking myself how I could promote their ideas while still remaining a true Christian, but I knew without a doubt that what they were teaching was completely incompatible with the Bible, so I had to make a decision.

I prayed and decided to wait to take action until God clearly told me what I should do.

One morning, I entered the gym, feeling good. I changed into my work clothes and was ready to go to work, but then thought that perhaps I should find Guard B and discuss the stoicism classes with him. I was trying to find a way to have my cake and eat it too, to be on their team and still remain a child of God.

After finishing my work, I prepared to start exercising. Going past the guards' office, I saw B alone, facing his computer. Seizing the opportunity, I stepped into the office and greeted him, but he did not respond; he seemed to be concentrating on something else. I greeted him again, to which he may have mumbled something in response, but he did not turn toward me. I then took two steps toward him, which placed me directly behind his chair, and, without trying, my eyes fell on his computer screen. I was shocked and horrified. Two pictures stared back at me, both of them depicting a Baphomet or a demon, and beside them was a text. I could read only the title ("How You Can Be a Disciple of Satan"), but the rest of the text was too small for me to read. It seemed to be a course of some kind. The guard seemed extremely focused on how he could become a disciple of man's greatest enemy.

Guard B jumped when he realized I was behind him, looking at his monitor. He tried to close the page as quickly as he could, but he was so agitated that he could barely find the X in the corner of the screen.

"George, what a pleasant surprise! What can I do for you?"

"Good morning, Sir," I stammered. "I wanted… I wanted…"

I looked at him, no longer knowing what I wanted. I was too shocked by what I had seen to organize my thoughts.

"I wanted the straps," I finally blurted out. "I would like to lift some heavy weights, and I need the straps."

"Sure! They are in the top drawer. Help yourself!"

"Thank you!"

Guard B knew that I had seen his screen. He said nothing, but his smile was forced, and he stared after me as I left.

I hurried out of the office, my heart pounding. I could hardly believe what I had seen, but at the time, I was glad that God showed me who I was working with. Now, as clear as day, I knew that there was no possible way that I could be a part of their team. I made a decision right then and there that I would never, never play around with the idea that I could be a part of a group that promoted anything other than Jesus Christ as Lord and Saviour.

No more discussion was necessary. God led me into that office at the right moment, when I could see with my own eyes what the most ardent proponents of the stoicism class were pursuing. I was horrified, knowing that these men were teaching the inmates the fundamentals of life. I realized that the spiritual battles would be fierce and that I would do well to strengthen myself accordingly. These men were sending inmates to hell; I had seen how intense they were in their studies. Now, more than ever, I felt I must do something about these stoicism classes. I prayed that God would show me what I had to do.

The Cross is Forbidden

An interesting occurrence from my time in Huntercombe—that was to have repercussions later—transpired as I was doing my weekly grocery pick-up on Friday afternoon. Shopping was done by filling out a form with the desired goods and their quantities; the form was given to a guard, who then passed it on to the proper parties to acquire the goods outside of the prison, and the money was debited from the inmate's account.

As I was picking up my order, I started talking with the guard that supervised the delivery of the goods. He asked what I ate that made me so big, to which I replied that I ate whatever I found, particularly since they fed us so little. He grinned and turned to help someone else bag their acquisitions, and I observed a strange tattoo on his leg. A black cross inside a red circle with a red slash diagonally across it was tattooed on the back of his calf—in other words, the "prohibited" symbol superimposed on a cross. It was the first time I had seen such a thing; I asked him, out of curiosity, why he sported such a tattoo.

"Don't tell me you're one of those religious Christians who are offended..." he growled, turning toward me.

"I am a Christian, but not religious, so I'm certainly not offended," I returned. "I am simply surprised."

"And why are you so surprised?"

"This Christian symbol, the cross, is an important emblem of Christians. Throughout history, hundreds if not thousands of Christians were killed for the simple fact that they believed in Jesus, who died on the cross. When I see a tattoo such as yours, I see it as a lack of respect, nothing more. You have not offended me; on the contrary, I will pray for you."

"That is not necessary," he snarled. "I am an atheist; for me, God does not exist; your prayers are useless."

"God does exist," I exclaimed. "Furthermore, He knows you personally. So personally, in fact, that He knows how many hairs are on your head..."

"Hey, that's too much," he replied. "I can't believe anything like that. You know what? I have absolutely nothing for religion of any kind. I am anti-religious, regardless of what kind or what it's called..."

"And you still chose to show the cross with the "prohibited" symbol? Why didn't you choose the crescent moon if it is that you dislike all religions?"

"Hey, cut all the blather," he barked. "I want nothing to do with religion. That's what I want, and that's all there is to it."

"Still, you chose the cross..."

"Shut up! Next in line."

"Perhaps it was fear," I persisted. "You know why? If you dared put the crescent moon there rather than the cross, you would not walk around here in shorts. Muslims don't joke about their religion. If you had the crescent moon on your leg, you would get a kick in the rear, at least, before you got from here to the prison exit."

That remark would end up costing me. He said no more, and I left, somewhat disturbed. I thought a lot about it and looked forward to the next week when I could possibly find the same guard and apologize. He was visibly upset by what I had said, and though it was true, it was not said in meekness and love as it should have been said. I did not lie when I said I was not offended, but I was very saddened.

The following week I did not meet him, but two weeks later, he was there again. I was happy that I had my chance to ask forgiveness, so when it was my turn to have my things bagged, I immediately opened my mouth to apologize, but he took me by surprise.

"What's up, bro?" he asked.

"I'm sorry if I made you upset last time," I said, smiling.

"I'm sorry if I offended you," he returned, also smiling, "by wearing shorts so my tattoo could be seen."

He winked at me, indicating his pants. This time, he was wearing long pants.

I tried to explain that I had not been offended, merely saddened because he was sending a message of deception to those around him. Without the cross, we cannot see heaven! He repeated that he would like to understand me but felt himself incapable of understanding "religious people." We remained on friendly terms from that day forward but never again discussed any religious subject.

A Direct Confrontation

There was a Russian in the prison with whom I developed a friendship. We exercised together, and in our free time, discussed life, family, or occasionally politics. He often complained about the political situation in his home country and how terrible it was that he would have to return there; I would then try to encourage him and, when I had the opportunity, would tell him how God had changed my life.

I discovered his birthday was approaching and thought that perhaps I should get him a gift, but I didn't know what to get.

One Thursday afternoon, when I was in the chapel, waiting for the chaplain to arrive for the weekly Bible study, I was looking through the library there and came across a Russian Bible. I instantly thought of my comrade; this would be a perfect gift! When the chaplain arrived, I asked him if he could bring me a Russian Bible sometime, and he did so. The next day I took it with me to the gym to give it to my friend; it was a bit before his birthday, but I was impatient to give him the book about which I had told him so much and that had changed my life.

"Happy birthday, Vitali!" I greeted him. "Look, I brought you something! It's not a big gift, but it is something special."

"You got me a gift? But my birthday is still four days away!"

"That's fine," I grinned. "I wanted to be the first."

Vitali smiled at me as I rummaged through my backpack, then I pulled out the Bible and handed it to him. He hesitated for a moment, then took it and looked at it, somewhat indecisively. He opened it, then forced a smile.

"Oh, yes, a Russian book. But, it is a Bible, isn't it?"

"It is! The book of books!"

"I see you wrote me a message," he murmured. "'This book will separate you from sin, or sin will separate you from it.'"

"So it is," I replied seriously. "This book can help you more than you can imagine."

"George," he said slowly, "we are friends and understand each other well. I do not want to offend you, but I cannot accept this gift."

Shocked almost beyond words, I managed to ask him why he refused.

"George, you always talk about God, heaven, and hell," he said, seeming to gain confidence. "But for me, those things are all just stories."

"You never told me that before," I said sadly. "I thought you were a Christian. Even so, please accept the gift, and maybe when you're bored, you can read a little."

"You're funny, George," he grinned wryly. "You're such a hulk, but you believe these stories. How easily men are manipulated!"

"I don't think I've been manipulated," I replied. "It's not that I just heard this stuff, but my belief comes from my own experiences with God. I have experienced things that no one can argue with because I, myself, lived through them."

"I used to believe those stories too," he said soberly. "I was raised by my grandmother, who always took me to church on Sunday morning, but several months ago, I took some classes on stoicism here in prison. Now I understand that the idea of God is nothing more than a way to manipulate the weak. I can be good by myself, without divine assistance."

I stared at him, unable to believe my ears. He, then, was a victim of those poisonous classes. He had been manipulated by smooth talkers and his own pride, believing that "the big I" can be good by himself.

In the end, he accepted the Bible to make me be quiet and took it to his cell, and I, sick beyond words, began thinking and praying about a solution to the problem of these classes. I had to do something, but I had no idea how to go about it.

Before I had spoken to anyone else, I spoke to the one responsible for it all, the senior guard at the gym. It was a spontaneous decision; one morning, passing his office and seeing him in it alone, I felt a strong compulsion to talk to him. I knocked on the door and, as soon as he gave the word, entered.

"Good morning!" I greeted him.

"Good morning, George," he returned. "Please sit down and tell me how I can help you."

"It's about..."

"Rick and the team of stoics, I know," he interrupted. "I have found out that you cannot work with them. They have told me that you do not share the same values. It's unfortunate; that teaching would have brought out the best in you. It would have transformed you into a real man."

"Mister A," I replied, "when I was a 'real man,' I did things that brought me here. Happily, Jesus turned me into a different man. He changed my heart, my mentality, my whole life. No earthly teaching can change a man as Jesus can. What do you say to promoting the love of God in this place?"

It was somehow very easy to speak; the words came by themselves, from somewhere inside of me. The guard looked at me questioningly but somewhat angry at the same time. The words I said seemed to unsettle him just a bit.

"George," he said, "I admire your courage for coming and saying those things, but I've heard it all before. Nothing is new for me. I grew up in the Anglican Church. From the time I was young, I went to church, and I saw things there that I don't want to talk about, but that made me no longer want to be a Christian. I want to believe in nothing but that which I can do myself."

"Yes, I understand," I sighed. "We have all been let down by others. We have all trusted other people, whom we thought to be Christians, but they proved themselves otherwise. Then we, in our turn, let others down because we are human. None of us are perfect. The only One that is always perfect, who walked this earth without doing a single thing wrong, is Jesus Christ. Therefore, if we look to Him rather than to people, then we can trust, we can have faith. Without faith, we cannot be saved, and every man needs salvation."

As I said these words, I noticed that the senior guard got rather red in the face; he nearly said something but stopped.

He fidgeted a moment, then ran his hand over his face and forced a smile.

"Why would I need to be saved?" he asked a bit too loudly. "Saved from what? Who will save me? I was never convicted of anything. Maybe you need to be saved, like others incarcerated for their crimes, but not me. I'm fine as I am. Now, please, go back to your work. I'm very busy."

"Fine."

"Hey, one more thing," he continued. "If you don't want to help the team, at least don't hinder them. Don't throw any more wrenches in the gears, and leave them alone."

It seemed that someone had already told them that I was telling inmates, particularly Romanians, not to go to those classes since they were spiritually poisonous.

"Thank you for listening," I replied. "If I have upset you, please forgive me."

He stared at his screen and said nothing more. Neither did I say anything more as I left his office and went to change into gym clothes. I had a strange feeling down inside of me. My pulse was fast, and my face was red. I didn't know what had happened, but I began to understand that the confrontation with the senior guard involved more than just what met the eye. My mind was not the only place where spiritual battles were being fought.

That evening, lying in my bed, I reflected on what had happened. On the one hand, I was glad that I had done what I had to do and spoke honestly with the one that was pushing all this toxic teaching. On the other hand, I thought of his attitude and how he had yelled at me, saying that he didn't need salvation.

Lord, I prayed, *there are so many in today's world that refuse your gift. Why do you not open their eyes to see the truth?*

Immediately after that meeting, Rick grew noticeably colder toward me. He did not come to the next meeting for stoic teaching, and when I asked why he was missing, he quoted personal reasons. I knew it was more than that; I knew that my opposition to the teaching before the other inmates, as well as my discussion with the senior guard, had made him want to stay away.

All this was obviously discussed among the other members of the team of stoics because when my relationship with Rick soured, so did my relationship with the gym guards, particularly Mister B. Suddenly, all his enthusiasm toward me and the stoicism classes evaporated. I was never invited to another meeting or to be of assistance to Rick. They never even mentioned the classes. Now, it seemed, everything would revert back to a normal inmate-guard relationship.

For that, I was happy. I had not expected to extricate myself from the situation so easily. Not knowing the future, I thought it had been pretty painless.

A Fictitious Friendship

Several days after my meeting with the senior guard, the attitude toward me of everyone from the gym, who was on the team of stoics, changed. Those with whom I worked and exercised before were suddenly cold and distant. I also noticed that this attitude was much more pronounced in the gym when we were under the watchful eye of the guards from there than it was otherwise. If we met in the halls or anywhere else, things seemed normal, so I inferred that their hostility was just a façade designed to stay on the good side of the guards from the gym. I didn't blame them; that is prison life. If you want to serve your sentence comfortably and be released as soon as possible, you take care to please the guards. At the time, this did not bother me, knowing that I had done the right thing.

One day, a colleague from the gym, one of the inmates who was the most chummy with the guards, stopped me while I was doing my exercise routine, looking surprised, and asked me, with a big smile, if I didn't remember him. He said that we had met in a London nightclub many years before. I looked at him closely, but nothing jogged my memory, so I told him that I didn't remember him, then excused myself because it was time to do my next series of exercises. I finished exercising, then sat up to continue my discussion with him.

"Sorry," he said, "but I think I must have gotten you confused with someone else."

"No problem," I replied. "If I remember you, I'll tell you..."

He withdrew slowly with a clearly artificial smile. I figured he probably had gotten me confused with someone else.

Several days later, another inmate from Austria, who was also in my group of friends from the gym, with whom I had exercised side-by-side in the last few weeks and had developed a friendship, accosted me in the hall.

"Hey, big guy, come with me to my cell. I want to talk to you."

I went with him and entered his cell, after which he shut the door and invited me to sit down.

"I want to ask you something," he began, "and whether or not you are honest with me, I want you to think carefully about what I say."

"Go ahead," I replied. "You've made me curious."

"Several days ago, you talked with X, who said he had met you in a London nightclub many years before and asked if you remember him. Is that right?"

"Yes, that's right," I replied thoughtfully, "but I don't remember him. I walked in a lot of places, and I met a lot of different people, but him, I cannot remember at all. Why do you ask?"

"I'm asking you in order to warn you: be careful how you resolve this situation. X is telling everyone that you had a group of guys that, many years ago, terrorized the nightclubs of central London. He says that you control a number of illegal activities in those nightclubs and that many of them paid you for your 'protection.' Furthermore, he says you kidnapped people to hold them for ransom and committed a lot of other crimes."

"Is that so?" I asked.

"Today, he was discussing it with one of the guards," he replied. "He thinks you know him but don't want to admit it."

"That is stupidity!" I stared at him in disbelief. "The guy's got mental problems! I really do not remember him. What should I do; lie and say that I do remember him, even if I don't?"

"I think he was a little upset that you, according to him, acted rather rude..."

"What?" I asked, shocked. "What is he saying?"

"He said you go around with your nose in the air and that when he was talking to you, you walked off and said you were exercising. He felt offended."

"Bro, I am shocked by all this, but I really have nothing to say to this guy. I guess I will just have to ignore him..."

"George," cautioned my friend, "Inmate X is known to be Guard B's right-hand man. He is very valuable for them, and he is one of those who are always helping the guards. I bet you know what I mean by that. B protects him. You would be wise to go talk to X, and clear things up."

"Okay, I'll think about it," I agreed. "Thanks for telling me."

I headed back to my cell, confused. I could not figure out what was happening.

What was he trying to do? What did he want from me? A simple discussion I had has turned into utter foolishness. How could he come to such ridiculous conclusions based on a discussion of a few minutes?

Why is he accusing me of keeping my nose in the air? Why is he saying I'm a liar?

I thought there must be some mistake. I sat all evening from seven when they locked our cell doors until about eleven when I turned in for the night, trying to remember if I ever met this man, but I could remember nothing that would even remotely make sense.

The next day when I got to the gym and saw X, I was going to speak to him to resolve the situation, but I suddenly changed my mind and ignored him. I noticed that he looked at me strangely, but I said nothing and went about my activities.

Several days later, I needed the wrist straps again since I was doing Romanian deadlifts. I gave the door a few quick raps and entered, only to see Guard B and Inmate X talking earnestly to each other. Shocked, it took me a moment to regain my composure. I then asked B if I could use the straps, but without giving me an explanation, he refused. I apologized for disturbing them and left.

I felt again a strange feeling as I left the office. I felt like those two men were discussing me and not in a good way. However, I went on to my exercising and tried not to think about it.

My fake friend, X, began acting more and more strangely. Every time I met him, he turned his head the other way as if trying to avoid me. I tried to greet him, but he acted as if I was invisible. Guard B acted the same.

One day I decided to go speak to B directly.

"Good afternoon, Mister B," I said, entering his office.

"Good afternoon, George," he returned. "How can I help you?"

"I only have a question," I replied. "Have I somehow upset you? I feel as if your attitude toward me has changed."

"Don't worry about it, George," interrupted another guard just as B started to speak. "That's how B is; every now and again, he's just mad at everybody."

I grinned and turned to go. "You bastard," I heard B hiss between clenched teeth.

I whirled around, but B was looking somewhere else.

"I'm sorry? Did you say something, Mister B?" I queried.

"No! I said nothing," he replied, somehow looking surprised.

I looked around, but the other guards and inmates present just shrugged. Though he had spoken in little more than a whisper, I had clearly heard him say it.

I smiled and withdrew, still knowing that something was wrong. Mister B was still very clearly upset with me.

One afternoon soon after, as I was cleaning the gym and B was doing his exercises near me, I again asked if I had upset him, but he simply turned and walked away without responding. I knew something was wrong, but I had no idea what would happen next.

The Calm Before the Storm

I met X at the gym every day. On the one hand, he seemed almost to fear me, but on the other, it felt as if he always tried to be around me, to be noticed. If I was at one end of the room, he found work there too, close to me, but if I looked toward him, he acted scared, looking away fearfully. It seemed he was playing some kind of game.

As he continued his strange behavior, I noticed that my relationship with the guards continued to get more strained by the day.

From previous experience, I knew the enemy was preparing another attack. Too many inexplicable things were going on, such as X's continued strange attitude. What would make someone ask me if I knew him and, when the answer was negative, go tell everyone that I was a proud liar? What did such a person think he was gaining? Why would someone throw mud for no reason?

Feeling that the devil was setting a trap, I tried to prepare myself spiritually. I felt there was a storm ahead, but I did not know exactly what kind of storm, so the best thing I could do was prepare my spirit.

I began praying earnestly. In my daily dialogue with God, I always asked him for strength. I did not know what lay ahead, but something inside told me it would be a fight to the death.

Some of my Romanian colleagues, seeing my deteriorating relationship with the guards and knowing about my refusal to join the team of stoics, wanted to help me. One of them, a truck driver who had been caught with several kilograms of cocaine in his truck, advised me to go and talk to them, to apologize for my stubbornness, and to accept all their propositions because the Stoic course was something they were proud of, and continuing to say to other inmates that it is not good for their souls would only make things worse for me. He told me that if you upset the guards, you are at their mercy when it comes time to be freed because they could drag out the procedure.

That conversation was not good for me. I was no longer as strong, emotionally speaking, as I had once been because of the constant attacks. In previous times, George would have said, "They'll have to release me at some point. It doesn't matter that much to me." But I was no longer that strong. Ironically, I worried over my worry, wondering what had happened with me. I blamed myself for my weakness, saying that I was not a good enough Christian and that all that was happening to me was because I did not love those around me enough. The evil one would whisper, "You should have accepted their propositions and joined their team; if you had, none of this would be happening. But you, big tough Christian that you are, had to stand up to them. Look at what is happening now; these guys will see to it that your worst nightmares come true."

Another battle raged in my heart: on the one hand, I wanted to find someone that I could get the message to outside the prison, to let them know of the danger to which this course was exposing the inmates. But on the other hand, I knew that if I did so, my relationship with the guards would get even worse, and I would certainly face some consequences for my actions. I prayed that God would help me find a solution.

I felt like it was the calm before the storm. For several weeks I did what I knew to be right: I warned other inmates to avoid the stoicism classes. When I did so, I could see the frustration of the guards, as well as those inmates that were involved in teaching the classes.

Adriana is one of those gifts you recieve from God and you wonder, "Why me?"

Behind me is the Freedom House building and the headquarters of Fight for Freedom ministry. Only God made this possible.

Days after I came home from Huntercombe, we were on vacation at the Black Sea by Gods grace.

Fighting for Romania in the sport called Sambo Combat.

Holding Joel when he was just a few weeks old, what a blessing.

I met all this guys in Botosani Prison, we were cell mates. Few years later when this pictures was taken, we were all working together for my packaging company Urspack.

I never thought I would speak in front of people in a Church. God made this possible.

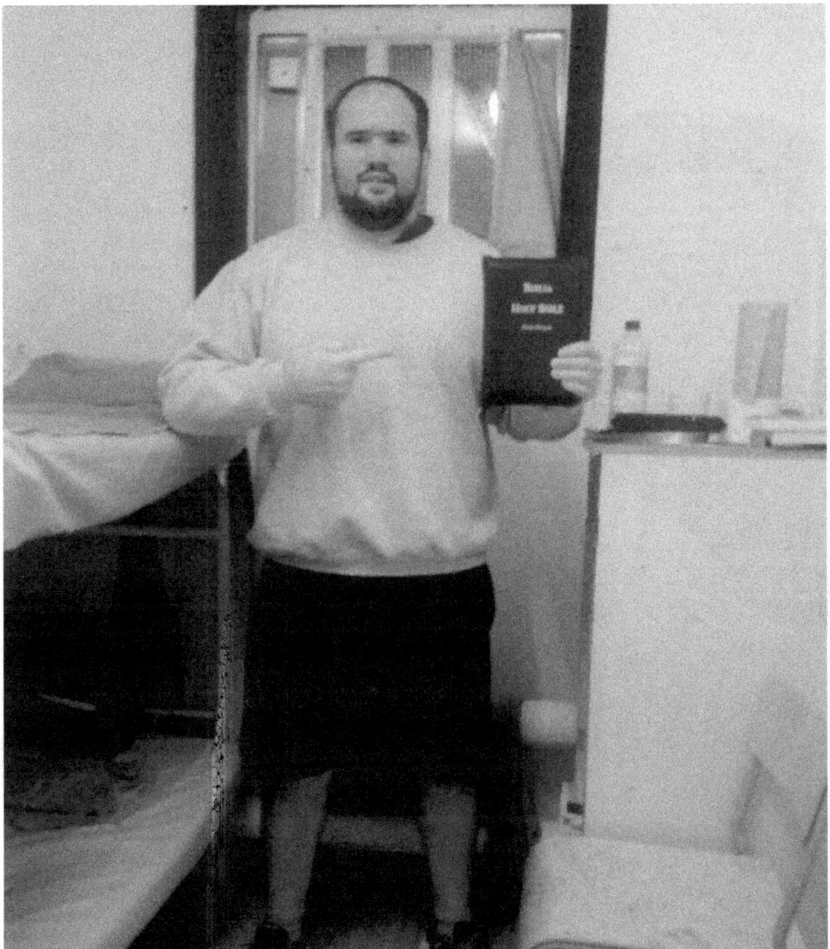

Inside a cell room in one of the UK Prisons I was in, pointing at The Bible. It was the only thing that helped me get out of there.

Sharing our testimony of how God put our family back together, with a group of families in Romania.

Speaking at the Home for Homeless.

The day David turned 14 years old.

Winning one of my MMA competitions.

With brother Puiu, my business and ministry partner, checking out the quality of the print for one of the orders at Urspack.

With my little brother Nicu, he was next to me at all the time.

With the National Grappling Team, representing my country as a heavyweight contender at The European Championship 2019.

This is who we are, a happy family under God's protection.

Part 5

Huntercombe Prison, United Kingdom

The Storm

The Storm Begins

Before long, one of my acquaintances from the gym called me aside and told me that he had heard two guards discussing a meeting that had taken place, in which the prison authorities had asked the police to open an investigation into my past activities. Supposedly, the way I had been acting made the guards suspicious, and, in their opinion, I was guilty of other—as of yet, undiscovered— crimes.

At first, I thought he was joking—he was known to be a prankster—but I saw that he was dead-serious and believed him to be telling the truth. Though it seemed strange, I was not worried since I knew there was nothing to uncover. Therefore, I put it down as another consequence of my conflict with the guards that promoted stoicism. I assumed it was simply an attempt at revenge. Still, I had to wonder, *Why did this colleague with whom I am not particularly close come and tell me?*

Soon thereafter, I was called to the office where they prepared papers for those to be deported, where they took my picture again, saying they had lost the one they took upon my admittance to that prison. It was a lie. An inmate told me several hours later that the picture was for the police since they were opening a case against me and needed a recent picture.

Strangely, even though I had been facing fierce, relentless attacks since I had arrived in England, this news did not bother me. For days, I felt fine, thinking, *What will the police say when they finish all this foolishness only to discover they were sent on a wild goose chase?*

One afternoon, being locked in my cell, I sat down on the bed to read, it being my custom to read for a while after they had locked our cells. I would then eat, then read again, or watch a little television.

Only this time, it suddenly felt as if, spiritually, all hell broke loose. I had only read a page or two when the evil one began whispering, "You see how I got you where I want you? You see how I can do what I want with you? I can use any person and any circumstance to accomplish my plan, and my plan is to destroy you. I promised you that you would never leave prison, and I will keep that promise. You will be imprisoned unjustly, just like that guy you saw on TV."

I leaped to my feet as if burned. I laid the book aside and began to pray, but the attack was one of the most intense I had faced to date. I knelt, but I could not connect with God. The thoughts were so aggressive that I could not turn my mind toward God, the One that could help me. The thoughts were from the devil; they were not my own.

Looking in the mirror, I saw that my face was again red; my heart raced, and my head felt as if it was about to explode. The evil one again whispered, "Where is the God you trusted in? If He existed, He would help. If He doesn't come to your rescue, it means He does not exist. Why did you have to stand up to those people? For what? For a God that does not exist?

"You alone are responsible for all that will happen to you. You are guilty because you trusted in a God that, if He exists, forgot you.

"He doesn't want to be bothered by you! He is tired of you! Do you understand?"

It was no longer just a whisper but a shout, a fierce scream that reverberated through my head.

I had a terrible evening. I went through some extremely dark moments as my body and mind reacted to the lies that the devil told.

I would get up and pace the room, occasionally looking in the mirror, scarcely recognizing the apparition that stared back at me. I felt so helpless I wanted to scream. "God," I silently shrieked, "will it really end this way? Must I arrive home in a body bag? Is this the end? Lord, don't allow the devil to take my life! Help me! I am loved by You! Lord, have mercy!"

Suddenly, the enemy was gone. Peace was once again present. I sat down on the bed. I could breathe again because, even in that hell, I had the strength to pray. God heard and gave me peace, so I lay down and slept.

At three o'clock the next morning, I awoke with a start. My whole body was shaking; I was in a panic and an extraordinarily great fear. I didn't know what was happening, I was very sweaty, and my heart was beating again; I thought it would come out of my chest.

I tried to kneel, knowing that, on my knees, I could find help. But there seemed to be a force that kept me from kneeling. With an immense effort, I managed to get to my knees, but when I tried to pray, I could not find the words. Fear had locked up my mind. I prayed for several minutes, then opened the Bible and read the first verse on which my eyes fell: "Behold, God is my salvation, I will trust and not be afraid" (Isaiah 12:2, NKJV).

Those words had a powerful effect. They brought my strength back, and the fear vanished. I was to discover in the months to come how powerful God's Word is. Leaving the Bible open beside my bed, I again lay down and slept.

In the morning, I awoke tired, as I had slept all night.

I was to discover in the months to come how powerful the Bible is. God speaks to us directly through the words written in His Word. Nothing, beginning with that night, would ever be the same.

The Rapist

The next morning, I went to the gym like normal. I knew that the guards had notified the police that they were suspicious of me, but I did not know if that was supposed to have been secret or if they wanted me to know it. While I was exercising, another Romanian asked me if I knew who had notified the police.

"I don't know, bro," I replied. "Probably the prison leadership or the guards..."

"Of course, it was the guards," he interrupted. "But I heard that it all came from X and from Guard B. They went to the prison warden and asked that you be investigated. It was they who registered the complaint because X feels threatened by you. They say you threatened them with death."

I was shocked out of my wits. I sat down on a nearby bench. "*Lord*," I said silently, "what is happening?"

It was shocking to see how the thoughts that the evil one had put in my head several months before seemed to be becoming reality. Until then, after every attack, I look back and see that everything had been bald-faced lies, but now the threats were not just in my head.

"What's happening, bro?" questioned my friend, pulling me from my reverie. "You feel okay?"

"Yeah, I'm fine..."

"But what was the deal?" he queried. "Did you have something against him that caused you to threaten him?"

"No!" I insisted. "I have nothing against him. Everything started as a simple discussion and degenerated into all this stupidity. I am shocked; I can't believe it. I don't understand what these guys have against me. Who told you all this?"

"X is boasting right and left about what they—he and B—did and how that, after a bit, all your muscles won't be worth two cents."

"Thanks for telling me," I managed. "If you hear something more, please don't hesitate to tell me."

"Sure, man, I'll do it," he returned. "But listen: whatever you had against him or whatever caused you to threaten him, I don't care; just don't do anything stupid. If you lay a finger on him, it'll be another prison sentence. You'll get another seven or eight years on top of your three years and four months. Besides, you're a Christian; you ain't supposed to be beating people up."

I started laughing. I had never threatened X and had no plans of any kind of retribution, but it seemed I was less credible in the eyes of the other inmates than X or Guard B. It was all made up. I had been a Christian for five years and for the last three years, had been going from one prison to another, but in all that time had never laid a hand on anyone, although I had had plenty of opportunities.

Nothing made any sense. *Why would someone complain to the police that they've been threatened if they have not been? Why would someone feel threatened by me? Perhaps because of my physique...*

It would not have been the first time that someone felt threatened simply because of my size, but this time there seemed to be more to it than that. If a person actually fears someone, he does not try to spend time with him, as it seemed X had been doing. There was something sinister at the root, but I did not understand what.

Arriving at my cell that evening, I felt sick, not knowing what to do. Should I contact my family? My lawyer? Should I go talk with the prison warden or get in touch with the police through my lawyer? Should I apologize to the gym guards, where the whole thing had begun? If I did speak with someone, would I be understood? Sometimes I hardly understood myself! What would my loved ones at home understand if I tried to explain it by phone? Probably nothing, I reasoned; it would probably just make them worry.

I was torn; something inside me wanted to seek help, but the fear of being misunderstood made me go on alone.

I was beginning to get an idea of who was behind all of this. I was just starting to realize who the real enemy was, but I was not yet totally convinced.

And now, all kinds of gossip about me began circulating through the prison: stories of how I had made death threats to X or that I was a hardened criminal. Many of the guards, and even some of the inmates, started viewing me with suspicion. I heard bits of talk, but I did not yet understand everything.

One afternoon, I got more details that made the whole thing more shocking and more chilling.

Another inmate, a Nigerian Christian, came to my cell door, saying, "Hi, Brother George! Do you have a few minutes?"

"Sure! What's up?"

"I came to give you a ticket for the Bible study next Thursday," he responded. In order to attend a Bible study, one had to be invited by the chaplain and could enter only with a ticket.

"Thanks a lot, Joe!" I exclaimed. "God bless you!"

"God bless you, too, George!" he replied. "Be strong! I'm hearing a lot of nasty things about you, but I don't believe them..."

He stepped into my cell and closed the door behind him, as if he didn't want to be seen speaking to me.

"George, I, too, was accused of being a rapist," he said, lowering his voice, "but in my case, it was worse. It was in another prison. Another man, believing me to be a rapist, came and punched me in the face. But, just as in your case, it was only a lie spread by other inmates. You know the opinion of prisoners in general regarding rape. But I don't think that will happen to you. No one would dare try to punch you in the face."

"Wait a minute, Joe!" I gasped. "So that is what they are saying? They think I'm a rapist? That's why they are acting so strangely? Who started that story?"

"George, I gotta go," he said hurriedly. "I have more tickets to pass out. Don't forget, God is the One that will mete out justice! I don't believe the stories anyway."

Joe's visit left me shaken but illuminated. Now it made sense: I had been accused of rape, and now the police were on my case, trying to prove it.

Only a person who has been in a similar situation can understand how I felt. Knowing what was happening only made my mental state worse. All of the devil's threats from months before were beginning to come true.

I felt it was just simply too terrible to be true; someone had to be told about the injustice of it all. But again, I had the problem of not knowing with whom to speak. It was a hard, terrible time for me. Making a decision was so hard, knowing you have the devil on your feet. It was not an easy thing, and I needed to be so careful of everything I spoke or did. It was so easy for others to wrongly interpret my words and intentions, as they, too, were also the subject of the same trick. Taking my courage in both hands, I called my wife. I told her that I had been actively working against some anti-Christian teaching and that it had gotten me into big trouble. I couldn't figure out any other reason for what was happening to me in there, but I did not tell her everything. It is difficult to make someone understand such things on the phone.

But I was enormously grateful for my wife's encouragement. She did not understand the whole situation, but her words strengthened me greatly:

"George, you did what you had to do. Regardless of what the consequences might be, you did the right thing. At the end of the day, it is more important to do what God asks of us than to comply with the demands of men."

Adriana's words gave me strength to go on.

The Brothers' Visit—Hell Opens Its Mouth

I felt I needed someone with whom to talk, so I called several brothers from the London area and asked if they could visit me. They were some trusted friends that I could talk to openly and who could strengthen me, or so I thought. They were pastors in the church of which I had been a part and were devoted Christian men who loved God. They scheduled a visit in roughly two weeks. I felt it was time to tell them some of the problems I was facing, to take my courage in both hands, and explain my mental state. I hoped that, with their wealth of experience, they could understand me and give me some advice on how to escape the mental pressure that had begun to be a constant companion. I was becoming more and more aware that it was a spiritual fight. I was beginning to understand that the enemy was using hostile people and situations to attack me from all sides. I couldn't fight him by myself; I needed help.

Finally, the scheduled time arrived, and several Romanian pastors from London came to see me. I was delighted, feeling that finally, I had someone to whom I could open up. Without much premeditation, I began telling them everything that I was going through, expecting a lot of help from them. I expected them to have a solution for my problem; I expected them to know a Bible verse or prayer that, recited for me, would instantly resolve all my struggles.

I took the courage to speak honestly to these men, assuming that our discussion would remain private. I had assumed as well that my discussions with my dear ones at their visits were private. How wrong I was!

Our visit lasted some over an hour, during which I told them of my struggles, the terrible fear, and times of panic that I went through. I told them of my precarious relationship with the prison authorities because of my refusal to propagate the teaching that they promoted. I had changed the stoics from friends to enemies, and they, along with another inmate who pretended to know me, had alerted the police that they had damaging information about me. And I told them that because of that, the inmates had begun gossiping, circulating false stories about me that were putting my life and health in danger.

To be called things such as a rapist in a prison puts one in grave danger since rapists are despised and beat up by the other inmates. Therefore, rapists and other such predators have their own special places in prison to protect them from the other inmates.

The time for our visit was rapidly disappearing, but these dear brothers were confounded by what I told them. They tried to encourage me with verses or stories from the Bible, which was great, but it was not enough.

Seeing this, I said, "Brothers, I know these things from the Bible. I read the Bible; I pray; I fast. I do all these things, but it does not seem to help. Rather, it feels as if, with each passing day, things get worse and worse. What can be done for this fear, this immense pressure that presses down on me, making my head feel as it will split?"

Looking at them, I realized that they did not even understand me. I had never heard of such things before and had never experienced fear, panic, or spiritual struggle. The thought that I could not find a solution, that no one, not even a pastor, has an answer, actually made me wonder if I am the only one in the whole universe who goes through such moments. This thought itself was a worrying one.

These pastors served in a number of London's prisons. They told me how happy they were that they could bring the gospel to the Romanians incarcerated in this prison; they told me of the sacrifices that they made, giving up a day of work each week to do so. I told them the needs were great and asked them to continue to spread the Good News among inmates.

I glanced at the clock and noticed that time was rapidly getting away, and I tried more desperately to get the help that I needed, but it was clear that, regardless of how well-intentioned they were, these pastors had never faced such things before. It was spiritual warfare, but they were not equipped to deal with it.

The good part was that I had finally gotten enough courage to tell someone about the spiritual battles that I was going through. I felt terrible, seeing the visit come to an end without having found a solution and not knowing how I was going to face more battles. I left the visit somewhat happy on the one hand for the fellowship that we had had, but also somewhat depressed, not knowing how I would be able to cope with my problems.

The Enemy Attacks from All Sides

I continued with my daily schedule, even though some nights, the enemy attacked me so severely that I barely rested. Each morning, I had to go to the gym, where I spent the day face to face with those people who were spreading false tales about me, and I was forced to smile and act as though I knew nothing about what was happening. I did my work smiling, then returned to my cell in the evening to rest—if I could—only to go repeat the torture the following day.

Our enemy is a skilled tactician, and when he is going after someone, he plans everything in detail. He will use everyone and every situation to fulfill his plan.

We need to be aware of his tactics, which Apostle Paul tells us in 2 Corinthians 2:11b (NIV), saying, "...we are not unaware of his schemes." A lot depends on how prepared we are when the devil is going to attack us. I think and know now, after lots of battles, that the best defense is to be hidden with Christ in God, as the Scripture says. Sometimes it seems to be a very long way to get there, but even so, we must not give up.

One day, I called my wife, Adriana. She rather hesitantly told me that she had dreamed something about me.

"It was a strange dream, George," she told me. "It was strange, but so, so real; as real as reality itself."

"Please tell me about it," I replied. "Don't keep me in suspense."

"Okay," she replied reluctantly. "I dreamed that we were both living with my mom in my parents' apartment in Suceava."

"And?"

"You know that they live next to a high school that has an athletic field surrounded by a high fence?"

"Yes, I know."

"Every morning, you would get up, get dressed, and leave the house, only to go straight to the athletic field, which, in my dream, was a prison full of demons."

"Wow!"

"You entered the enclosure every morning and fought with the evil spirits. After you beat them, you tied them and locked them up. There were some small cages, like prison cells, and you would throw them in to keep them permanently confined."

"I was doing a good thing," I replied.

"Yes," she continued, "but listen. You never wanted to fight with the little spirits, only with the big ones."

"You know how I am," I replied, with just a bit of a smile in my voice. "I'm never satisfied with the little ones. Go big!"

"It's just that one day, you got up and went to do the same thing, but evening came, and you failed to return. Someone came and told me that the demons had ganged up on you and that this time they tied you up and refused to let you come home. Furthermore, after that person left, I was very upset and was seized with terrible fear. The next moment, I heard a noise at the door, and I went and peeked out through the blinds. At the door was an evil spirit pulling wire after wire out of the breaker box in the hall, intent on leaving me in the apartment with no power and no lights. Then I woke up."

For a moment, I was at a loss for words. A lump came into my throat, and I fought to keep my composure. I didn't know for sure if or how this related to what was happening with me every day.

"Calm down, Adriana," I finally said. "That dream was from the devil; he was trying to scare you. We need not fear him."

"I know that, sweetheart," she replied, "but please be careful what you do. You want to serve the Lord, but it's a big fight. We pray for you; the church prays for you. There are brothers that call me occasionally, and they said that they received a prompting from God to support you in prayer. You are being prayed for..."

"Thank you," I choked, barely being able to speak since the lump came back into my throat and my eyes welled up with tears. I didn't know what more to say. The Lord had shown me clearly that I was indeed engaged in a spiritual battle.

People in that situation need someone to talk to that will try to understand them. Those spiritual fighting battles need the listening ear of a friend that wants to help. But in my case, with all the gossip going on, I trusted no one anymore. There was no one to whom I dared open up, though I was glad I had taken one small step in that direction when I spoke to the brothers that came to visit me. I knew that they would take my case to their churches and would pray for me. I believed I had done the right thing, but I couldn't know that everything I had said would be twisted and used against me.

The Word of God sustained me. I read from it every day, receiving strength to love those around me and to pray for them. There are times when we receive strength from the Lord—and it can only come from Him—to pray for the good of those that are doing us harm.

Misery at Another Level

One day, upon returning from the gym, I heard someone whistling. It was M, sticking his head out of the laundry room of Patterson section. I entered, and M, dressed in his best, asked me to sit down. I immediately asked if he was expecting a visit since he was dressed up. He said he was, but it was not family coming to visit.

"George," he began seriously, "I must tell you something important. I would keep my mouth shut, but it seems something strange is going on."

I saw fear on the man's face. He first made me promise that I would not disclose where I got the information he was about to give me, at least until I was out of Huntercombe. I assured him that I would not betray his trust and that he could speak in full assurance of confidentiality.

"George," he began again, "today I was called to the warden's office. There were a number of guards present, as well as someone dressed in civilian clothes, whom I think was a police officer."

"And..."

"They told me that they have observed that you and I spend a lot of time talking. They asked what we talk about and exactly what you spend so much time telling me about. I told them that your favorite subject is God, but we discuss sports, politics, and other things as well."

"There's no harm in that, M," I replied.

"In that, no," was the rejoinder. "But after they inquired into several things about which I knew nothing, they told me that I had been summoned to speak with them because they suspect you of some crimes, among which are rape, violent crime, and since they think you're a religious fanatic, they wonder if you maybe committed violent acts in the name of your religion, something like terrorism.

Suddenly, my eyes and ears ceased functioning properly. I could barely see or hear M anymore. I felt as if I had taken a hard blow to the head.

"Hey, George, are you okay?" I barely heard M, as if he was speaking from a great distance.

"Hey, man, wake up! Are you okay?"

"Uh, yes," I stammered, "I'm fine. Continue. It's just the devil. M, that villain said he would destroy me, but I didn't know how he would go about it. I think I'm beginning to understand..."

"What? What devil? What are you talking about? It was people; it was guards, police..."

"I know, M, I know. Sorry. Please continue," I said, though I was still hearing M as if from a distance.

"They made me an offer, bro! They said that if I provide them with compromising information about you that allows them to convict you, I will be released early. They would annul the rest of my sentence. Can you imagine?"

I looked at M. He, naturally, would have loved to get out of prison early. Suddenly, my thoughts flew to X. Perhaps now I could understand what would motivate a man to accuse me of making death threats. Now it was clear why he would play so dirty and who was, in fact, behind all this. Still, in M's eyes, I could see his disgust for the proposal he had received and his wish to not get involved in their plotting.

"Sounds like a good offer, M." I tried to smile, but it didn't come.

What I heard from M nearly knocked me down. I tried to be myself, but it was not easy. For months, ever since I had seen the interview of the man that was unjustly convicted, I had been attacked by thoughts of the same thing happening to me. Until recently, I had considered them nothing but the devil's lies and had tried to just go on, but now there was some substance to those thoughts. I saw that the evil one indeed had a plan that he was trying to implement and make those thoughts become reality. I could scarcely believe what was happening.

"M, do you think that they made that same proposal to other inmates?" I asked.

"Of course they did! There's talk about it throughout the prison. It's a subject of gossip, largely among the inmates that hang out a lot with the guards. All that talk goes to the warden and to the guards 'responsible for you.' It's a group composed of security guards and guards from the gym, and they are in touch with the police. They tried a number of different ways to get me on their team. They told me that I had better tell them if I know anything about your past, since there may be families that are suffering as a result of your actions, and it would be the right thing to fight for the truth alongside them."

"Now I understand why some inmates that I had talked with before suddenly started ignoring me," I sighed. "I thought I was imagining things. It is not safe to have prisoners talking about you as a rapist. You know what I mean. Do you think I should notify my family, M? Should I call a news outlet? Should we make it public? What should I do?"

"I think you should stay calm and do nothing," he advised. "You are in their power. I know you want to right all these wrongs, but even if it's hard, you must have patience."

"M, it feels as if these men know everything I say. I can't understand it. Do you think it's possible that the devil tells these people what I say in private? Otherwise, how would they find out everything I say?"

"Don't ask me about that, bro!" he exclaimed. "This devil talk gives me the creeps. I don't know what you are going through, but what's happening now is too much for me already."

M told me more of what these men had discussed with him. It seemed to me that, for some of the things they knew about me, they had no other source than the brothers that had visited me several days before. The discussion with those brothers was the subject of the debate between M and the guards. While not containing anything that could potentially get me in trouble, I had told them some personal information, such as my emotional state. It was things I discussed in private with three other servants of God, never with the guards or prison warden.

All these discoveries made my condition worse. Please, dear reader, try to put yourself in my shoes, if only for a moment. After months of being mentally attacked with the possibility of being unjustly convicted and given a long prison sentence, to talk with someone who had just come back from a meeting in which those present had discussed the possibility of making those negative thoughts come true, it was nearly too much.

Still, I did not want to consider the possibility that the brothers, themselves, had divulged some of our discussion to the prison guards. I thought that perhaps another Romanian had sat unnoticed at another table within earshot and had overheard, or perhaps that the devil was making my private affairs known to the guards. This last thought troubled me considerably since I knew that there are people that communicate directly with the spiritual world. With what I had seen Guard B studying several weeks before, I felt the possibility of information being conveyed by spiritual means could not be excluded.

M again asked me not to tell anyone what he had told me, and I promised again that no one would find out.

I went to my cell and fell to my knees. For two hours, I knelt before the Lord.

"Lord, You are the One who has sustained me until now. You have done so much for Your servant. Lord, You know all the battles that I have fought over the last few months. Only You know the whole truth about what is happening. You know who is behind all this. Lord, You know that Your servant is guiltless; would You allow something so unjust to take place? Would You allow Your servant to be overpowered by these men? Please answer me, Lord!"

Dear reader, I reached for my Bible and opened it, continuing to pray. The Word of God opened to the prophet Isaiah, and my eyes fell on verses 4–7 of chapter 7: "Take heed, and be quiet; do not fear or be fainthearted ... thus says the Lord God: 'It shall not stand, nor shall it come to pass" (Isaiah 7:4–7, NKJV).

Instantly, my spirit was overcome by a profound calm. I felt as a small child might after having been pulled away from great danger by a parent. I cannot fully describe what came over me, but I felt victorious, like a winner! I no longer feared anything. How good was God to give the exact words I needed in that moment of intense tension! The Word of God is alive!

Though my situation was becoming precarious, God continued to sustain me. I tried to follow the example of Saul in 1 Samuel 10:27. When some rebels despised him, he said nothing.

One rainy day, feeling very, very low, I went for a walk in the prison yard. I looked at the sky and asked, "Lord, I know the Bible says that all things work together for good for those that love You, and You know that I love You. Still, how can all that is happening to me now, all that these men are trying to do, be for my good?"

The answer came in a quiet whisper, "This, too, George, is for your good!"

Though I will never forget that experience, it did not end my struggle.

More Details Emerge

Though the time of my release was nearing, my situation became more and more critical. I asked myself if I would ever arrive at home with those I loved or if something bad would happen to me, exactly as I had been envisioning.

For some days, all I heard from others in the prison was something in the order of "Hey, George, is what I hear about you true?" or "George, I heard a lot of bad things about you, but I don't believe them." This troubled me enormously. *What is these people's motivation?* I wondered. *Are they sincere, or are they just playing with me? Do they have a purpose for all these questions?*

Later, I understood that these things were not happening by chance.

When the prison chaplain visited me, he had one goal: to convince me to confess my sins. He would tell me that if there is something on my conscience, or something that is robbing my peace, that I should confess it, so I didn't have to bear the burden alone. While he acted as if he was ready and willing to help me bear my burdens, his eyes were devious. I felt sure that he was fake and had been sent to obtain information that could be used against me. It was true that I lacked peace, but not because I had done something wrong.

What could I do? I had no one to go to since everyone assumed I was guilty.

One day, M pulled me aside.

"Let me tell you a good one! I see you are feeling better, and you can take it."

"Go ahead," I replied, somewhat hesitantly.

M worked in the offices and heard a lot of the discussions of the guards. Every day, he heard all kinds of gossip. He had told me a lot of rubbish that he heard when they were discussing my situation.

"I heard a discussion in the offices today. Two security guards were talking about how they were going to be promoted because they were working on your case."

"They are expecting promotions? For what? Are you serious? They are getting rewarded for destroying a man's life?"

"George, I heard it with my own ears. You know that they are working with the police and they opened an investigation. So they are quite happy to be working on your case because they are sure they will uncover some incriminating evidence against you. Their reward will be a promotion, a larger salary, and other benefits."

"You know, M, if they are expecting to be rewarded for finding evidence of my guilt, they will get nothing."

"I know that, bro. I see how all this is affecting you. It's a crime, what they are doing. I will stop telling you what I hear about you from the guards or from other inmates over a coffee. I will stop because it is doing you more harm than good. But what can I do? I am an inmate like yourself. They trust me because I've worked with them for a long time. I'm trying to help you. I've been telling you what I heard at the office, but I'm wondering if it's the right thing to do. But because of all the sick things they are trying to do to you, I had decided to hide nothing from you."

"M, I have no doubt that you are sincere. I want to ask you something: do you believe that in 2018 it is possible for someone, regardless of who it might be, to get someone else wrongly imprisoned? Is it possible that something like that can happen here in England as it did back in Romania during communism? You know, it happens all the time in my nightmares..."

"George," he sighed, "we live in a world where anything is possible, but we must keep one thing in mind: those that are in charge of the investigation are not the same ones that you upset here in prison. Those here with whom you had some conflict tried to find something against you and started all this foolishness. But a prison guard is really quite powerless. Investigations are run by agents of law enforcement, by experts in criminal law. Besides, regardless of how ill-intentioned some people are, you will still find, even among that same group of people, those that say, 'Hey, this is not right. You cannot do that; it is not just.' An investigation goes through many people, and, believe me, many of them are good men, people of integrity."

"M," I replied, "I know that some of them are professionals and good people, but, though it may be difficult for you to believe, I know who is behind all of this."

"Serious? Who?

"The devil."

"I don't know what to say," he replied. "You've told me that before, and I find it hard to believe. It seems more likely that these men's evil nature is behind it."

"Their evil nature and their determination to destroy me can have but one source," I said earnestly. "My nightmares, the attacks, the fear, and panic—all these have a single source. That source is the one that declared war on the day that I chose Jesus Christ as my personal Lord and Saviour."

"What are you trying to say? Who would believe that? I know that you are sincere, but if you told that to them, they would consider you a fool. They don't believe your mental health to be outstanding the way it is."

"But what do you believe, M?" I queried.

"I believe God exists," he parried. "Even though what you tell me feels strange, from what I have seen happening here, I think it's a plausible option. But can you please tell me why you threatened X?

"M, I have tried to remember anything in our discussion that could have caused him to think that I was threatening him, and I can think of only one possibility: when I handed him a Bible as a gift, I said several words that, at the moment, I thought had moved him."

"What did you say?"

"I asked him if he is prepared for eternity. When he heard the question, his eyes got wide, and he stared at me. I told him to think well on what would happen to his soul if, for example, he would die the following night. At the time, I thought that those words had left a deep impression."

M roared with laughter and, for quite a spell, seemed unable to stop.

"Please stop, George," he finally gasped. "My stomach hurts from laughing."

I stared at him, unable to comprehend what he found so immensely funny.

"What's so funny, M?" I asked. "That's a question that every one of us should ask ourselves every day."

"Bro, I find it so funny that that question would be the reason that he would run to the guards, saying that you made death threats."

"But I didn't threaten him! I didn't say anything bad!"

"I know, George. But when a man with your physique comes into a prison and asks you if you're prepared for eternity, believe me, that it scares a man that doesn't understand where you're coming from. It scared him so badly that he went and reported you."

"Maybe there is something in what you're saying," I admitted, "but I had the best of intentions. But still, I don't think that's all. I think there's more to it."

"Whatever it is, it's funny. Listen to you: 'Are you ready to die? Are you ready for eternity?'"

M burst out laughing again. He found it exceedingly funny that I should ask X these questions that, from my point of view, were absolutely normal.

M seemed to be a sincere person. I knew that he worked on a team of inmates that worked for the prison and assisted the guards in the relationship with the inmates. He knew much more than he told me. He told me later than many times they asked him to tell him everything that I said to him. They asked him to give me messages, then relay my reaction to them. They had even asked him to try to make me say certain things. But M was a man who had seen much and was not that naïve. He saw that things did not add up and that they were trying to implement some diabolical plan, so he did not go along with their schemes. He was a good man.

At the same time, M began to know God more personally. He was a religious man, but he didn't understand that Jesus didn't want our "religion," but rather a relationship with Him. I talked about that to him a lot, hours a time, days on end. I was glad to see him begin to understand what the Bible said, but my situation made me sick at heart. "Lord," I said, "what kind of witness am I for this guy? I tell him about You, and the next minute I'm all panicky. I tell him I have a powerful God, then shake with fear. Lord, I'm bringing shame on You too..."

Face-to-Face with the Enemy

It was a Friday afternoon when a fellow inmate who was well-connected with the leadership of the prison security team came to the gym and asked me to come to speak to the chief of prison security.

Several minutes later, I was seated and talking with the chief guard. In the discussion, I tried not to let on that I knew what was happening, though I doubt it made much difference since it was freely spoken of throughout the prison.

"I'm glad you accepted the invitation to come and talk, George," began the chief, smiling.

"You called me," I replied. "Has something happened?"

"I wanted to tell you that you will be going home soon. Your documents have been prepared for your deportation."

"That is good news," I smiled. "One of your colleagues said something to the contrary several days ago, but that does not matter. I believe what you are telling me now.

"George, you hear all kinds of talk, but you must learn to ignore it. I know you had some encounters with the Romanian authorities a number of years ago. I don't know how things are done there, but here, we do our work seriously and correctly."

I did not ask him how he knew that I had had some encounters with authorities in Romania. The fact that I had been serving a term in Romania and had been sent directly to England from the prison in Romania was well-known, but he was referring to more than the legal proceedings. Later, I remembered that I had told a "friend" in Huntercombe about what the guard asked me, so no wonder he was asking this question. It is certain that those who spoke with me were interrogated and asked about what we had spoken. I later understood that in these interviews, some of the prisoners, in an attempt to get or stay in the guards' good graces, exaggerated what they heard.

I knew that they were investigating me and that they said all kinds of things about me. I felt the hate of these men that worked "seriously and correctly," but I could say nothing. I was afraid to say that I knew what they were doing. I didn't know what to expect from them, and I simply wanted to finish my sentence and go home.

"I would like to believe you, Sir," I finally responded, "but many times, here, I don't know what is happening to me. Some things have happened in this place that don't add up. I know that it may be difficult for you to understand, but I have had times of other-worldly fear and panic. Furthermore, some things have transpired in this prison that amplified the effects of this fear. It seems that there are people here who are seeking to verbally attack me."

I was referring to what they were doing, but I didn't want to say it directly.

He looked at me, and it appeared as my words had had some effect. He colored, then said very bluntly and somewhat forcefully, "No one has any reason to fear if he has done nothing wrong. He that is afraid is hiding something. He is afraid of"—he grinned sarcastically—"of losing his family, his life, his liberty. You understand, George?"

"I understand, but I don't think you understand me. I warned you that I am a difficult person to understand."

I knew that this man, even if he had wanted to understand me, could not. He was too far along in an investigation doomed to failure. But he still did not know it and was hoping to uncover something that existed only in his head. Why was I afraid? They were so frustrated because things were not turning out as they had envisioned that I feared they might make things even more difficult for me. Though this fear was tied to the mental attacks that I had been experiencing, this fear had a basis, in fact.

Our discussion culminated in the guard wanting to know more about my dealings with the Romanian authorities. I didn't know why he was so interested. I had no way of knowing that our discussion would someday land on the desks of those about whom I spoke. At the time, I thought that the man only wanted to hear about my experience in Romania.

"I don't mind telling you, Sir," I began, "that, had I wanted to avoid being extradited to Great Britain from Romania, I could have done so. Had I chosen to do so, I would not have had to answer for the crimes I committed here. I accepted the extradition because I was willing to own up to what I had done and face the consequences."

"I am surprised!" he responded. "How could you avoid extradition after the British authorities sent a warrant for your arrest?"

"It's quite simple," I replied. "When the warrant for my arrest arrived in Romania, I was arrested and taken before a judge that had to decide whether to have me sent to England or not. I accepted my extradition; I did not fight it, as was circulated in Romanian mass media. Who did fight it? It was the Romanian authorities who had opened another investigation into my background in cybercrime. They did not want me extradited until they finished their investigation in Romania, a process that had not yet even begun. Though the charges from England were much more serious and, therefore, had priority, they still tried to block extradition. That suited me fine at the time because it meant that only six days after being arrested, I could go home to my wife and kids. It was time of great happiness, but it was terminated rather suddenly when a businessman that I had known and who was friends with the prosecuting attorney that was working on the investigation asked me to stop by his office. I went to see this man who was reported to be a Christian. He greeted me warmly, saying that he had heard that I had been arrested for some rather serious crimes in England but that through a miracle, I was to be freed in several days. This news, though it should have made me happy, did not surprise me. 'George, it all has to do with people,' he told me. 'I have a proposition for you: would you like to avoid extradition altogether? Would you like to remain free forever? There is that option. You know that the prosecutor working on the investigation is a good friend of mine. Put something appropriate, such as euros, into an envelope, and I will send for one of his employees to come and get it. Do this year after year, and what do you get? You'll be free! The investigation about cybercrime will never go anywhere, but it can block your extradition to Great Britain indefinitely! Still, you will have to remember one thing: you can never leave Romania. Our country is so beautiful that you have no need to go anywhere else.' I told him bluntly that I had no money for bribes because I had a family to support; I had two children with another on the way. I refused to be enslaved to unscrupulous individuals that would flash extradition papers every time they needed more money. I refused to play games with gangsters disguised as Christians on the one hand and as public servants on the other. It was during that time that God began working in my heart and life. I had begun to put my hope and trust in Him; otherwise, I may have given in and paid it."

"Interesting tale," he grinned.

"It's not just a tale; it's the truth," I told him. "Is that not what you wanted to hear? Perhaps you would like to know what transpired next?"

"Sure! What happened next?"

"What followed was a trial in which the judge, quite unlike my experience in England, failed to take into account all aspects. Nothing that my lawyer brought to my defense was accepted; the court steadfastly refused anything that could be to my advantage. The only things taken into consideration were the things put forward by the prosecution. That all culminated in a sentence that even those who worked in the justice system considered overly harsh. How could it be otherwise, after I had refused the generous offer of the prosecution?"

He looked at me as if watching a captivating movie. He hardly even breathed.

"I will tell you only one more occurrence. I hope that that will completely answer your question."

"Sure! I am listening."

"Have you ever heard of finding out what sentence you will receive before the end of the trial? You have no reason to have heard of it: you have not gone through such a thing and doubt that it is possible in England."

"How could you know your sentence before the judge pronounces it? The sentence is given at the conclusion of the trial."

"Six months before the end of the trial, I was at a sauna. I went somewhat regularly because I worked out a lot, and the sauna helped me recover."

"And?"

"When I was there, a school friend of mine who worked as the chauffeur of the chief prosecutor that was working on my case entered. He sat for a while, then looked at me and came over close to me and said, 'George, we have known each other since childhood.' I acknowledged that that was true, and he continued. 'I respect you for your athletic prowess, but our life sometimes takes us where we do not wish to go.' I nodded again. I was eager to hear what he had to say since I knew who he was and where he worked, and I knew he had not come over just to say he respected my athletic accomplishments. 'George, I'm telling you this for your own good. Give no more money to any lawyers. If you do, you are only throwing it away. It has already been decided that you will get four years of prison time.' I was shocked and told him that he must be mistaken since the trial was still in process and that it would continue for at least six months, in which time anything could happen. 'If you believe me, fine, and if not, that's also fine. I'm just trying to help. Two evenings ago I was at a party with my boss. They were having a barbeque, and there were present a number of high-ranking people in the justice system, authorities in matters of law. They discussed your case and decided on a sentence: four years of prison time.' I was shocked. I don't know what caused him to tell that to me. Perhaps it was a last-ditch attempt to get some money out of me. Perhaps he thought I would ask him to use his position to intervene. I don't know, but I did begin preparing myself psychologically for what was ahead. On the day of the sentencing, roughly six months after that discussion at the sauna, I smiled. It was neither more nor less than four years, exactly as my friend had 'foretold.'"

"Are you serious, George? Romania is that corrupt?"

"The corruption of my home country is well-known," I sighed, "but I do believe that a new generation is coming that, when they get into places of authority, will not follow the lead of the older ones that have been influenced by the heritage that communism has left us. I would like to ask you, Sir, from your point of view, what is the difference between a pickpocket or a burglar and a corrupt police officer, prosecutor, or judge?"

"There is no difference," he replied. "Oh, wait, yes, there is. When those that represent the law are corrupt, they are guiltier than those that break the law by other means. He that steals does not always know exactly what the law says, but those that work in the courts know perfectly what is legal and what is not."

"I agree with you. Stealing a man's liberty unjustly is equal to a crime, don't you think?"

"George, I must go," he said, "but I would like to talk to you more at some point. What you have told me is very interesting."

I did not know that what I had said would arrive, several months later, at the offices of those in authority in Romania, those in my hometown of whom I had spoken. When I arrived home, there would be another battle to fight.

My Dear Wife's Visit

I was surprised to receive a visit from Adriana and my brother, Nicu. I think Adriana knew that I was having some problems, so she made the effort to leave the children at home and come to see me. It was a pleasant surprise that did me much good. My spirit was uplifted when I saw my wife. I spoke to her of what was happening at home, in the free world. I told her some of what I was going through, but not too much. I tried to protect her from the indignities that were going on there.

At one point, Nicu left, and I was left alone with Adriana. I then asked her to pray for me and, when back home, to ask the church to pray since I was going through some things that I had never experienced before and that I did not completely understand. I explained to her that sometimes, out of the clear blue, I would be struck by panic attacks. As I was talking, I saw tears in her eyes. I understood that I should say no more, so I stopped. I assured her that I was fine and that I would be coming home shortly.

I then changed the subject, talking about our marriage, our relationship as a couple, our children, and our future after I served my sentence. We also discussed personal issues, things that should stay only between a man and his wife. I did not realize that our discussion would be made public.

We discussed her health. Adriana had given birth to three children, and after the birth of the last one, Philip, she had gained weight and, though she had tried to lose weight, could not get rid of the extra kilograms. I encouraged her to do more physical activity, but, at the same time, I assured her that I loved her regardless. But I knew that Adriana had some medical issues, and it was therefore important that she lose the extra weight. I encouraged her that, when I got home, I would help her, we would start a regimen of diet and exercise, and, together, we would succeed.

We encouraged each other, reflecting on the goodness that God had shown us in years past. If, after all we had gone through, we were still a family, the Lord Jesus certainly deserved the credit. Earlier, things had been very strained in our family. Before we became practicing Christians, before we began taking the Bible seriously, we were near divorce. When we received Jesus Christ into our lives, the first thing He did was to put our family in order. I had not known until that point how to properly appreciate, respect, and love my wife, but from that moment, everything changed completely. The Lord Jesus did not only enter our hearts, but He entered our family and repaired the relationships that I, in particular, had damaged.

The visit lasted two hours, but it passed like two minutes, after which I took her in my arms and wished her a pleasant flight home. I asked her to kiss each of the children for me and to not forget to ask the church to pray.

The "Private" Discussion with the Pastor

Though I struggled each day on two fronts—my inner battles and my struggles against the injustices I faced—I had not given up on my idea of finding someone that could sound the alarm on the stoicism classes, so I approached a Pentecostal pastor. This man inspired trust. He seemed to be a man who fulfilled his responsibilities with integrity, preaching with much passion and energy and rejoicing when an inmate responded positively.

"Hey, brother, can we speak for a few minutes?" I began.

"George, I'm sorry, I can't today, but Tuesday I can promise you that we will speak."

"Thank you!"

"You're welcome!"

That was the sum of our conversation one Sunday afternoon, so I had to wait for another two days for a few minutes with the pastor. I wanted to discuss spiritual things with him, things that influenced my spiritual state at the time. I wished to tell him about my battles and ask him to support me in prayer, but I also wanted very much to tell him about the stoicism classes that were poisoning some inmates with lies about the existence of God. Perhaps because of his position, I reasoned, he could do much to sound the alarm and stop the classes from taking place.

I was surprised when the pastor showed up at the gym at ten o'clock on Tuesday morning. I had never seen him there before.

"Hello, George! I came to get you so we could talk for several minutes. Come to the chapel!"

"We can speak on the volleyball court," I suggested. "There is no one there."

"No, come to the chapel. I insist!"

I went with him, impatient to talk about my problems. I hoped for some support. My colleagues watched us go with some surprise. As we were leaving the gym, an Albanian stopped me.

"I can see you're a good Christian," he grinned. "The priest follows you even to the gym!"

Entering the chapel, I sensed that the pastor was somewhat tense, but I did not give it much thought. He asked me to sit in a different chair than the one I had first chosen, then looked at me and said:

"So, then, George, you said you wanted to speak with me. I am listening."

"Sir, there are so many things that I would like to discuss with you..."

"No problem. I'm here to listen."

I began to talk about me, how God had changed my life, and about my family. I then started to open up more, talking about my problems, my sleepless nights, my panic attacks, my fear, and my depression. I had the sensation that he was listening and that, at long last, I was before the only one in that place of harassment who could sit and listen.

I continued opening up more and more, telling him about my plans for the future and the "Freedom House" center that I wished to start. It was a place I had long dreamed of starting after my release where newly-released inmates in Romania who had no support group and were at high risk for re-incarceration could go. For these men, liberty could be dangerous since, for example, many of them risked freezing on the streets during the winter. These men have no chance of being employed because wherever they go, they must do a background check, and when their potential employer discovers that they were in prison, the door is closed in their face. Romanian society, in general, is quite suspicious of these kinds of people and, unfortunately, rarely gives them the helping hand that they need to rehabilitate. Therefore, a large percentage of them—over fifty percent—prefer to return to prison, where the state provides them with a bed, food, medical care, and a weekly shower.

I told the pastor about our family business, where we produced packaging for fast-food restaurants in Eastern Europe. I told him how that since 2016, when I was incarcerated in Romania, my business partner and I had begun to employ ex-inmates that were released from the prison where I was staying and who, I knew, had no place to go. If I knew of an inmate that was to be released but no one to whom to go, I would call my business partner and ask him to come to pick up the man, find him a place to stay, and employ him in our business. I had done that a number of times, and until that moment when I spoke with the pastor, we already had six ex-inmates working at our company that had successfully reintegrated in society.

I told him about my wish, when I was released, to serve in the prisons of Romania. I told him how I would like to start an organization that can support both ex-inmates and those working with them.

I recounted my experience with a guard who had a "forbidden cross" tattoo on his leg. In addition, I made a grave mistake in telling him about my discussion with the guard and how I had told him that he dared to put it there because it was a Christian symbol and that if he put the crescent moon there with a red slash through it, he would be kicked out of the prison since the Muslim inmates revolt when their religion is mocked. That remark put my life in danger later on.

It all culminated with a discussion on the stoicism classes that some inmates in Huntercombe were obligated to attend. I was surprised to learn that he knew nothing about the classes. I told him that what was taught there was completely opposed to what the Bible said. I then told him about the posters on the prison walls and how some of the quotes spoke of non-existence of deity. I asked him how it was possible for all these things not to distress him. He said again that he knew nothing of the posters on the prison walls. The fact is that I should not even have had to tell him about them since the posters were so large as to be seen from the next postal code, and the lettering of the quotes was large enough to be easily read from a distance.

We ended the discussion on a positive note, with him telling me that he and the church he pastored would pray for me. He promised me that he would do everything in his power to find out more about the stoicism classes. In addition, he told me that he is totally opposed to the display of any quote that speaks against the existence of God and that he would ask the prison warden to replace those quotes with Bible verses. His assurances made me enormously happy, and I told myself that I had finally found someone that understood me.

Only that, on the day after our discussion, "the war" began. Whereas before, the guards at the gym had shown their dislike for me by denying me some rights that the other inmates enjoyed, now they openly showed their hatred of me to my face. When I entered the gym and greeted everyone, not one of the three guards present returned my greeting. I didn't think too much about it, since I was getting used to their ignoring me, but what surprised me was the attitude of the head guard. When he saw me enter the gym, he came immediately and summoned me to the area where the toilets and showers were located.

"Ignat," he hissed. "I want you to get busy cleaning these toilets right now! You hear?"

I will never forget that day. I stared at him, shocked. I had not even had time to change clothes. For a second, I considered simply turning my back and returning to my cell since he had no way of obligating me to do what he asked. It felt degrading to do as he asked, particularly since all the inmates had gathered and were watching as if we were a circus. Still, I felt I must show by my actions that I am a disciple of Jesus, so I humbled myself and did as he asked.

That section of the gym was taken care of by two Polish prisoners. I had never been asked to clean the toilets before; my job was to clean the exercise room. What he had asked me to do was completely outside of my normal responsibilities, but I got the necessary tools for the job and got to work.

But just as I was getting started, the Pole that was normally responsible for that job intervened and told the head guard, "I am responsible for this area."

"Put your mop down," rasped the guard with rage-filled eyes. "Today, I want to see Mister Ignat clean the toilets."

So it went the rest of the day and the next day. And so on, day after day, the guards' attitude toward me became more and more hostile. I put it all down as stemming from the old conflict that we had had and accepted it all. I spent a lot of time in prayer before God, daily asking him for strength and wisdom to show, through my actions and attitude, that I loved Him.

Brother Mike

Several days before I was to be visited by a man that was coming from America, especially to see me, I was stopped by a guard in the hallway.

"Hey, George, you're getting a visit in a few days? Someone from America is coming to see you, no?

"Oh, yes! Brother Mike—an extraordinary man—is coming! But why do you ask? Did something happen?"

"No," he replied, "This morning, I was just looking over the visits planned for this week and happened to see your name. So, the man coming to visit you, he's someone important?"

"He's important to me because he's a part of my family," I grinned. "Why do you ask?"

"Just out of curiosity. Is it true that he has a TV station?"

I stared at him. No one, outside of a Romanian to whom I had mentioned Mike's upcoming visit several days before, knew that he had a TV station. The guard's interest in Mike's coming raised my eyebrows somewhat.

I thought it odd that the guard would even mention it, but enough odd things were happening that I did not think about it much. I was looking forward to a visit from a dear brother from Arizona who had remained close to our family during my time in prison and who had answered my wife's prayers a number of times by sending her financial assistance.

Brother Mike had had an unusual experience with his son, who had been imprisoned in the USA. The young man had had a lot of problems because of an explosive temper, but in prison, he turned to God and came out a changed man, a man born-again.

Brother Mike did not often speak of the anger of his son in bygone years but rather of the joy he was experiencing now. He once told me, "Brother George, it's like looking at a rose and being charmed by its beauty and pleased by its smell. You don't think about the manure with its strong odor that was put at its roots and helped it grow. That's how it is with people, my son, in particular. I now rejoice that he is a man transformed by God and no longer think about what has been."

On the day of Mike's visit, I found out that my brother, Nicu, would be coming to visit as well. I was delighted; I needed encouragement so badly!

The two hours passed quickly. Brother Mike, a man who knew his Bible well, spoke from the Word, encouraging me enormously. God spoke to me a lot that day through him. At one point, Mike brought to my attention a chapter from Revelation.

"Brother George, do you know what the 'works of the Nicolaitans' were? It is speaking of homosexuality."

We discussed this problem some from a biblical perspective, but Mike spoke with much love of all men's need of salvation. Further on, we discussed some of the Lord's work that Mike wanted to work on in Romania. All too soon, the visit was over.

I remembered something Mike told me, that he, though he is an American citizen, was rudely received by the authorities at Heathrow. He was placed in a tiny room and left there until they had checked every piece of his luggage. They asked where he was going, to which he responded that he had come to visit a friend in prison. They then bombarded him with questions about his relationship with this friend, plus other questions. Mike was surprised since he thought he had been expected. *Did Mike's problems at the airport have anything to do with me? I wondered. Will the authorities go that far? Was my conflict with the prison guards somehow connected to the questioning he received at Heathrow?*

Two days later, the prison chaplain knocked on my cell door.

"Hello, George!" he greeted me. "May I come in?"

"Hello, Sir! Of course, have a seat!"

"George," he began, "I came to see you because I feel it necessary to tell you something."

"I'm all ears," I replied, greatly interested in what he might want.

"You know, there are people among us who are different than we are, who think differently, who have different views than we..."

"Of course," I replied, even more puzzled.

"I'm referring to... well, you know, those that choose to live differently, in which a man marries another man or a woman another woman."

"Oh, yes, I know. That is their choice. I thank God for my wife, and I want to stay that way!"

"Of course!" he responded. "And me too! But that is not what I am referring to, but to the fact that we must accept those people."

"Are they making you problems because of me? Do you feel that I am not able to accept someone that is not like me?"

"No... I'm just saying."

"You are asking what my attitude is toward such people?" I asked, still somewhat puzzled.

"Yes. What is your opinion of them?"

"I am of the opinion that God loves all people, just as he loves you and me. I believe that God wants all to be saved."

"Yes, I know that is God's attitude," he insisted, "but what is yours?"

"Who am I to have a different attitude toward someone than God does!" I exclaimed.

"So you love those people?" he queried.

"With all my heart!"

"Great! I am glad for that response," he said, rising from the edge of the bed and making his exit, seeming greatly relieved. It seemed as if he was expecting a different response. I had simply told him what was in my heart, which is, by God's grace, love for all such people, though not, of course, for their sin.

Several days later, something else occurred that I thought strange. It happened while I was attending a class about exercise and its positive effects on the body. Roughly twenty inmates were present, and we were listening to one of the gym guards who was teaching the class when I heard off to my right:

"Hey, George, did anyone ever tell you that you look like a homosexual?"

I looked at the man without knowing what he was talking about. It was a young black man, twenty-two years old, who was in the gym guards' good graces.

"No one ever told me that, but I would need to think..."

"Shut up, homosexual!"

I shut up.

"Shut up, homosexual! You're a gay! You and all the other Romanians in the prison!"

At that, two Romanians seated next to me wanted to stand up. I quickly motioned for them to remain seated. The other inmates were laughing. I just sat there, knowing that this young man was trying to get a rise out of me, as was the devil.

"You know what is interesting, young man?" I asked. "What you say does not affect me at all. Gay people are people just like you. God bless you."

At that point, the guard intervened, though he acted as if he had not heard the exchange, even though the young man had been speaking loudly. I wondered then if my private conversation with Mike just a few days before was the reason I had been approached by the pastor, and now, on the same subject, I was the target of attacks that were meant to be offensive. By the grace of God, I was not offended at all. I love gay people, and I pray for them just like I pray for my family.

I saw again that the devil, through other people, had been trying to get me to react in an ungodly way. Praise God that He, at that moment, gave me the patience and strength necessary to remain calm.

A Disagreement Among Friends

I noted that these people became even more hostile after my meeting with the Pentecostal pastor. I thought that perhaps he had already taken some measures, such as speaking to the prison leadership about the removal of the posters and the termination of the classes. But that was not it at all; my hope was in vain. I was soon to find out what had happened. M, very upset, called me into his cell.

"What happened, M?" I queried. "Why are you upset? Did someone make you mad?"

"Yes!" he sputtered. "It's you, George! You made me mad..."

"Why?"

"Good grief, man, when will you ever learn to shut up? When will you ever keep your big mouth shut? Don't you know that all that is happening to you is because you keep opposing those that can eat you alive? You're in a foreign country, with foreign laws and foreign people. You're only an immigrant! Your kids are looking forward to your return. Does that not matter to you? Forgive me for saying so, but I thought you were smarter than that! Let the people offer whatever classes they want! Let them put up their posters and put on them whatever they want to write! Let it go and say nothing to anyone!"

"May I ask you what happened?" I asked, shocked. "What have I done to make you yell at me like that?"

"George, who did you talk to in the last few days?"

"With you, with other guys from this section, with my family on the phone..."

"No," he insisted, "think harder. Did you talk with anyone else, such as a guard or someone in the prison hierarchy?"

"I spoke with a pastor," I said after a moment's thought. "He's a good guy. I told him how things are with the classes and other things. I think he listened and will try to do something to put a stop to courses. That's good news, isn't it?"

"Perhaps you haven't been very observant," M returned sardonically, "but everything you told that pastor is on the desks of those that are trying to figure out what to do with you. They are having meetings specifically to figure out how they can pin some incriminating evidence on you. You know they have people specially trained for that? You, in their eyes, are guilty, and that is all that matters to them! Be aware that all that you discussed with the pastor they have in writing and what you said has been twisted to be used against you."

"Wow!"

"Yes, wow!" he snapped sarcastically. "Don't you realize that these people think you are crazy, and they care not one bit what happens to you? They don't care if you live or die, if things go well for you if they don't. If they cared, they would have come to talk with you and tried to help. They are well aware of your emotional state and your problems, but they prefer to spy on you in whatever way they can and find you guilty of something. You managed to make them hate you the maximum amount possible and now somehow found a way to make them hate you even more! You are only a man, and from now trust no one, and keep your mouth shut. Don't you see that everything you say is used against you? All your good intentions mean nothing to them. I understand that they are on a witch hunt, and the timing of your release depends on them. Don't you understand?"

"But, come on, bro, I didn't mean to upset anyone!" I returned. "Don't you understand that people from this prison are condemning inmates to eternal death by teaching that God does not exist? They would send them directly to hell!"

"Okay, so they send them directly to hell, so what?" he rasped, now even more upset. "They can do whatever they want! What does it matter to you?"

"I..."

"You are up to your neck, and you still care that who-knows-who is going to hell? Please understand that until whoever it is gets there, it will have cost you your skin. Believe me: these guys don't play games. What they are doing costs a lot of money, which they must somehow justify. They have their superiors to report to, so they will search the moon and stars to try to find something more that you can be charged with. What will your kids say if their dad never gets home because he was trying to save people from hell?"

"I'm clean, M," I responded. "I have paid for my deeds. What they are doing is no more than a waste of money and time. But that is not what bothers me; what plagues me is my own condition that seems to get worse by the day. They will not keep me in prison; they have no grounds for doing so. But understand that they can destroy me psychologically and would not care if they did so. That's what worries me. As for my kids, I am sure they will find someone that can tell them the truth if something happens to me. M, the souls of men are of utmost importance; by comparison, everything else is of little worth."

M slapped his forehead with his palm and sighed. To a degree, M was right, and that saddened me. I was already in a delicate situation that seemed to be getting worse. I didn't know what to say or to whom to say it. Everything I said was used against me. Where could I find someone that could understand me?

I had thought that the pastor would understand me, help me, and offer support. But how? Everything I did came back at me. I was disoriented and had no idea what to do. But I had still not lost the motivation to tell the truth that they were, in this prison, actively trying to convince people that God did not exist.

"Hey, George, another thing." M's voice broke into my thoughts.

"Go ahead."

"Don't tell anyone anymore that you would like to serve in a prison, that you would like to start a Christian organization for ex-inmates in Romania. Those dreams are good, but they are seen as foolishness by the people here. They laugh at those dreams, thinking you're off the deep end."

"M," I replied seriously, "if it is God's will, those dreams will come true. But if they are only human ideas, they will come to nothing. Time will tell."

My discussion with M worsened my condition. Before I arrived in Huntercombe, I had no reason for fear but still panicked; now, I had some reasons. It was real; he that had dogged me months was putting together a well-laid plan. Using people, he was orchestrating events in order to bring all my fears to fruition.

But I still had God's protection, for which I was grateful. No longer only attacked on the level of the mind, I was now being "attacked" by people, but when I would allow myself to wallow in the misery that they caused me, the Holy Spirit would urge me to pray for them. Therefore, evening after evening, I brought them before God in prayer, each one by name, from the prison warden to lowest inmate, anyone that I knew was in any way connected to my present condition. There is a profound joy, a deep beauty found on one's knees in prayer for one that did him wrong.

One day, it happened that another inmate made a gesture that took me by surprise. He worked in the offices and, being around the guards all day, observed the misery that I was mired in. He, therefore, brought me a complete list of the leadership of Huntercombe prison, which he had found in a folder in the office and made a copy. I stared at him and at what he put in my hand.

"Take it," he hissed. "One day, you will need it in order to take all these bastards to court."

I took it, not to use it in court but in prayer whenever God gave me the impulse to pray for those that were making life hard. I now had a complete list of prayer requests!

Several days after he had given me the list, that inmate was transferred to another prison because he had gotten into a fight with one of his countrymen.

The Pastor Caught in the Middle

In the middle of all this, I was looking forward to the following Tuesday, when the pastor was scheduled to visit again. I wanted to talk with him again; I could not believe that everything I had said had been transmitted further.

I was disappointed. I had thought I could trust the man. Besides, while I do not know what the law in England says about private discussions between a man and his pastor, in most countries, such discussions remain confidential. In my situation, it proved to be otherwise.

Tuesday arrived, and upon arrival at the gym, I asked the guard—a young man who seemed to care less about what his colleagues said about me and the only one I ever dared asked for help—to call the chapel and tell the pastor that I would like ten minutes of his time to talk. The guard made a call, whether to the chapel or the front office I could not ascertain, and told me that the pastor would either come to see me or would summon me to the chapel.

An hour passed. I finally went to the guards' office to ask him to call the pastor again. Arriving at the office, I was surprised to see Guard B talking on the phone with someone, seemingly a colleague of his. His tone was harsh and angry as he asked where the pastor was and why he was not showing up. He seemed quite upset. When he saw me, his tone changed, and he smiled.

"I'm trying to get you the pastor, George," he said. "See how hard I'm trying to help you? I have not gotten through to him yet. He should be here somewhere, but no one seems to know where he is, and his radio is not turned on. I'll tell you when I find out anything."

I was shocked that Guard B had even spoken to me. He had not even returned a greeting for quite a long time, but now he makes a call to try to facilitate a meeting between me and the pastor. *How nice of him!* I thought but then immediately replaced that thought with the assumption that he probably had an ulterior motive for it.

Lunchtime arrived, and we went for lunch. We had an hour and a half in which we were locked in our cells. The guard to whom I had spoken that morning came to me and told me that he had not yet gotten through to the pastor, but by that afternoon, he was sure to speak to him. I thanked him and left for cell. In the hall, lo and behold, who should I run smack into but the pastor!

"Be blessed, Pastor! I was trying to locate you all morning!"

"I know," he returned. "I was busy and forgot to turn on my radio. They didn't get a hold of me until ten minutes ago. They told me that you were looking for me. How are you? Is everything okay?"

"Well, that is the problem: I'm not okay. From the time I had that discussion with you one week ago, things have become more and more complicated. There's more hate, more pressure from the gym guards, and not just that. I don't know what happened, Pastor, but it seems our whole discussion in the chapel, which had been confidential, is now known by all, guards and inmates alike. How could that happen?"

The pastor was visibly panicked. He looked one way, then another as if he was afraid to be seen speaking to me.

"George," he said, leaning in and speaking quietly, "I think you are sincere, but this situation is much more complicated than you think. You are too young and ill-equipped to understand some things. You need experience. I cannot give you an answer today; I am rushed. I have already had a rough day so far, so please understand me. Earlier today, I, too, was cussed out by someone in the prison hierarchy; I tell you that so that you know that there are some here that hate me too. You are not the only one."

"You were cussed out? I'm surprised! How is it even possible? Maybe because you didn't have your radio turned on?"

"Yes, who knows?" he replied. "I don't really know the reason, but it is certain the man tends to hate those he does not understand."

I tried to think quickly. The pastor was between the proverbial rock and the hard place, with the wishes of his boss—to relay information—on the one hand and his desire to do what was right on the other. I later heard rumors that the pastor had had some heated arguments with those in leadership because of what they were asking of him. Still, they had managed to convince him that I was nothing but a nefarious prisoner who was trying to hide his past, and, in order to find the "truth," he had to do as they wished.

"It's fine, Pastor!" I finally said. "When can we meet again?"

"Next Tuesday," he said hurriedly, "or perhaps this Thursday if I have time."

He hurried off, and I continued to my room, stopping along the way for my lunch. After arriving at my cell and eating, I lay down for a half-hour, but sleep evaded me. A thought kept nagging at me. *Why would the pastor be sworn at by a guard in the prison leadership?* I wondered. *Yes, he had his radio off and would not respond to their calls, but all that fuss over something so small?*

I remembered Guard B's tone of voice when he could not locate the pastor. Putting everything together, I thought that perhaps I should take M's advice seriously, keep my mouth shut, and trust absolutely no one.

I met the pastor the following week. In the interval, I had an accident at the gym. My foot had slipped while doing squats with a large amount of weight on my shoulders; I had fallen and hit my lower back on the weights. The accident meant that I was off of work for a while; I could barely walk and spent a lot of time in my room, M or another inmate helping me when I had to go to the phone or the doctor's office.

The pastor came to my section and found me, wanting to talk as he had promised. I invited him into my cell where we could sit and talk, but he insisted we go to the chapel. I tried to explain that I found it painful to walk, that it would take me long to get there, and that we could sit at one of the tables scattered throughout the prison where they served meals, but nothing but the chapel would do. So we started toward the chapel, with me using the walls for support and being assisted by the pastor.

Having arrived, I began to tell him how that after our last discussion, the guards' dislike of me seemed to increase. I knew that they had had access to everything we discussed, but I wanted to hear an explanation from him for how that could have happened. I did not get one; he only said that when I was older and had more experience, I would understand such things.

I finally understood that something was not right. There were only two possibilities that I could think of: either the pastor was passing on what I said, or our discussions in the chapel were being recorded. It seemed the situation was too difficult for the pastor; he was caught in the crossfire without knowing what was going on. He acted defeated. I don't think he wanted to dance to their music, but he felt he had no choice.

Now, knowing how things stood, I tried to discover more. As far as I knew, the only man who worked there that could be of any help to me was the pastor, but now he, too, was compromised. M was only an inmate with no more information than what slipped from between his bosses' fingers and what he heard the guards discuss.

One day, I asked a Turkish colleague who worked in the offices if he heard how that the police had opened an investigation into X's complaint. He said he didn't know but that he would check it out. Two days later, his attitude toward me changed radically. He was no longer the man that had said he would check things out. I sensed that he had passed on to his superiors what I had asked.

When such things happen, your natural reaction is to protect yourself. I knew no better way of doing so than going to God. The Lord was good. When the devil's attacks became too severe, He began to whisper, giving me peace and the strength to go on. Praise His name!

I felt the pastor did not want to be involved in what they were doing. He stopped by my cell one day and made me understand that God was using me to raise awareness about what they were doing in the prison and that prisoners were, many times, "educated" on God's non-existence against their will. He did not say much, but later I found out that he had done some research and discovered that the stoicism classes were indeed being done surreptitiously and that those responsible had not met the necessary requirements to make them legal. I understand that those in charge at Huntercombe were forced to terminate the classes and take down the posters negating the existence of God. That made me very happy, it was a victory, but I still wondered about the pastor. Was he really there to strengthen me, or was he sent by others with baser motives?

Another strange moment happened on a Sunday morning when I was in the prison chapel. A servant of God who served in Huntercombe Prison once every two weeks (whose name and position I will not write here) came close to me and said, "George, in this place, people are hating you, so be very careful. I don't know exactly what is happening, but my advice is to try to please these people." Then he came back and left. I tried several times to get details from him about what he told me, but I couldn't. I understood that, before this moment, he was also called for a meeting with the prison management in which aspects regarding my person were discussed. Things were becoming clearer and clearer. There were no people following in my footsteps but the devil himself.

My Friend, the Cashier

The prison's visiting room had a store where visitors could buy food, sweets, and drinks, including some things that we, prisoners, did not have access to except during a visit. When my brother came to visit, I would ask him to bring plenty of coins; the store only accepted coins—they could be caught by a metal detector—in case any of the cashiers, who were also inmates, would try to steal anything.

A Romanian worked at the store at Huntercombe. He had committed some kind of bank fraud and received a severe sentence. When he was not at work, he liked to exercise, and since I was in the gym all day, we became friends.

Whenever I was expecting a visit, I asked him to set aside something that I particularly liked; if it was something in high demand, it would not last long, and if the visit was in the afternoon, the pickings were usually slim if you didn't know the cashier. This particular young man was an agreeable guy, and he always, when asked, put aside a portion of spicy chicken for me.

At one particular visit, my brother went to buy the food I liked but returned, saying that they were out of it. I was surprised; I had told the cashier two days previous that someone was coming to visit and asked him to keep a piece of spicy chicken for me, but nothing was left in the store but bread, soft drinks, and coffee. I had some bread and coffee but did not understand what had happened.

The store always closed fifteen minutes before the end of visiting hours. On that particular day, my friend exited the store, dropped what was left in a cart, and left, along with an Arab friend. They walked directly past our table, but they ignored us completely. He was a good guy, and I was surprised by his actions. I resolved to ask him about it the next day at the gym.

At the gym the following day, I saw my friend, but he motioned me with his eyes to follow him to the dressing room. Once there, he looked around furtively.

"What happened with you, bro?" he asked

"Uh, what do you mean?" I replied, puzzled.

"Man, you're in a mess! I'm sorry I didn't say hi yesterday and didn't save you any chicken, but I was afraid a guard would see me, and I might lose my job.

"Oh, that's no problem," I returned. "I wasn't trying to do anything crooked. I asked nothing out of the ordinary. My buddies always pay for the food when I buy something. They would have no grounds for kicking you out."

"That's not what I'm talking about. I don't know if you found it out, but every visit you get, regardless of who the visitor is, is intercepted. Every conversation, every word that comes out of your mouth or the mouth of your visitor is recorded and listened to. Some guys from London came and installed some technology to listen in, man. They're saying bad things about you. I don't know exactly what they're saying; I don't want any trouble. It would be best if we were not seen talking. I have only two more months, and I'm going home. My family is waiting for me."

"Be calm, man, nothing will happen to you! I'm sorry if I wronged you in any way."

"It's okay, but I can't stay and talk with you more. I can't even save some food for your visits. I'm very sorry, but I'm off to finish my exercise."

"Okay," I replied, somewhat confused. "We'll be seeing you. Be cool."

"Okay, all the best."

He headed for the door, and I turned to sit on a bench. I did not feel well. What he said had troubled me to the point of dizziness, and I felt the need to sit down.

"Hey, another thing." My comrade stopped and turned toward me once more. "I'll say it fast."

"Go ahead," I replied somewhat wearily.

"You know that I work with an Arab that is also my roommate?"

"Yes, I know. What happened?"

"I don't know where this comes from," he sighed, "but they say you have no respect for Muslims and have said nasty things about them and their religion."

"What?" I gasped. "I am what? Disrespectful? To whom? To the Muslim religion? Well, I respect anyone's belief system!

What more is there? Who told you? Where did something like that come from?"

"I know no details. I'll find out more and tell you in the coming days. Take care of yourself. The Muslims in here are livid. I'm sorry. Take care of yourself."

In the days that followed, I tried to talk to him more, but he avoided me. In the last few weeks, before he was deported to Romania, he didn't even come to the gym. He seemed afraid that if he was seen talking to me, there would be consequences.

As my colleague had said, the rumor spread that I disrespected Muslims. The next day, Abdul, an inmate from Chechnya, a region in southern Russia bordering Georgia, came to me to ascertain that the rumor was false. We often worked out together, and he could not believe that I could say objectionable things about Muslims and their religion, yet exercise with him week after week, talking about all manner of things, and never show any lack of respect.

I assured him there was absolutely nothing to it, but even so, beginning on that day, my relationship with Abdul began to go south. He would politely refuse when I proposed that we exercise together. I understood that there would be no point in pressing him; though I had assured him that the reports were completely false, he could not completely ignore everything he was hearing.

Still, I do know that as the report circulated throughout the prison, Abdul came to my defense when other inmates spoke ill of me. I found that out from another Muslim soon before I left for Romania.

Let the Blood Run

Now things were much clearer. On the one hand, what was happening saddened me, but on the other, I was happy to have a better understanding of what was transpiring. I had at least put to rest the theory that the devil was directly involved in the transmission of information. It may sound like an outlandish theory, but there are people in the world who are in direct contact with the powers of darkness. I was glad that, in my case, it was simpler; they were using technology to capture my discussions.

Now the question was, what were they after? If they were only after incriminating evidence, why would they construe the mention of a tattoo as Islamophobia and then spread it throughout the prison? There was more to it than a simple search for truth, I decided. They had declared war on one who dared to openly criticize some of the things they promoted. Their goal was to destroy me emotionally, if not physically. Accusing someone of Islamophobia in a prison where nearly three hundred of the inmates are Muslims is no small matter.

One day, something else happened that disturbed me considerably. M came to work, upset. He told me that he had gotten into a heated argument with two other inmates and a guard, and he feared that its repercussions might affect his job. The argument had stemmed from my discussion with my wife, Adriana. While I will not go into details out of respect for her, M had overheard the three men making crude jokes about my wife and her extra weight. While I could have overlooked even that when I understood that every word of my private discussion with my wife had not only been recorded but spread throughout the prison for everyone to hear and make jokes about, I wanted to go straight to the prison warden, but M stopped me. Of all the things that happened to me in the prison, I consider this to be one of the most unjust.

Wow! I thought. *What does that have to do with finding the truth?*

I thought that regardless of what I said or how well-intentioned I was, it would do no good because they would just distort what I said and either use it against me or make jokes out of it, whichever best served their own interests. That day, I decided to call home and ask my family to get in contact with the press, with the human rights services, or with anyone that would be interested in the fact that in 2018, in a prison in England, an inmate was systematically put under intense psychological pressure. I had thought that such things could only happen in communist countries and other dictatorships.

But whenever I would put my hand on the phone to make the call, something in my spirit said, "No, George! It's no use. You will accomplish nothing but to disturb your loved ones." I knew it was of the Lord, so I never made the call.

One day, on my way to the gym, I stopped outside the office of the security guards. I wanted to scream as loudly as I could about the injustice of it all. I wanted to protest, to refuse to enter my cell, to do anything that showed that I had had enough. But again, the Lord warned me. "No, George, it's no use. You are only an inmate, and you would accomplish nothing but to give them more reason to call you crazy. Besides, that's not My way. Come to your cell. We must talk."

I bowed my head and walked toward my cell. There, within the four walls of that tiny room, I met with my Lord. There in my cell, we talked. Often there, during the night, I had won some of the sweetest victories of my life. No medal or trophy of any athletic career can compare with the victories that I won there, in the midst of intense personal suffering. I stayed on my knees for hours on end, talking with God and telling Him all that was happening. Had I not done so, had I not let myself fall into His arms, I doubt I would be writing this book; I may not even be alive. But the most wonderful thing of my entire prison experience was that I saw, with my own eyes, that man's help is fallible, but God's help, in times of need, is never lacking.

Who is, in Fact, the Enemy?

After my original discussion with M, when I found out that the authorities suspected me of serious crimes, and even more, after my discussion with the cashier who gave me more details on exactly what was happening, I did a lot of reflecting on the position in which I found myself. It was clear to me that this situation involved more than met the eye; this case was being influenced by the powers of the spiritual world that surrounds us. It was clear that I had to win the war, and in order to win, I had to stop fighting strictly defensively. I had to launch a counter-attack, which would be done on my knees. The most important thing that I now understood more clearly than ever is that I had a very real enemy and that behind all the evil that those around me were doing, there was one that was controlling it all. Nothing happened out of pure chance.

The fact that I finally understood that was very important. It cleared my mind, and things began to make sense; and in a battle, when things make sense, one begins to think he may actually be able to win.

I also understood that the devil was trying to neutralize a threat to him and his kingdom, and he would destroy me if necessary and if I allowed him to do so. He does not always try to destroy a person physically; a young person's seeming inability to stop wasting time on YouTube, a lady's habitual neglect of her time with God, a man's addiction to pornography—these are all symptoms of spiritual warfare, the devil's attempt to neutralize a threat. A life transformed through the power of God is a menace to his power, and he will do anything necessary, including taking a life if he is allowed to do so, in order to remove a threat.

Another one of his tactics was to make me be misunderstood by those around me. The attitude of those around me, the prison authorities, was not so much a result of their being evil people but of their believing the devil's lies. Just as he lied to me by putting those thoughts in my mind, so he lied to them about me.

Knowing these things gave me the strength to go on. I knew that Jesus Christ had defeated this enemy two thousand years ago at Golgotha, and I, believing in that sacrifice, could be victorious as well.

I knew that the most important battles in history were won on the knees; I knew that prayer was the way Satan could be defeated, but I had not been prepared for this fight. I had been a practicing Christian for more than five years, and I had some extraordinary experiences with God. These experiences helped me tremendously, serving as reminders of God's power, but I had not been prepared for a fight with the devil.

I did not know how to fight because I did not know who I was in Christ. I did not understand my identity in Christ. I was a born-again Christian, a child of God, as the Bible says, but I did not understand how my identity as a child of God could be of assistance in this fight. This made me a loser from the very beginning.

What makes so many Christians fall victim to the attacks of the devil is the fact that though they love God, they don't fully know how to exercise their rights as His children, bought by the blood of His Son.

God Sends Me an Angel

I must write briefly about a person that I came to know whom I considered an angel, sent by God to me particularly for this time.

One Thursday afternoon, soon after I arrived at that prison, as I was standing in the lunch line with other inmates, I saw the door open, and a lady of diminutive stature walked in with a handbag on her shoulder and several magazines in her hand. She stopped and tried to talk to an inmate, but he excused himself, saying he was busy. She went on to another, who talked with her briefly and accepted a magazine.

What caught my attention was the glow that emanated from this lady. She had a gentle face, like that of a mother, and a smile that inspired trust. When she came closer and stopped near me, I knew she was a child of God.

I started speaking with her, but after only a few minutes, a fight started among some of the inmates, and the guards asked everybody to go to their cells. Because of the incident, I did not get to talk to that sister for more than a few moments. Even so, in the few minutes that we did speak, my heart was filled with joy. She gave me a Christian magazine and promised that she would be back the next Thursday.

I waited impatiently for the chance to talk to her again. When she came, we sat at one of the tables where the inmates ate their meals. I was told that she was a volunteer and came every Thursday to speak with the inmates for a specified period of time.

Every Thursday, I tried to finish my work at the gym early in order to be at the section before 5:00 p.m., so I could meet with S. This sister came at a real time of need for me. The moment I saw that she was a born-again Christian, a relationship of brotherhood was established, and I could share with her the problems I was facing and the fear in my heart.

The sincerity with which she listened to my questions and the fact that she was willing to pray with me specifically for those situations convinced me that, at last, I had found an honest person in the prison who was not sent to spy on me, as had the chaplain and the pastor. She was sent by God to support me.

Once, as we were talking, S said she had a surprise for me. She reached into her handbag and pulled out three books: a book of meditations in English by Richard Wurmbrand, the famed Romanian pastor—a book that encouraged me enormously; *God's Smuggler*, by Brother Andrew, the founder of Open Doors; and *The Steps to Freedom in Christ* by Dr. Neil Anderson, an American brother.

God's Smuggler is the account of the smuggling of millions of Bibles through the Iron Curtain to the Christians under communism for whom the book was forbidden. I was fascinated by how God worked through and with Brother Andrew. *The Steps to Freedom in Christ* helped me understand that being a Christian entailed victory over the powers of darkness. It helped me understand what Paul wrote in Ephesians, chapter 6, about spiritual battles and the weapons of defense and attack that we have at our disposal.

These books, particularly the last one, shed a lot of light on the darkness around me. When I discovered that Neil Anderson wrote more books about spiritual warfare, I immediately called my brother, Nicu, and asked him to buy all the books he could find that were written by this man and send them to me as quickly as possible.

Within a week, I received the books and devoured them. Of course, the Bible was still the food of which I ate every day and without which I could not have survived spiritually, but these books helped me tremendously.

The evil one still attacked, but I began to score small victories; they were small, but victories nevertheless, and they encouraged me and gave me some time to recover.

It felt as if I had found a recipe for success in my battles. The meetings with S were extremely important; every week, she would see how I was and how I was progressing.

One Sunday afternoon, when the cell doors were locked and I was engaged in one of the fiercest battles I had yet faced, there was a knock on my door.

"Hey, George!" I heard S's voice from the other side of the door.

"S! God bless you!" I responded happily.

I went to the door and managed to see through the crack between the door frame and the door itself.

"George," went on my friend, "I came with another lady, also a volunteer, to bring you some books."

I could see the other lady through the crack as well.

"God bless you!" I said again. "How did you manage to get in?"

"I think it was the work of God. There is no other way to explain it, but at any rate, the important thing is that we are here. How are you? How are you feeling?"

"I'm not very well, S," I murmured. "I was again hit hard by that condition that you know about. But now that you have come, I feel much better! Praise God!"

"George, I brought you some books as I promised, but I don't know how to give them to you. I'll go see if the guard will unlock your cell for a minute."

She returned a moment later.

"I'm sorry, he refused," she reported. "But I'll put them here on the floor beside the door so you can get them in the morning."

"Thank you, S!" I said fervently. "God bless you for your efforts. Thank you with all my heart!"

After a short dialogue, which encouraged me a lot, these two ladies prayed for me and left, about twenty minutes after their arrival, leaving me in a completely different state than that in which they had found me. I had gotten the strength to go forward, though I knew the enemy would attack again. For at least a full day, I had what I needed to win. How important it is for those that face depression or other demonic attacks to have support from other people! For me, access to people that understood and could help me was very limited. On that day, though it was not Thursday and the inmates were locked in their rooms, God opened the prison doors for those two angels to come to my cell.

After they left, I got a songbook and began to sing. I sang with my whole heart, loud and full of joy. I sang till the hallways rang! Why would I care what the inmates or guards said! To them, I was just a crazy inmate, but I rejoiced in my God and thanked Him for the miracle that He performed for me.

Later, things began to get worse again. S offered me a large percentage of her time within the walls of Huntercombe, time in which she would normally have been in other sections of the prison. But when I was in need, and she could see it, she spent all her time with me, reading the Word and praying. Of course, that did not go unnoticed by the guards and the prison leadership, so one Thursday, S told me that her boss, the chaplain, forbade her to bring any more books for the inmates.

"But, S," I protested, "you promised me that book..."

"I know, George," she sighed, "but these are the new rules."

"Do you think the chaplain saw you bringing books on occasion?" I asked.

"I don't know, but it seems strange to me," she mused. "In all my time as a volunteer here, no one said anything about it. Another thing: the chaplain told me that I am spending too much time in the Patterson section and that I should divide my time equally among all the sections, but he did say that I still have the right to spend more time where I think the need is greatest."

"Thank you, S," I said, "but what about that book? Do you think you will manage to bring it in?"

"I don't think so," she replied. "I'm sorry; rules are rules."

"Yes, I know," I sighed. "When rules are made unscrupulously, as we both know that this one was, I don't think it's wrong to break them. Remember Brother Andrew, God's smuggler? You brought me his book."

S smiled gently. "We can pray, George. God will make a way."

S was right; God did finally get that book to me. I found it in the chapel next to some other Christian books. It was another book that helped me a lot in my daily battles.

One day, returning to the gym from lunch, I was surprised to see S coming out. I had not known it, but she sometimes came to the gym while the prisoners were at lunch and exercised.

"Hey, S, I'm delighted to see you! I see you have your training equipment with you. I didn't know you enjoy that sort of thing!"

"George," she responded warmly, "God bless you! I'm happy to see you too! Of course, I enjoy exercise; it keeps me in shape. Exercise equals health."

"Oh, how glad I am to see you," I exclaimed. "The last book you gave me was excellent! It helped me to understand some important aspects of the Christian life. We have much to talk about; I'll be expecting you in the Patterson section!"

"Of course! I'll come this afternoon, but until then I must tell you about a victory that I think we will win. You remember that we discussed the posters in the prison halls, and I promised that I would try to find a way to put some Bible verses on walls?"

"Yes, I remember," I said eagerly.

S motioned me to step to the side, more out of the public eye.

"George, I petitioned the head of the gym guards, Mister A, and he told me very politely that he could not help me, that I had to talk to the prison warden. Two days ago, I sent him an email with my request. So I hope we'll get four or five Bible verses on walls! What do you say?"

My heart nearly exploded with happiness. *What a sign of victory! I thought. After all that suffering, the Word of God will be displayed for all the inmates in Huntercombe to see on these very walls!*

"What can I say, S, but 'praise the Lord!'" I exclaimed. "That makes me so happy! I'll look forward to the reply; I think it will be positive."

As we were rejoicing and praising God for S taking the initiative to send that email, Guard A, the head of the gym guards, came out of the dressing room. He stopped, looked at S and me, and frowned. He looked at us rather strangely when he saw we were talking to each other. I greeted him respectfully, as I had always done to all the guards.

His frown did not disturb me; I was used to that, but S shrugged in a puzzled way when he greeted us so coldly.

The next Thursday, S did not come, nor the next, nor the next. I asked the chaplain what had happened. He said he didn't know, that perhaps she was sick. I prayed for her, thinking that was the case. I prayed that God would bring her back; she was great spiritual support for me. I could not get used to the idea that I may never again have someone like her to pray with.

My friend M asked me what happened to S. He knew her too and had many times discussed the Bible with her. He was seeking God during that time, trying to learn more of Him, and S was a great help. I asked him to try to find out what had happened; perhaps he could learn something from the guards while he was in their office.

One afternoon, M came to me. "It's exactly as I suspected," he told me bitterly. "S has been prohibited from volunteering in the prison on the grounds that she brought books to the inmates and converted prisoners of other religions to Christianity."

I smiled, but it was a bitter smile. I knew that it was because she brought me books and because she had the courage to petition the warden to put up posters with Bible verses on the prison walls. I am convinced that was the true reason.

When people are filled with the Holy Spirit and willing to be used by God, He will use them even in their absence. Exactly one month after S was banned from entering the prison, M received a letter from her. He came to my cell happily, and we excitedly read the few lines written by S.

She said that she no longer had permission to enter the prison without a specified reason. They said that her access to the prison had been suspended for a specific situation, but she did not disclose what that situation was. She then wrote some encouragement for both of us, then at the bottom of the page, in small letters: "For George, Acts 25:24–27." I immediately opened my Bible and read the passage, how the Jews accused Paul and tried to kill him, but how the authorities found him not guilty of anything, much less of anything worthy of death.

That evening, I wept before the Lord and thanked Him for S. Though she no longer had access to the prison, I knew she was praying for me. Furthermore, God had prompted her to write that letter, through which God had spoken to me: "Don't worry. Just as the Jews wanted to kill Paul, so there are people here that want to destroy you. Just as Paul was innocent, so are you. And just as Paul escaped from their hands, so you will escape the hands of those here."

S's letter brought me peace for several days.

I did not meet S again during my stay at Huntercombe. After I was freed and deported to Romania, I found out that she was again allowed to enter the prison as a volunteer. I assume they "resolved" the situation that had her banned. May God bless this lady and her family!

New Information Appears

"Good morning, George!" M greeted me. "What are you doing?"

"Good morning!" I returned. "What is there to do? I'm going to call home. What are you up to?"

"I'm making you a coffee. Come over when you've finished your call. We'll drink a coffee and talk."

M inviting me to his room for a coffee was not unusual, but I could see in his eyes that he had something important to tell me. We had to be careful where we spoke because we could be overheard anywhere in that closed and well-controlled environment. I had nothing to hide, but I was sick of having more words recorded and reinterpreted in order to be used against me. After my phone call, I went straight to M's cell.

"You want to play table tennis, George?" he asked.

"Sure, let's play," I replied. "But I got whipped last time we played."

He grinned. We always encouraged each other that way. Sometimes one of us won, sometimes the other, and we always ribbed each other good-naturedly over our games. I need to admit M was the better player.

We started our game and our coffee. M was known for the coffee and milk concoction that he made. He had a lot of patience. It took him quite a spell to make it, but he produced a terrific coffee.

"George," he finally began, "I heard a few more things about you and the investigation..."

"I'm all ears," I replied, greatly interested.

"All this foolishness started, they say, because of the way you act," he continued. "They became suspicious when they saw the fear and stress on your face. They thought that perhaps you were hiding something, so they started investigating."

"What do you think, M?" I asked. "Would it not have been simpler if they had just come and asked if something happened? Would it not have been easier for everyone if they had started on the premise that I need help? Maybe there is something behind my emotional state. Sure, that is the 'official' reason, but we both know the truth."

M shook his head. "Anyway, this investigation that they are doing into your past is starting to look like a big circus. Some of the guards are starting to shrug whenever the subject comes up."

"It's no wonder, M. They were filled and inspired by too much hatred. They were so upset at me that they thought no one could stop them, but in the end, the truth will stop them; it is the only thing that can."

"I don't know what to think," M replied thoughtfully. "I must admit that at the beginning, I, too, thought that what they were saying about you was true. It took me a while to figure out what was actually going on. You should know one thing: if you had not spoken against them and what they are teaching here, they would not have had the motivation to put so much pressure on you. I'm still wondering who is profiting from this circus."

"No one is! Sooner or later, they will have to admit they're on a wild goose chase. The biggest problem is the pressure that they have put and are continuing to put on me. They wanted so badly to find something that they never considered the possibility that I was hiding nothing. But what will happen if they break me, if some night, I finally snap? What if tomorrow morning you have no one talk to. My parents lost a son; my children lost their dad... Who will answer? Who will care?"

"The situation truly is serious, George," sighed M. "But the truth is, no one will answer, and no one will care. They will say that it was unavoidable; you had some emotional problems and that finally, you snapped. Do you think that anyone will realize or care what they did?"

"Of course not," I replied. "But there is a sense of justice that God has put in this fallen world. The Bible says that what is done in secret will be revealed. Someday, their injustice will be found out."

"Who would believe that, George?" M shot back. "They are betting on the fact that if you say anything, they will say you're crazy, and no one will believe the story of this guy with mental problems."

"M, I believe in God, and I really don't care if someone else thinks I'm crazy," I returned. "I'm trying not to be upset with any of them because I know that behind them is my real enemy.

So I trust in the only One that can really help in this war: God. Behind all injustice is someone planning it, and that someone cannot be defeated with a fist, an army, or a lawyer. He can be defeated only in the name of Jesus Christ."

"I never thought that deeply about it," replied M thoughtfully. "I always thought that behind anyone's bad actions, even my own, was human hatred and nothing more. But it seems that perhaps there is something deeper and more sinister..."

"I have often asked myself, especially as I've gone through this time, how many people throughout history have suffered unjustly. How many people have had everything taken, from their material possessions to their liberty, their family, even their lives, because those in power misinterpreted their emotional state or the expression on their face and assumed they were guilty. Do you understand the seriousness of what is happening? These people nearly destroyed me because 'it seemed to them I was guilty.'"

"They say your expression led them to think that."

"M, does that seem right to you?" I demanded. "Because someone's expression is one way or another, you then have the right to destroy them? For me, body language no longer exists. I will no longer judge another, as long as I live, based on what people call 'body language,' so help me God. The facial expression, gestures, and the rest can be influenced by many different factors. But I must admit that, before this experience, I have been guilty of doing so, just like these men."

"Well," admitted M gravely, "I, too, many times, judged people based on how they act..."

"There are times when I start sweating profusely; I blush, my heart pounds, the veins on my temples stand out, I'm enveloped with fear and panic, my heart feels as it will jump out of my chest... Now I ask you: does it mean I am guilty of something, just because I experience such things, a condition that I cannot control?"

"It's your battle, George, and you are probably not the only one. But," M brightened, "I have some good news for you too."

"At last, good news!" I exclaimed. "Bring it on!"

"Those in charge of this investigation have gotten in contact with the authorities from Romania to ask them about you. They told them of your emotional state and asked them to do some digging and see if you didn't commit some crime there. Several days ago, the answer came back, and they say they have found nothing. So the British authorities got back to the those at Huntercombe, saying they can indict you for nothing, that there is no evidence that you committed any of the things that have been circulated. I suppose the guys here were pretty disappointed. All their dreams of catching a great criminal or rapist simply collapsed. What do you say? Ain't that good news?"

"Why would I call that good news?" I asked with a wide smile. "The good news that happened here is that God strengthened me and helped me through this time. The fact that they didn't find anything does not surprise me in the least. After all, it's difficult to find something that's not there."

"At any rate, I wanted you to know it," M replied. "I thought it was important for you to know and that you would find it helpful."

"M, at the risk of being redundant, the only One who helps me is God, though He often uses people. He was the One that really took care of me. People should not be feared; they want trophies, recognition. These people dreamed of praise and awards for cornering me. M, a God exists that will allow nothing to remain hidden; everything, even the best-kept secrets of men, will, at the appropriate time, come to light."

"George, another thing..."

"What is it?"

"They told me this morning that they consider you... I don't know... They used a funny word. Let me think. Oh, yes, they called you 'schizophrenic.'"

"Okay, what does that mean? Is it good or bad?"

I am embarrassed to report that, at the time, I did not know what the word "schizophrenic" meant. I did some research and discovered it is not a good thing. If they reached that conclusion, perhaps I should have been sent to a psychiatrist. That may have been good for me, but it would not have helped their investigation.

"George, yet another thing: you sing pretty often; I hear you from my cell. It's okay to sing in your cell, but not throughout the prison. The guards say you sing loud wherever you are, the gym, the halls, the library. They say it's suspicious that you are forever singing that Jesus forgave you, He helped you, He healed you. They say you sing about forgiveness and that it's a sure sign that you did something wrong and feel guilty. Try to sing less throughout the prison, and try to keep it mostly to your cell."

"M," I grinned, "I sing so badly that I thought for sure no one listens. You've just given me more good news: people are listening! That's great!"

"Come on, George, it's no joke. I think you sing too much. I think there are a number of Christians here, but you don't hear them singing in the halls."

"I sing to God," I responded, "because of what He's done for me. How can I keep from singing? Look, I'm here, alive, with you, healthy! Don't you see all the reasons I have for singing? And another reason is that I am encouraged to listen to God more than to those around me."

"Okay, okay, whatever." M rolled his eyes. "But at least change the songs because those that say 'God has forgiven you' sound suspicious."

"M, whatever I sing, whatever I say, I will make these people suspicious. They're on the hunt for blood, and therefore everything they hear makes them suspicious. But seriously, bro, do you think I have a wealth of songs that I can choose from? I don't know many, only a few, and I must sing what I know. They will not stop me; I will keep singing about God's forgiveness. Oh, if only they would know how much they, too, need God's forgiveness, they would help me sing!"

M and I went our ways. Arriving in my room and thinking about our discussion, it occurred to me that those songs of praise to God disturbed the devil more than anyone else. That was the problem! I resolved to never stop singing. "Be swift, my soul, to answer Him, be jubilant, my feet, our God is marching on!" It's a song dear to my heart, and day after day, you could hear me belting out the chorus from quite a distance: *"Glory, glory, hallelujah!"*

I learned that, in the fight with the enemy of our souls, there is no room for compromise. You compromise just once, and it will be much easier to do it the second time. The devil knows that if he can get you to compromise once, he has you on his hook.

My discussions with M helped me so much. There were not many that were readily disposed to talk to me, particularly after all the gossip. The news he brought should have made me very happy, at least that was what M thought, but the news was not the cause of my joy. Why should I be happy that they found nothing against me?

The fact that they got a negative result from the authorities in Romania as well as in London changed the attitude of those in Huntercombe. I felt it. Frustration was written on some faces, and they did not hesitate to express it if the occasion arose. Others looked at me and spoke, for the first time, in a friendly way. The prison chaplain, out of the blue, told me that he was working hard to find a Romanian pastor to come in weekly and preach to the Romanian inmates.

The pastor looked me up and told me to be strong and not give up on my ideas, even if some people think they are far-fetched. I was surprised when he grabbed me by the shoulders and said, "George, you are healthy! Don't give up, but preach the Word of God without fear!"

His words were a great encouragement, and I could see on his face that he felt bad that he had had a hand in all the foolishness. I am convinced that he is a man of God but had buckled under the pressure from the prison leadership and danced to their tune. I saw all these changes in attitude and thanked God.

Even with all of that, the attacks of the evil one did not slack off. All the pressure to which my mind had been subjected made my condition much worse than when I first arrived at Huntercombe several months before. I continued, nevertheless, to fight for life, hour after hour, day after day, night after night.

The Madness Begins

Rumors had been circulating through the halls of Huntercombe for some time. It was a delicious tidbit, so it became a subject of wide discussion. They said that that big Romanian, the ex-MMA fighter, is under investigation for all kinds of crazy things. It was a subject that caught a lot of attention in a prison where nothing of note had happened for months. Since there is little to do in a prison, juicy gossip is in high demand, and something like this, worthy of Hollywood, fits the bill perfectly. What R had told me had ceased affecting me since it was several weeks past. I decided I would keep to myself and no longer let the lies that were circulating affect me.

I didn't feel free to speak my mind anywhere. My life was a strange mixture of the love of God keeping me afloat and the hatred of Satan pulling me down. Had it not been for God's sustaining me, I cannot imagine what may have happened with me.

I was extremely frustrated during this time. As I watched the lengths to which they went to close me in, I could not help but get frustrated. Soon after, I was told by a person whom I was not sure if I should trust or not that even in the gym, they were recording and looking for me to say something that could help their case. I had an idea to try to verify that they could hear whatever I said. I knew that if I said something that interested them, I would be able to tell if they heard it by their actions.

Therefore, one morning as I was working out with R, I began accusing myself out of the blue.

"R, you know, they are right. X has every reason to be afraid of me."

"What are you talking about?" R was puzzled.

"About X. He didn't go to the police for nothing; he should be afraid of me."

"What are you implying? What in the world are you talking about?"

"Well, he's afraid of me, and he has a reason to be. Years ago, I was a tough one. I beat people up left and right until they were strewn all over the floor. There were a lot of them, all of them idiots."

R stared at me. The expression on his face was priceless, and I nearly burst out laughing but restrained myself.

"Why are you telling me that?" he finally managed. "That's the past; let's exercise. Let the past lie, and let X and B do their thing. Let's get some exercise done."

"Sure, let's do it! But be aware that I was a tough one. Everyone was scared of me. Bro, you don't know what I was. You don't play around with me."

R continued staring at me even as we began working out again. He did not understand what I was up to, and I could not tell him at the time.

"Hey R," I continued after our workout was over, "do you think someone could hear what I told you about how tough I was? Do you think anyone was listening?"

I said that to make the circus more interesting for them.

It was enough to shake something loose. The next day nothing happened, but the following morning there was quite a commotion. They said they had long been waiting for the moment when George said something that justified their investigation, which I do not avoid calling a masquerade. The guards were clearly thrilled, as was X. Starting that morning, X was again under my nose when I was working out. If I did chest exercises, he did them as well. If I worked on my legs, so did he. He was constantly beside me, waiting for me to say something to R again which they would find interesting.

That day I said nothing of interest. When I was finished, I headed upstairs, and perhaps for the first time since my arrival at Huntercombe, I was not depressed when I got to my room. It was comical, the way I had made them so happy. I could see the glee on their faces.

The next day their composure was returning, so I thought I should give them a reason to get worked up again. I motioned R over.

"And so what if X called the police? If he says something about me, I'll tell them something about him."

I thought for a moment, then continued.

"X sold drugs. I should tell the police that. Good, I'm prepared if he tells them anything about me."

Again, they were all animated for several days. Poor R was so surprised he didn't know how to respond. I played the role of a person going completely bonkers, and I began to enjoy watching their excitement.

I continued doing it for several days. *You think I'm crazy?* I thought. Here, let me give you a reason to think so.

"R?"

"Yes, George."

"Long time ago at the nightclub where X was present, I beat up one hundred and fifty people in a single night, all by myself."

R was lifting weights and nearly dropped the bar on his feet. "How many?"

"One hundred and fifty. They all had sticks and stones in their hands, but I jumped in and knocked out five with one blow. They were all over the floor. They had no idea what happened."

To this day, when I remember R's face, I grin. Poor R no longer knew what to think of me. He had heard I was crazy, but now he could see and hear himself that I was completely nuts. I couldn't tell him what I was doing, at least not in the gym.

"One hundred and fifty people is a lot, no joke," he finally managed.

"Keep your mouth shut, and don't tell anyone," I warned. "Make sure no one finds out. I would like to write that in a book sometime, but until then, don't tell. If you let out my secret, I'll write a few lines about you."

God helped me keep my word, as I have written a few lines about him. R was more and more perplexed. He didn't know what to say to all this foolishness, but he did listen and kept his mouth shut.

The next day: "Hey, R."

"Yes, George."

"You know that we are poisoned every day?"

"We are *whaaaat*?"

"Poisoned."

"How?"

"They put poison in our food," I said as seriously as possible. "They do it every day. I'm not going to eat anything except what I buy at the store."

"Wow!" he replied. "That means I should buy some stuff myself."

Shortly thereafter, the chaplain came to see me. He seemed very eager to help me.

"George," he told me, "if something is heavy on your heart, don't forget that I'm here to help you. You don't have to go through anything alone. You can tell me anything. You can confess anything, no problem. I know how to keep secrets, and you can be certain that no one will find out what you said."

"I'm fine," I replied. "I have nothing to confess."

He looked at me narrowly. "I want you to know that sometimes we get the impression that someone is trying to harm us when, in reality, it's not really true."

I said nothing, just looked at him in puzzlement, so he continued. "For example, sometimes we may think someone is trying to harm us by poisoning our food or drink. Such things are just in our heads." (Of course, it was not the case; the food was not poisoned in any way. I just wanted to check if the rumors of being recorded in the gym were true.)

When he said that, I could not keep the smile off my face. *Bingo!* I told myself. *So the person who told me they were recording in the gym was right! They are indeed listening in!*

So, I kept up my role of psycho for a period of time. I saw how it stirred them up, and I figured after the difficulties of the last few months, it was my turn to smile.

Later, I explained to R the games I was playing. He laughed, too, and thought it a great joke, but I have since wondered if I did the right thing. Was I led by the Spirit of God, or was I simply venting my frustration and resentment?

Regardless of how they treated me, I, as a Christian, should not have acted that way. I believe that God has shown me since then that I did not do the right thing; even if it did improve my condition, I was somehow trying to, in some small way, get even, something a Christian should not do.

After several days, M came to me and told me that he could no longer tell me much of what he heard since the guards were starting to avoid him, but he saw that they were agitated every time the subject of "George" came up, and he did not understand what was happening. There were periods of time when they had meetings to discuss me. The guards seemed happy that I was finally starting to talk. They never suspected that George, in his terrible condition, would prank them. They took everything seriously and were happy that all their work to get an investigation started seemed to have been justified.

One day I was out in the exercise yard when a prison officer that was involved in my investigation appeared at the window of one of the administrative buildings nearby. He smiled at me in a rather self-satisfied way, and I smiled back. He raised his middle finger, but I kept smiling. He then gave me the finger with his other hand as well, and I kept smiling, though it was a little forced, to be honest. He seemed to be trying to communicate, "At last, we've got you. You are ours." It didn't seem to occur to them that I could play pranks.

I do have a side that enjoys jokes, but it was not often seen in prison. In my younger years, I loved jokes, pranks, and all manner of foolishness, but when I became a Christian, I had to repent of those kinds of practices. The Bible warns against foolish and crude jokes, though a good clean joke is still something I enjoy.

I do somewhat regret the way I pranked the guards. From a human point of view, perhaps my actions were understandable, but they were not justifiable from a Christian standpoint. A child of God should not deceive anyone, whether in-joke or not, and when I understood that, I stopped my antics.

The Last Attacks Before My Departure

I knew that the Lord would give me victory in my struggle with depression. My freedom was nearing. The pressure was greater than ever, but I was beginning to be battle-hardened. God was giving me the strength necessary to pass through any attack more easily. It was the last day before my departure, and I felt that the devil was ready to play his last card.

It was a Wednesday morning, and a "well-intentioned" inmate whom I considered a friend came and told me that in Huntercombe prison, there were three detectives from Scotland Yard posing as inmates. These three, two men and a lady, along with the prison warden, some of the guards, and Inmate X, were discussing the subject of "George Ignat."

"I don't know what they are discussing, George," my friend told me, "but it doesn't seem good. The whole prison is talking about it. I came to tell you because I consider you a friend."

"Thank you, bro," I replied, "but even if they've hit the road and come all the way over here, it was a fruitless exercise."

"I don't know that," he responded. "You know. I'm just doing the duty of a friend."

"That's fine," I nodded. "Thank you!"

It wasn't the first time he had brought me such news, and I knew another mental attack was coming. I tried to stop every thought that would bring me fear. *At the end of the day, I know I am not guilty of anything,* I told myself. *I have nothing to fear. God will not let such injustice happen to me.*

There was never a situation of guilt or a true desire to find the truth. It was just about the sick desire of a group of people who, being deceived by the devil, had no limit in exerting extraordinary pressure on my psyche. This story would not stop here but would continue beyond Huntercombe prison, even beyond the borders of England.

Arriving at work that afternoon, I again had another terrible mental fight because of what my colleague had said in the morning about the three detectives. Regardless of how hard I tried to get rid of the thoughts, I could not succeed. The belief that I would be accused and imprisoned unjustly was more real now than ever. Who could call that a lie after all I had gone through? I could see that exactly the three men my colleague said were talking with the police detectives were missing from the gym that afternoon: the head guard A, guard B, and the inmate X.

I started exercising. Many times I found my refuge in doing sports, so I will suggest that people facing what I was facing try to exercise. I truly believe this helps a lot. Soon after I started my training, another prisoner approached me, "George, the whole place is talking about a few detectives from London police being present here in Huntercombe. I found out they are coming after you." That was enough to put me in one of the worst situations I had been in up to that moment.

At one point, Guard B, Head Guard A, and Inmate X came through the door, laughing and having a good time. They had not been at the gym all afternoon, and I assumed they had been at a meeting with the detectives. Now they were laughing, their faces covered with smiles. They seemed to be quite happy about something. After taking several steps into the gym, they stopped and looked at me for a few seconds, then continued their noisy discussion.

Guard B approached me and raised his right hand. "Give me a high-five, George," he grinned. "It was a great day, a day of victory!"

I straightened up and looked at him. To me, and this is no exaggeration, he looked like a demon. His face was as red as a cooked crab, and his smile was demonic. "Come on, George, give me a high-five," he repeated. "Don't be shy."

I stood, unmoving, looking at this man that seemed to be trying to give me the idea that he was coming from a meeting that had had a very favorable outcome, which would mean a disastrous outcome for me. They knew very well that an informant had been sent to tell me of the meeting that was being held. If the meeting actually took place, I have no idea, but standing before the guard that day, this verse from Psalm 39 came to my mind: "...I will restrain my mouth with a muzzle, while the wicked are before me. I was mute with silence, I held my peace even from good; and my sorrow was stirred up" (Psalm 39:1b–2, NKJV).

He dropped his hand and left, still grinning. All the other inmates noticed that I had not given Guard B a high-five even though he had invited me to. Perhaps they felt that it was rude of me, but I simply could not give him a high-five; I could not lift my hand. All afternoon, things continued the same way; those two guards and X would watch me, nudge each other, then laugh. I cannot describe how I felt; words cannot convey the pain that went all the way to my heart. There are times in life when we go through the valley of the shadow of death. We need not describe how we felt but what we did and how God helped us to get out. Whole books should be written on the subject because those that are there must know that there is a way out.

What else could I do but go to my Father? Arriving at my cell, I took my Bible and knelt, then prayed and cried. Yes, that's exactly what I did. I had lived a quiet tough life, a life in which crying was forbidden, but now I was living so differently. Now George, who could throw destructive punches in a fraction of a second, was on his knees, not because of man, not because of the devil, not because of pain, but because I understood that winning has a name, and that name is praying. I was there to get the highest form of victory in the name of Jesus Christ. By the way, I will tell you a secret right now: there is a beauty in crying before God. I always find something extraordinary in doing that. I think every Christian should cry before God once in a while; it feels heavenly. After I had told my Father about everything that had happened that day, I asked Him to give me a Word from the Scriptures. After I told Him what had transpired, it was my practice to ask Him to bring a conclusion and tell me what to do, and I listened.

That evening, in His goodness, God replied to me through the prophet Isaiah,

> You shall be far from oppression, for you shall not fear; and from terror, for it shall not come near you. Indeed they shall surely assemble, but not because of Me. Whoever assembles against you shall fall for your sake. [...] "No weapon formed against you shall prosper, and every tongue which rises against you in judgment you shall condemn. This is the heritage of the servants of the Lord, and their righteousness is from Me," says the Lord.
>
> Isaiah 54:14–17 (NKJV)

I closed my Bible, stood up, and washed my face, then lay down on the bed and continued talking to God. I fell asleep peacefully. What a great God we have! What a good and caring Father!

My time at Huntercombe could have been a great curse. The terrible attacks of the devil, combined with the hostile attitude and evil intentions of those in charge, could have destroyed me. My only support was God, but He was enough. He made me able to survive without losing my mind or my life. I am convinced that neither I nor anyone else, regardless of how strong they are, could survive the pressure put on me by the devil and the people there without divine help.

Part 6

Home, Romania

At Home

The release day has arrived; I had to leave Huntercombe early in the morning in order to be repatriated to Romania. Several friends wished me farewell, and I was taken, along with my belongings, to the reception desk, where I was welcomed by several guards. One of them shook my hand heartily.

"You were one of the best inmates I've ever had," he told me.

I smiled and thanked him, but I could not believe him. Not that I had been a bad inmate, but I believed he was speaking in irony. Huntercombe was a trap for many reasons. I fell into this trap the moment I chose to ask to be transferred from Wormwood Scrubs. I acted under my very poor emotional condition when I took that decision; it is very important if under such pressure not to take immediate decisions, but rather, even if it seems hard, just try to pray and let God decide for you. After my release, I met a person who was one of my colleagues in Huntercombe. He knew all about what happened to me there, and he told me, "George, the God you love so much helped you to be able to leave that place in good health; they could have easily destroyed you."

I think it is important to mention what's coming next, a somewhat strange occurrence that happened several days before my release. It was eight o'clock in the evening, and I was lying on my bed when I was again attacked. I rolled over to drop to my knees beside the bed when a perfectly clear voice in my head whispered: "You can easily get out of this battle. All you must do is to want it. I'll make you a deal: if you promise me that you will no longer talk about Him (he didn't say a name, but I knew Who he was talking about), I will leave, and you will have peace."

It was very clear and convincing, and it felt friendly, as if it really wanted to get me out of this war.

I thank God that I did not take time to think. I acted immediately, rebuking him in the name of Jesus. I was so furious at this enemy that at that moment, I would have liked to see him in front of me physically so I could beat him up. I rebuked him again and again until I was completely at peace, then I began to sing.

I was surprised at his nerve. I was shocked at his brazenness in trying to make a deal with me, but when I looked at the Scriptures, I saw that his audacity knows no bounds. He went straight to the Son of God and offered Him all the riches of the world! What impudence!

In the end, his plan backfired: I was more determined than ever to share the Good News of a new life in Jesus Christ. I wanted to tell everyone that the only solution to our problems, and the only defense against our enemy, is Jesus. I pushed all my plans and dreams down the list to make room at the top for the sharing of the Gospel. I pray that I can do that regardless of the times or of the circumstances of life. I want to do it out of love for my Lord and love for those around me. Every man has greater value than we can ever imagine. Interestingly, we, as people, see differences between us, but we are all of equal value before God. The druggy in the alley and the President of the United States will both stand before our great Judge. If I would truly see people through God's eyes, I would be more concerned with their end than with their clothing, their smell, or how they may be of use to me.

In my time at Huntercombe, I saw that all these attacks had the goal of snuffing out my burning desire to tell others that a God exists that is ready to forgive us and rebuild our lives, regardless of our past sins, our nationality, our religious background, our skin color, or anything else that, in the end, doesn't matter.

The devil had a good strategy because when the rumors about me began to circulate, the number of inmates with whom I could speak decreased significantly. In prison, no one spends time talking to a rapist.

I left Huntercombe in a prison van bound for Heathrow airport. There I met my brother, Nicu, and another dear brother in the faith, Ovidiu. They had bought tickets for the same flight so we could fly together.

I was thinner, significantly weakened from my nightmare. Since I had had a few extra kilos on me, I saw my weight loss as a good thing, even though it didn't come from a diet. Nicu, seeing my weakened state, asked me if I was okay, but I told him that we would talk when we got to Romania.

We had a layover in Warsaw, and while there, I had a terrible panic attack. I was grateful that Nicu and Ovidiu were with me. I had not yet managed to totally escape my tormentors.

After a few hours in Poland, we boarded our late-night flight to Bucharest, where we were met by my father and Brother Puiu despite the lateness of the hour. When we got to our vehicle in the airport parking lot, I, having always loved driving, went straight to the driver's seat, despite not having driven for over three years. After nearly six hours of driving, we arrived home.

We entered the house about seven o'clock in the morning. My dear wife, Adriana, was awake and waiting for me. I hugged and kissed her; then we exchanged a few words before going to see the children. All three were sleeping. I kissed each one, one by one. Levi opened his eyes, and I will never forget the happiness on his face when he recognized me.

"Daddy, Daddy!"

He grabbed me around the neck, and we stood for a few minutes in a tight hug. Then Philip and David awoke, and we had breakfast together. We hugged; we kissed; we cried. We prayed.

I arrived exactly on Philip's fourth birthday. We grilled, ate cake, and enjoyed our family time. Several days later, David turned eleven, so we celebrated again. They were wonderful times, times that we had missed in the last several years, but now, by God's grace, we could again rejoice together.

For the first few days, I barely left the house or the yard; I just wanted to stay with my family. After several days, we borrowed Puiu's vehicle, and our whole family went to the Black Sea. We enjoyed the sun, the water, the peace. I could hardly believe it; from the hell of Huntercombe to the beach of the Black Sea, healthy and whole. It was only the unspeakable grace of God.

One afternoon I went out to the beach alone. I sat down near the surf and began praying and meditating on my future. I was certain that God didn't bring me through all that He did just so I could enjoy liberty. I felt a responsibility to continue serving.

"Hey, I see you're deep in thought." My dear wife had come out to see where I was. "What are you thinking about?"

"Adri... A lot has happened. I need time to tell you everything. There may be things that you find hard to understand, but we'll take our time as we go through it.

"I believe you," she replied. "I felt that you were having a very difficult time. I felt every battle with you. We'll discuss them all."

"But," I said, somewhat soberly, "I'm thinking about the promises that I made to God. I need to tell them to you because some of them involve our life as a family, not just me, and I want to keep every promise that I have made.

"Dear," she replied, "I am with you in every decision you make. I know that you love God and will make wise choices. I will support you."

"Thank you!" I responded gratefully. "That's what I wanted to hear."

Now I faced another question: had all that I had gone through disqualified me from preaching the gospel? After all the fear, all the depression, was I fit to stand up and teach others?

Again I faced a battle, the devil trying to discourage me. I remembered what M had told me, how the guards had laughed and joked about my desire to serve, calling me a schizophrenic. They said the chances of me preaching anywhere were virtually zero. Knowing the problems I had had and how many people knew about my emotional issues, I thought it possible that I was not qualified to serve God in the way that I would like.

I felt that I had brought reproach on God and His people. I felt guilty that I had not shown enough fortitude when facing the attacks. I tried to disconnect myself from England, but I couldn't. The wounds of the soul still hurt and would continue to cause pain for some time.

Still, I had the ambition, stronger now than ever, to preach the gospel, particularly in prisons among the outcasts of society. I asked the Lord to show me what He wanted me to do, and the answer was not long in coming.

Several weeks later, my phone rang. At the other end of the line was a sister, Tamara, who had served in the prisons of Bucharest for many years since 1990. I did not know her personally, but she was wondering if I would go with her to speak in several large prisons at different places in the country. It was the answer for which I had been waiting.

Enthusiastically, I went and told Adriana immediately. She was somewhat less excited.

"But you just got home," she said slowly. "You are already returning to prison?"

"Sweetheart, I will only be gone for a single day, max two," I replied.

"But you just got here!" she repeated. "We haven't gotten enough of you yet."

"I know, and I haven't gotten enough of you all yet either," I agreed. "Nor will I ever get enough of you, for that matter. But please let me go anyway. People behind bars have a great need of God. They cannot come out to go to church when they need to, so someone must go and tell them who God is. I am willing to do that."

Adriana kissed me on the forehead. "Go with the Lord Jesus," she said softly. "We will pray for you."

Adriana's acceptance made me very happy. I had promised that I would never upset her again, so I was unwilling to make a decision without her consent.

"The following day, Puiu and I left for Bucharest to meet Tamara and go to the first prison. Leaving my ID card and being given a badge that said "VISITOR" gave me a strange sensation. I remembered seeing men come into the Botoșani prison with that badge. "Lord," I said at the time, "when will the day come when I can wear that kind of a badge?"

By God's goodness, the day had come!

When we left that first prison, I had an even greater eagerness to serve God. "*Lord*," I prayed, "what You did for me at Golgotha was much, much more painful than my experience in England. You conquered anguish, shame, hell. You overthrew all the powers of darkness. Lord, I am Your child, Your heir. Give me Your strength to do what You want me to do in Romania."

What Happened with Urspack?

After several weeks with my family, I had to return to work. The Urspack factory is in the village of Bosanci, the village my mom grew up in, a few kilometers away from Suceava. As I said earlier, God had worked in my absence. When I left, we had one or two employees, one client, and a small work area, but when I entered the new factory, I could hardly believe the spaciousness and thirty-five employees that were now working. I praised the Lord for what I saw.

I felt strange and out of place, though as I timidly went through the factory, I met G, a fellow inmate from Botoșani Penitentiary. Puiu had agreed to employ him since he had no family, making reintegration into society difficult. A man that had a job was much more likely to stay out of trouble. As I saw inmates' needs, God made the factory grow, giving them a place to work.

Though we had started out as fifty-fifty owners, I felt Puiu, having done all the work in my absence and having overseen the tremendous growth, deserved much more than a fifty percent share in the current business, but he would hear none of it.

"No way," he told me. "What we agreed on still stands. We are Christians and love the Lord; we don't change with any wind of feeling. An agreement is an agreement; "'Let your yes be yes, and your no, no.'"

I hugged my dear, sincere partner in business, and we knelt to thank God that we were once again a team. Though I had been in partnerships before—many of which left a bad taste in my mouth—I was thankful for a partner like Puiu and partnership that had begun with prayer and fasting.

The business continued to grow after I arrived at home, God making it a blessing for more people. We acquired more equipment, hired more people, and rented more space. Though we had a rough year during the COVID-19 pandemic, and I thought it might spell the end for Urspack, God once again came to send us the help we need by sending us brothers and a sister in the faith from America—Jim, Leticia, and Steve. Brother Puiu and I would someday like to write a book about the business that we started by faith, and in that book, I would like to write more about these three brothers in Christ, about their involvement in helping us run the business through the very hard times of the COVID-19 pandemic period.

I am eager to share about the miracles that God worked in our business.

I believe that God will continue to make Urspack support for ex-inmates and other outcasts of society who are looking for a place to work. To Him be all the glory!

The Bullying Begins

I had been home for some time. I had begun some mission work, though somewhat clumsily; my recent emotional injuries were still smarting. I had organized a prayer group among the ex-inmates at Urspack, as well as giving my testimony in churches and prisons around the country.

One Saturday, returning from a meeting in a prison, I thought I should call another Christian businessman in my hometown who I had known for several years, asking if I could meet with him to learn from his business experience.

He answered the phone and seemed glad that I had called but said he was not home at the time and asked me to call back two days later. I tried to call back, but he did not respond. Several hours later, I tried again with the same result. I sent him a message asking him to call me, but he didn't reply. Three days later I tried calling him again, but it said that my number had been blocked. I was surprised, thinking it was some mistake; it never occurred to me that he might be avoiding me.

This occurrence did not discourage me. I was at home with family, friends, and church, and my emotional state was improving by the day. I saw God restoring George Ignat, and I rejoiced. The attacks were lessening in frequency and intensity, but the enemy, our ever-present foe, was formulating a new plan.

People from the area, some of which I had known for years, began pulling me aside and telling me things that showed clearly that the devil had not given up. Some seemed to be worried and asked me how I was and if it was true that I had difficult times in prison and such things. Some even asked, "I heard you went crazy in prison. How are you feeling now? Are the things I hear in town true?"

"I heard gossip that you told everyone in prison that you're a child of God," one told me. "I understand the road you've chosen and that you want to draw closer to divinity, but calling yourself the brother of Jesus is too much."

"It's not me calling myself a child of God," I grinned. "The Bible says that."

It was interesting because I hadn't talked to anyone until then about the problems I faced in the UK, not even with my wife, so it was easy to figure out what actually happened.

I knew that the Romanian authorities had had access to my private discussions and to everything that happened to me in England, and they were the only ones who could spread such things about me. Were they now attacking my credibility through gossip? Looking back at the way they treated me in Huntercombe, I said to myself, "There is no way these people here will do the same." My attacks were seen as emotional meltdowns; calling myself a child of God was interpreted as ego, if not outright lunacy; my visions for the future were considered delirious nonsense. I was labeled an emotionally-unbalanced, starry-eyed, dreaming megalomaniac.

One day, after telling someone how God worked at my trial, he said that he heard a different version. He had heard that I acted insanely in order to gain clemency. "People are saying very bad things about you, and even among Christians," he warned me. "Beware."

Soon after my businessman friend blocked my number, I was stopped on the street by one of his employees. "George," he said, "I must tell you something. My boss sends his apologies for not answering your calls, but he sent me to tell you that he has reasons for not wanting to get in contact with you. He asked me to not be upset, but until a few legal things are clarified, he cannot talk with you."

"What?" I asked, confused. "Did I upset him somehow?"

"No, I don't think he's upset," my friend replied. "I don't really know much, but he thought that as a well-known businessman, it would be wise to keep his distance. Sorry, Brother George, that's all I know."

Knowing the devil was circulating lies again, I thought about doing some investigating on my own but felt that God was telling me to mind my own business.

Things began getting more complicated when an inspection was done at our business by the authorities. Our accounting firm told us that the revenue service had confiscated our documents. Puiu and I immediately went to see what the matter was. Our accountant told us that the men that had stopped in for the documents had decided to do a thorough audit, from the start of our business, five years ago, to the present.

I looked at Puiu; he was calm. He told me that he had taken great care to pay all taxes, salaries, and other expenses and, if anything was left over, to take our salaries from that. Puiu understood that a spiritual battle was being fought and knew that Christians, especially outspoken ones, were being attacked, so he had tried to ensure that there could be no cause for complaint.

Days, then weeks, went by, but those that had taken our documents did not return them. Our accountant was getting worried; she said that in the many years that she worked with many different companies, nothing like it had ever happened.

Though Puiu was in the dark, I was starting to suspect that it had something to do with me.

After a few months, they returned our documents, saying that they had been delayed. An audit that should have taken no more than a few weeks had dragged on for months. Furthermore, they told us that they were fining us twenty-five thousand lei (about six thousand dollars).

"Why a fine so large?" asked Puiu, shocked. "What mistakes did we make? We would like to right our wrong if you tell us what we did."

"Sirs," he replied, "you have been in business for over five years. Five thousand lei a year for five years equals twenty-five thousand. Does that seem like too much?"

"It's quite a lot if you don't tell us what we did wrong," replied Puiu.

"I thought you were smarter than that," he replied. "It is not that you did anything wrong; we just have to fine you, that's all."

"I understand," said Puiu, with a shade of sarcasm in his voice. "We didn't do anything wrong, but we still get fined. Thank you very much!"

There was nothing we could do. Going to court meant risking another audit, plus a lot of time and cost. We looked at each other and shrugged.

Several weeks later, having paid the fine, other men came to do another audit. These men were much more belligerent, threatening us with prison time. The accountant called us, so scared she was nearly crying, asking us to come at once. All the documents were in order, but they still threatened us.

People were starting to avoid me. Friends that I had known for years no longer answered when I tried calling. The business began suffering because of people avoiding anything having to do with me; it was now affecting more than just my family, but my employees, though we did manage to keep paying them. I knew gossip was flying, and I felt sure that it had come from the only source possible, though exactly what people were saying eluded me.

Puiu observed as well that strange things were happening since my arrival, but he did not blame me. He simply said that the devil has always attacked true disciples of Jesus. Besides, the devil hated what we were doing with ex-inmates at our business, so attacks were to be expected.

If there was one person I had wanted to protect from the rumors, it was my mother. She was getting elderly and had some health problems, so I did not want to add another burden, but one day she told me, "I have seen the change God brought about in your life over five years ago, and it makes me very happy. I've prayed for you since I was pregnant with you, and some of the decisions you made earlier upset me very much. Now please tell me the truth: have you left that all, or are you still involved in crime?"

I could not believe my ears. She had tears in her eyes, telling me that she had a deadly serious reason for asking me.

"My dear mother," I replied, "I can tell you before God that I try to ensure that every decision I make is in accordance with the Bible; I would never do something illegal. It has been many years now since I met Jesus. I have had some tough times, but I never walked away from God, and I will never do so."

"I know you love God," she responded, "so I did not believe anything I heard. Stay with Him whatever happens. I thank God for you."

"You said you heard something about me; can you tell me what you heard?"

"I'll tell you, but don't tell anyone."

"Deal," I replied. "It will stay between us."

"My sister invited me over one day and told me that her sister has a neighbor whose son is a police officer. He said that you would be arrested again. He said they were working on a case against you and that you would be arrested again. He said it repeatedly. I cried so much. I did not want to tell you, but I wanted to hear the truth directly from you."

I assured her not to worry. "I am here with you. No one, nothing will take me from you. They have no grounds for arresting me."

Though my mother was comforted, I was troubled. Who would say such things to my aunt, knowing that I would find out? I tried to determine the devil's next move in order to be ready for it. Though I was now with my family, my church, my brothers, though we now had our regular prayer meetings and other times with God, he had not given up. But I knew that I was in a much better position to stay strong.

A Dream Becomes a Nightmare

I was driving towards a business meeting in a rush when I received a call from a Christian guy. He told me that he had dreamed something about me but was afraid it might upset me. He had dreamed it several nights in a row, and the Lord had told him to recount it to me. I assured him that if it was from the Lord, I would not become upset. He told me that, in his dream, two police officers arrived at our business in a plain white Dacia Logan. Though it was an unmarked car, it had a police license, which in Romania began with MAI. The two officers were very rough with me, and in the end, they arrested me. He said Puiu was there too and was very upset.

He then asked me if perhaps I had committed a crime. I assured him that if I went to prison, it would be just for a visit or because they started arresting Christians for their faith as in the communist days.

I tried to understand what the Lord might be telling me, but it didn't seem to make sense.

Four or five days passed. Puiu and I had left work for a bit to do some other things when an employee called me.

"Come to the factory as soon as you can!" His voice trembled.

"Did something happen?" I inquired.

"Yes, the police came. They questioned me."

Puiu and I rushed back to the business. The employee was still outside, even though it had been nearly thirty minutes since he had called, but there were no police.

"What's happening?" I demanded. "Why are you outside? It's cold."

"I want to talk to you." The man was clearly on the verge of panic.

"Please tell me what happened."

"Boss, I was taking some of the cardboard cut-offs out to the dumpster when a white police car appeared. A police officer got out of the car and yelled at me, asking who the owner of the business was, where he was, and what he was doing. I told him that he should ask you or Puiu all those questions, that I am just an employee. He scared me. I'm sorry. I didn't know what to say. I hope what I said was okay."

We assured him that he had indeed answered wisely. I looked at Puiu, and he looked at me. What in the world was going on?

"Please tell me," I said, turning again to our employee, "was the vehicle an unmarked white Dacia Logan with an MAI license plate?"

"Yes!" he exclaimed. "How did you know? Do you recognize the vehicle?"

"No," I replied, "I was just checking."

It was exactly like the man said he had dreamed about several days before.

The employee went inside while Puiu and I discussed the occurrence. Puiu was somewhat more baffled than I. He admitted that the first time I told him about the pressure I felt, he thought it was all in my head, but now he was feeling it too. He wondered how I knew the vehicle.

I recounted the man's dream to him. Not only did the vehicle match, but the officers' attitude matched as well. Puiu grinned. It was evident that the devil was up to something.

"I can hardly believe my ears." He shook his head.

"It's simple, brother," I told him. "There are two options: either the man who called me was put up to it by someone else, probably the officers that came, or else the man dreamed it just like he said he did. It is possible that my phone is tapped, so they may have decided to make the dream come true after he told me."

Puiu found it hard to believe that a fellow believer could be a willing accomplice to such a scheme, but I assured him that the police had often used Christians to bring me messages. The Christians usually did not understand all the implications of what they were saying or its effect on me; they were simply cooperating with authority.

"I hardly have words." Puiu shook his head in disbelief. "Is such a thing possible in Romania in 2019?"

"If they can do it in a strong democracy such as England, what keeps them from doing in Romania?" I asked. "Our liberty is relative, Brother Puiu. These 'occurrences' are designed to finish my psyche off, just like in England."

We could do nothing. Everyone shrugged when we asked what to do. No one wanted to get involved.

"Puiu," I said, "there is only one thing to be done. This evening I will call a prayer meeting. I will tell God what is going on and ask Him what to do. I don't think the devil will quit anytime soon; God is the only One that can stop him."

That evening, I asked Adriana, along with some others, to pray with me. We had an evening of prayer like we often did: a number of brothers get together at the church or at someone's home. We talk, we sing, we read from the Bible, we spend time in prayer. While praying, if God gives a word to anyone, the rest listen to what the Lord is telling us through that person.

On this evening, I brought all my frustration and problems to the One who knows all. I felt like the man described in Lamentations 3:52–63.

Suddenly, the Lord spoke to me.

"Listen, O Man, this is what the Lord says: 'There are many that evaluate you in one way or another. There is a fight going on that is too much for your strength, but I will humble those that are troubling you, and I will strengthen you. You will understand that My Word is just.' Hear, O Man: this is what the Lord says: 'You will emerge victorious like David, not by your wisdom, not by your strength, not by your abilities, but by Me.'"

I cried not because I was afraid, not because I was hurt, but because of the goodness of the Almighty God Who created the universe just talked to me; isn't that amazing? I had been reminded again that there was someone who understood me completely. He would give me strength.

A Friend Willing to Help

Still seeking answers to my many unanswered questions, I wanted to enlist the help of someone of repute in town to help me find out what was being said about me and from where it was coming. Though it had to be someone "in the know," it also had to be someone whom I could trust and who trusted me.

I decided to stop in to see a childhood friend who was now an important businessman. I did not call ahead but simply stopped at his office one day. He acted nearly fearful when I walked in but soon warmed up, and we discussed families and reminisced over bygone years.

After nearly thirty minutes of small talk, my friend suddenly stood up and picked up his phone, motioning to me to give him mine as well. He disappeared into another room and soon returned without them. He then shook my hand again, saying, "You're normal, man, you're absolutely normal! I'm so glad to see you like this!"

I understood that he had been told some information about me; I was curious to find out what he had heard.

"Why did you take the phones?" I inquired. "Do you think someone is listening in?"

"I don't know about me," he replied, "but I know for certain you are being listened to and closely monitored. You don't move a finger without them knowing it."

I asked him to tell me all that he knew, but he responded by asking me to tell him all that had transpired in England. He wished to know what I had done to upset so many people, so I told him about the panic attacks, my opposition to the stoicism classes, and how they had opened an investigation. I told him how I had discovered that I was being monitored during my last few months and about the pressure that that discovery put me under.

"Now I can tell you what is happening here," he said. "The British authorities sent everything from their investigation to Romania. Everything they recorded, everything other inmates said about you, everything. Listen: everything, absolutely everything came to the prosecutor's office in Suceava."

"Are you sure?" I asked in disbelief.

"Absolutely certain," he affirmed. "I had wanted to look at the information more closely since it involves you. I know that since you repented, our paths have not often crossed, but I'll never forget what you did for me in the past and will always consider you a friend."

"So, what is happening?" I asked. "I hear all kinds of things, and people I've known all my life avoid me. Someone is spreading all kinds of gossip."

"George," he responded, "a lot of stories have been floating. Someone is spreading misinformation, especially among people of influence. You are said to be psychologically deranged, a schizophrenic, and a dangerous man, so don't be surprised when people look askance. I was told personally to be careful around you because you are now a violent man. But I have not heard of anyone being beaten or of even feeling nervous around you."

I hardly knew what to say. "I am shocked! I've gone through some rough times, but this is ridiculous!"

"Furthermore," he continued, "they say you have committed serious crimes and are trying to uncover them. We are talking serious crimes, bro, very serious crimes. That's why people are avoiding you. Even though I realize that it is just gossip, and many of those in authority know that, they keep pushing the narrative."

"As you know, I was no saint," I said a bit ruefully. "But I neither was I the man they are trying to paint me as. These men are trying to live in a movie. What should I do? Should I go public with all this? There are surely some media outlets that would be happy to carry the story. But who would believe me? I am an ex-con, and those making accusations are people of high repute."

"George, calm down," my friend advised. "We'll find a solution, but you can't go public. It would be too easy to use what you say against you. Then the accusers would look like the good guys, and you would be the fool. They have recordings of you discussing, with a pastor in England, your fears and your fights with the devil. Forgive me for saying so, but I think going public would be a mistake.

"What motivates these people?" I wanted to know. "How did I make them mad? Can I make something right?"

"There are two reasons," he responded. "One is that those who worked on your case here in Romania hoped you would get a long prison sentence in England. They worked hard to bring you to justice, and in some ways, feel cheated that you were only in prison for several months. Many of them are upset to see you walking the streets, a free man; they consider it an injustice."

"That was the Lord's work," I murmured. "He told me to tell the truth; then He did the rest. I, too, was surprised by my light sentence, but that is no reason to hate someone and try to make them miserable."

"It may not be a good reason," he replied, "but it did frustrate them. I don't want to scare you, but they don't like to see you on the streets and will do everything in their power to put you where they think you belong. You must be very careful in your work, your business dealings, and with the people that you meet. You must stay perfectly clean; they will not forgive the smallest offense."

"God changed me; they will find nothing out of order," I declared. "I'm a different man than the one you once knew."

"George, George," he inserted, "you were much better liked before you came around with this faith stuff. Fans of contact sports were in love with you, no joke. Everyone admired you; even when you were arrested for the first time, some said you were a modern-day Robin Hood who stole from the rich and gave to the poor. You had sympathizers all over town. But now you've walked away from that, you've changed, and people's attitudes toward you have changed as well. With all that happened in England and all that you said there, you do not have a good reputation, especially among powerful people in town.

"The road of faith is not always easy," I mused. "There are wonderful times with God, but there are also difficult times when people hate you, as they did Jesus."

"Would you like to know what people say about your change?"

"Of course!" I exclaimed. "I am quite curious to hear it!"

"No one believes one bit of what you say in public. Some say you're a dangerous criminal; some say you're a deranged nitwit; they all say you're hiding it behind a religious façade. They see you as a con artist who decided to stop being a gangster and prey on religious folk, who are often seen as gullible. They see nothing but a talented actor playing the role of a pious Christian sidling up to naïve religious simpletons, and they would love to expose you. I've heard discussions about how you will not play this role all your life; you will commit the long-awaited crimes, then everyone will see your true colors. Furthermore, they don't like your public speaking. You go speak in churches, and the recordings are on the internet. There are many people that listen to what you say, and they can't stand it. In their eyes, you're just a cretin who should have nothing to say."

"The role of a true Christian is a difficult act to play," I responded. "Even we, Christians, don't do so well at it. God knows my life; He knows my heart, so I don't need to worry. Those people cannot believe that what I say comes from a sincere heart; they are deceived. Only God can bring light into such hearts."

"You shouldn't worry," he agreed. "You do what you believe to be right. I've seen some of your clips on the internet, and your sincerity is real. But I do have some advice: go and apologize to those that you have upset. Try to make peace with them. That would help a lot."

"To whom are you referring?"

"Those that you have offended," he replied. "The rumor is that, in a discussion with different people in England, you told them that the authorities in Romania are corrupt, that they tried bribing you. When that recording got here, many of the people to whom you referred were still in their position; many still are. We live in Romania; we've all worked with corrupt officials, but I don't think it was wise of you to say such things there. Can you imagine the effect it had on those people here? How they reacted should be no surprise!"

"First of all," I countered, "I told the truth, and secondly, it was in a private discussion. I did not know I was being recorded and that the recording would be sent to Romania. How could I know that my private discussions in Huntercombe prison would make their way to the authorities in Romania? And even to those working on my case who expected cover-up money! I can't believe it!"

"I haven't finished yet. Here's what you must do: keep from saying anything on the phone about anyone or anything that can be used against you. Remember: say nothing about anyone or anything that can get you in trouble! Suceava is a small town. If you want peace, you must be wise. Things you say can be interpreted many different ways, and they will not be interpreted to your advantage; you can count on that."

"Please explain yourself when you say I should say nothing about anyone or anything," I requested.

"George, a phone can be a great tool. All this technology can be useful in running a business and connecting with people, but all these benefits come with a darker side. This technology allows people to invade our private lives, to follow our most personal moves. You can be listened to when you're talking on the phone, and you can be listened to when your phone is lying on your desk and you are not using it. You can be filmed using your phone's camera. This is by people who are paid to protect the population, but they are curious too, if you understand me. I would advise you to carry a phone without a camera, one of those old ones. They are more difficult to track."

"I know what you mean. I had used a smartphone when I got home because they are easy to track. I have nothing to hide in my private life or in my business. If someone wants to track me, that's not my problem."

"I know you are sincere, George," my friend countered, "but we are not talking about truth or justice. The fact is that there are powerful people, men of influence, who hate you. It's personal for them, or they wouldn't have gone to such extremes. I've tried to help you; I tried to explain to some that you're a good guy, but they laughed in my face. I don't understand how you could get so far under someone's skin."

"You've heard of the devil?"

"Yes."

"He's the guilty party," I told him. "You'll probably think I'm crazy, but he is the one that tries to destroy people. But God still has the last word."

He looked at me skeptically before finally speaking. "George, I can't say that I understand you, but I will think about what you said. Eventually, though, people will figure out it was a farce."

"I'm sure they will," I replied. "But tell me, do you think they can invent something to pin on me?"

"In the past, people here in Romania could fabricate anything whenever necessary, but it was usually for political purposes. It might be wise for you to leave the country for a while, perhaps a year or two, to give them an opportunity to forget."

I had discussed that with my wife since she was also suffering, but we had not reached a conclusion yet. I told him that we would consider it, thanked him for his help, and took my leave after he brought our phones back.

The discussion had helped clarify so much, and though some of the things I learned were unpleasant, I left with a lighter heart.

God Wants Us in Romania

My wife and I seriously discussed moving out of the country. The pressure was affecting her, and she was concerned about our kids. She was optimistic about starting again; the children were young and could integrate well, and she was convinced that I could find a job as a sports instructor or trainer.

One morning, she told me that she would like to discuss it, so we sat at the kitchen table. Everything we discussed pointed toward our leaving, but I wanted to ask God. I told Adriana that we would ask the Lord to give us a response by that evening. We prayed throughout the day and continued discussing it off and on; though everything appeared to point to relocation, we waited for a direct answer from God.

Late that evening, still lacking clear direction, we knelt to pray. I asked the Lord to speak through His Word, through a dream, through a thought, or however He wished, but I asked Him to make it clear.

After we prayed, I opened the Word of God and began reading the first verse that I saw. It was Jeremiah 12:5.

> If you have run with footmen, and they have wearied you, then how will you contend with horses? And if in the land of peace, in which you trusted, they wearied you, then how will you do in the floodplain of the Jordan?
>
> Jeremiah 12:5 (NKJV)

When I finished reading, Adriana had tears in her eyes. I took her hand, saying, "The Lord wants us in Romania!"

I read verse 6 as well, which also had a powerful message for us:

> For even your brothers, the house of your father, even they have dealt treacherously with you; yes, they have called a multitude after you. Do not believe them, even though they speak smooth words to you.
>
> Jeremiah 12:6 (NKJV)

The Lord had spoken so clearly that there remained no room for doubt, and several weeks later, God worked some miracles that confirmed His will even more clearly: we were to remain in Romania, at least for the present.

The Fight for My Human Dignity

Having settled the question of where we were to live, my vision for a Christian center for ex-convicts again felt more possible, but I was busy with the business, speaking in churches, and—the most important—being a husband and father that my family had missed.

The devil tried to drag me down using whatever means he could. He especially tried to discourage me. I received messages of discouragement from him and from other people. Messages on social media often implied that I should leave the public sphere since I was nothing but a bandit, criminal, con artist, etc. The devil did a lot of damage to me, but he was not happy. I could feel that he was upset. I was still standing, and that was not something he would agree with. For months, I felt like my dignity was gone. I felt like garbage; it was the feeling the enemy wanted me to have.

I became so discouraged that I nearly gave up on my dreams, but God brought a thought to my mind. I remembered David in the Valley of Elah. His brothers saw a shepherd, King Saul and others probably saw a victim, Goliath saw nothing but a kid, but God saw a victor. It occurred to me that what God sees in me is what matters. He will use what He sees; what others see is of little significance.

The devil was trying to bring me to nothing, but it occurred to me that that is the material that God can use. When I am nothing, God can use me. He made the world of nothing; He doesn't need our wisdom, our abilities, our material resources, our relationships, or our position in society.

"God," I said, "I am nothing, but I am willing nothingness. If you can use me, here I am."

God then began to work with the nothingness He had, offering me my dignity back. "I can do all things in Christ" (Philippians 4:13) is not just a verse of the Bible; it is the reality I chose to live by. It is the place where I get my energy, my power, my strength. I take everything that I need from the Lord Jesus Christ in order to succeed in fighting the good fight.

Freedom House Christian Center—a Miracle

God gave me the vision for a Christian center for ex-inmates while I was incarcerated. While in the Botoșani prison, I was acquainted with a man who had been freed but was back behind bars several months later. Knowing that he had been in and out a number of times, I was curious to know what always brought him back. His response surprised me.

"George," he told me, "you and many others here have a family waiting for them with open arms when they are freed. I have no one. I have spent a total of twelve years in prison in seven different segments. Every time I'm freed, I have the same problem. There is no one to give me a helping hand. No one will give me a job; they want a police report, and when they see I was in prison, they show me the door. The government has nowhere to put us when we get out of here; we have no food..."

"What do you do when you get out?" I wanted to know. "What did you do last time you were out in the few weeks you were free?"

"What is there to do?" He shook his head. "I loitered in parks or on the street. I ate about once every three days. I stayed in the train station for a while, but it was getting cold. To keep from freezing, I stole five loaves of bread and some meat, not necessarily to eat it, but so I would get caught and brought here."

I could hardly believe it. I didn't think that such things happened in Romania anymore. We were always told that we are in the European Union, poverty is decreasing, and people are doing well. I couldn't imagine that someone would steal something so they would have a bed and daily bread.

"Well," I finally managed, "how does it help to be here? You're locked up without liberty. You're just a prisoner. Most people here long for freedom, and you always return to prison? It doesn't make sense to me."

"Perhaps to you, it doesn't, but to me, it makes all the sense in the world. If I stay on the streets, I risk freezing to death when winter comes. Even if I have no friends, I don't want to die. Here I have heat, a bed, and a loaf of bread every morning at nine. Ever since I've been in prison, the bread was never more than thirty minutes late. Prison means survival. Unfortunately, this is my lot."

I have seen a lot in my short life and have experienced some tough times, but I never thought I would live to see something like that. Unfortunately, there are many more like him. There in prison, God gave me a thought.

"How would it be to find a place where you could build a center where people like that could go? They could have three meals a day, their own room with a bathroom, toiletries, a change of clothes. For a year or so, you could prepare them to be accepted by society. You could teach them a trade, proper etiquette, and some basic knowledge of computers and other things that would help them in society. Furthermore, they could get in contact with the Bible, through which they could get to know Me. What do you say, George?"

I grinned. "Lord, that would be hard to pull off. Who could do it? It would require enormous amounts of money. But, God, what is impossible for You? Anything is possible when You are involved!"

I called Andrew, a dear brother in the faith, and told him. Andrew had started a blog for me, where I would write letters and send them to him, and then he would transcribe them into digital format and upload them. He told me that when I got out, we would see about it.

I was so excited that I told everyone of my idea: my wife, Brother Puiu, other brothers in the faith, and fellow inmates. They all shrugged, saying that if it was the Lord's will, it would happen.

Now a free man, I started looking for real estate outside town where I could build something. I prayed that God would make it happen if it was really His idea, but if it was just a result of my own stupidity, that He would show me. I met with several Christians, some of whom said they would help me find land, while others said they would help to build something once I had the land. But when it actually got down to helping, only a few were courageous enough to step in and assist.

One Wednesday, in Cluj-Napoca with Puiu, where we were visiting two prisons, my phone rang.

"Brother George Ignat?" said the voice at the other end.

"Yes! How can I help you?"

"God bless you!"

"Thank you, and you too!" I replied. "With whom am I speaking?"

"I am Brother Ionel, and I understand you've been looking for a place to build a Christian center."

"That's correct; I'm looking to buy some land," I responded.

"I have some land," he told me. "But I have something that I would like to give to you in the name of Jesus. It is something I think you could use—a building with forty-four rooms."

"I don't know what to say," I stammered, shocked and nearly speechless. "You took me by surprise."

"Just say, 'Praise the Lord,'" he replied.

"Amen!" I nearly shouted, finding my voice again. "All praise to Him! I am astounded. I am in Cluj currently; I'll call you when I get back."

"Call me, and we'll go look at it."

Immediately upon arriving home, I called Brother Ionel, and we went to see the place, about fifteen kilometers from Suceava, in Verești.

Looking at the building, I told Ionel that it was exactly what I needed. It was much better than I had anticipated. He sighed, and tears came to his eyes. I wondered what was happening.

"George," he finally said, "I waited twelve years for the Lord to send someone that could use this building. When I bought it twelve years ago, I told the Lord that it is His to use. It makes me weep with joy that He finally sent someone that can use it for His glory."

I found a lawyer to help me get the organization set up legally, but he soon came to me and said that it was not possible for me to set up an organization because of my record. I explained to him that this organization is for ex-inmates like me and that the vision for it was born out of situations exactly like this—society doesn't want to have anything to do with ex-convicts. He understood but said that the law is the law, and the law says no one with prison on his record could set up a nonprofit organization.

I considered setting it up under the names of other people close to me, but I felt the Lord saying that it must be under mine. I then considered using Adriana's name, but I wasn't at peace about that either. I finally left the idea in the hands of the Lord and went about my work. Ionel had called me, telling me the building was mine if I paid for the paperwork. I told him what I was up against, and he simply asked me to call him if I resolved anything.

Time passed. I still thought about the project occasionally. "Lord," I said, "I was so sure the idea was from You, but it started to look as if I was mistaken."

One evening when I was at the sauna, I met a brother in the faith who was a lawyer, practicing in another city. We exchanged some small talk, and then he asked me about my mission work in prisons. I told him of my dreams and how they had been dashed because the law would not allow a man with a prison record to set up an organization.

"What law?" he demanded. "Who told you that?"

"A lawyer from Suceava. Why do you ask?"

"I specialize in setting up non-profit organizations, and I am aware of no such law," he told me. "Come to my office on Monday, and we'll figure it out."

That discussion again brought hope. Perhaps the Lord would do it after all!

On Monday morning, I arrived at my new lawyer's office.

"It is exactly as I told you, George," he beamed. "There is no law in Romania forbidding a man with a bad record from setting up a non-profit. Whoever told you that either did not know the law or was lying."

"I am surprised! I don't understand what happened!"

"I don't know his reasons, but I do know the law does not exist," he told me. "Look, I have an idea: to avoid working with the court from your town, we will submit the request in the town where I work. The courts here will not throw wrenches in the gears. What do you want to name the organization, brother?"

"I was thinking about the name 'FIGHT FOR FREEDOM.'"

"It sounds good, but why that name?"

"Our life is a continuous fight for liberty," I replied. "To be freed from prison is a struggle. To be freed from the prison of sin, of drugs, of alcohol, of a depraved life—it all requires a fight. Every man fights for a better life. Through this organization, we want to be a support to those who want true freedom and are willing to fight for it."

"That's great, George! I'm glad this is started, and I pray it will work out. I will do everything I can for you."

"Thank you," I responded fervently.

Four weeks later, he called me and told me to come to pick up the documents for the new Fight for Freedom organization with me as president, Puiu as vice-president, and Andrew as secretary. My dream that had been called idiocy was taking shape!

Several days later, the organization possessed what was formerly a dormitory for student workers on the farm in Verești, near Suceava. We went to the immense building immediately after signing the papers. Puiu, Andrew, and I knelt in prayer, thanking God for the building. We had seen God's hand at work in making my vision become reality. Looking at the huge building and estimating the costs to remodel it, we again knelt in prayer.

"Lord, you gave us this building, but without Your continued help, we cannot do much. We need you every step of the way. Amen!"

The Promises of God

Several weeks later, a businessman from London named Peter called me. He had heard that there was a former MMA fighter who had changed his life, and he wanted to learn more. He came to visit me in Romania, and we discussed the vision of Fight for Freedom. As he was an experienced Christian businessman, I asked if he would be willing to serve on our board of directors. After weeks of thoughtful prayer, he agreed to join our board. We were delighted; his background in business would be a tremendous asset.

"What will you call the building?" he asked me. "The organization's name is Fight for Freedom, but what will the structure be called?"

We decided on the name "Freedom House." Initially, we wanted to call the Christian center "Second Chance," but even here, God helped us find the most appropriate name. Leticia, our dear sister from America, called us one day and told us that she had prayed for this project and that God had given her a specific name for this place, namely the Freedom House. We liked the name and immediately began using it.

Peter was a great help from the outset, suggesting things such as organized prayer times and fast days. For him, as for us, the spiritual aspect was of supreme importance.

We found another board member, a man named Robert, who was the logistics manager at Urspack. I had gotten to know him at the Botoșani Prison, and he had later become our employee, as well as becoming active in mission work.

Brother Peter called me one day, wanting a meeting with just the two of us. We met at a restaurant where he told me that some businessman from the area had told him that he would be wise to not get involved in our project. They told him that I was an ex-convict, a dangerous man, and that I was not a Christian at all but just playing the part. I appreciated Peter's being blunt with me, not hiding anything.

"Brother Peter," I told him, "there are two ways to find out the truth. One is to wait a while; the truth will come out. The other one, the better one, is to ask God to speak to you and let you know the truth."

"I will do that, George," he agreed. "When I get back to London, I will spend time in prayer, asking God specifically to show me if this project is based on truth or if there are other interests involved."

Three days later, my phone rang.

"George, I am amazed how quickly God answered!"

"What happened, Peter?" I asked.

"A brother called me last evening. I met him just once, eight months ago, and he still had my phone number. He said he had received a word from the Lord for me. He sent it as an audio message, and I will send it on to you."

"Please do! I am eager to hear it!"

The voice was unfamiliar, but the message was similar to those I had heard before. The Lord had spoken powerfully.

"Listen, My son! The work before you is built on truth. There is no deception or duplicity involved. The one on whose shoulders I have put the work will be strengthened because whatever starts with Me will be blessed. See, I have prepared the place, I have prepared the souls of those who enter, and I will make something great out of nothing. Get involved and do your part. Do not listen to the voice of the enemy nor to the words of people who are but dust."

I sometimes ask myself, "Why do I cry when I hear the voice of God? Is it because I am weak, or is it because I am overwhelmed by His love?"

The Freedom House continued taking shape with each passing day. God brought a group of men from the city of Arad to help with the work. They volunteered their services, traveled over six hundred kilometers, and worked for a week to get the remodeling project started. God then sent me two of my former colleagues from prison who were construction workers. They needed a place to work, we needed builders, and so we employed them.

We eventually needed someone that could stay at the site every day and act as on-site foreman. I soon found out that Vlad, a man who ran a construction business in England for twenty years and who had had a positive influence on my life, had recently moved back to Romania with his family. When I called him, he said that he had been waiting for God to show him what he should do in Romania. He took the call as God's answer, and he became a great blessing to us and the Freedom House project.

I don't know what the future holds for the Freedom House and Fight for Freedom, but I see the dream that God gave me while still in prison being realized, and that is a great source of happiness. My dream now is that God would use this organization to support men who have a high chance of re-incarceration. As long as there are men that are in and out of prison, we will fight to give them a chance. As long as there are young people who grew up in orphanages and are turned out onto the street when they turn eighteen—many of whom end up in prison—we will work to find a solution for them to break the cycle. But above all, I know that God can do more than I or our team can ever ask or think. To Him be the glory!

The Home for the Homeless

In November of 2020, a person I had never met before called me. He recommended himself as a Christian named Liviu, a Romanian who lived in Great Britain.

I was going to learn that God has much more work in store for us than we initially thought.

This guy told me that he had found out how the Christian organization Fight for Freedom was working to help disadvantaged people in society. I replied that it was true and that we were doing it wholeheartedly as for God.

This gentleman told me that he had recently bought a former hotel in the Burdujeni district, right next to the main train station, where most of the street people in our city gather, and his intention was to make it available to a Christian organization. This location was to be used for charity, and he told me that he had discussed selling it with three such organizations and that he was praying for God to give at least one answer.

He asked me if we were interested in using that building. I did not give him a direct answer, as I preferred to have time to think and to meditate on this opportunity to serve God by serving the people of the street.

I spoke with the board of the Fight for Freedom mission. There were both pro and con opinions due to the fact that we were at that time involved in several charitable activities that required both sustained time commitment and financial resources.

I called him and told him that we did not have a very clear answer for him, but we were going to pray. Personally, I put a sign before God. It was November, and this gentleman from London told me that he would come to Romania at the end of March. I said in my heart, "God, if this work is not for us, if the Fight for Freedom mission is already too crowded with too many projects, then please do things in such a way that by March, one of the other two Christian associations that were contacted by him will have already made contact and will have already started working in that location."

Time passed, and on the first of April 2021, Liviu called me to tell me that he was in Romania and that he would like to see us. I have to say that I kept hoping for a call that someone else had been found to take care of this project since we were already so busy. Liviu visited me at the office and told me that neither of the other two Christian associations wanted to get involved and that he wanted an answer from us. I knew it was God's will to get involved in this social work, so together with my brother Andrei, I went to the notary public where I signed a five-year contract with Liviu for that hotel.

I understood that a bigger team was needed than we had and that I would have to ask for the help of a church to form a new team of volunteers. Two weeks later, God put in my heart the thought of going to one of the churches in the area where this hotel was located. I preached in that church, and then I presented the project of our mission to help the street people in that area. I received a positive response, above my expectations and those of my colleagues on the board of Fight for Freedom. In two weeks, a full-fledged team was formed, and people with a heart for the disadvantaged came to help us in this beautiful work.

Now, as I am writing this chapter, it is the autumn of 2021, and we have already started serving a hot meal to the street people of Suceava seven times a week. We have a canteen with a fully-equipped kitchen and a hall that can accommodate over seventy people. It is a great opportunity for us to tell these people about the great love of Jesus Christ. We believe with all our hearts that God loves these people as much as any man. Every soul is important in the eyes of the One who created it; a man of the street is equal to the president of the country, equal to the richest or most influential man on earth in the eyes of God. God loves the troubled and miserable man so much; I believe this with strength.

At this point, Fight for Freedom is more than I could have dreamed, and I know that God plans to do even bigger things.

From the middle of 2020 to the autumn of 2021, when I wrote these lines, we managed with God's help through Fight for Freedom to donate a significant amount of food to more than 600 needy families. I came with my colleagues to help several people who asked us for support (people with disabilities, orphans, the elderly without opportunities), and it is an honor for us to be able to serve those around us. We always do this in the name of the Lord Jesus Christ, and all the merit belongs to God.

I pray that Fight for Freedom will have the greatest impact and be as relevant as possible in the society in which God has allowed us to live. The desire of our heart is for God to have the glory and honor from everything that He will help us do.

Would He Ever Stop?

After being harried by the authorities, after hearing my name defamed, after seeing our business suffer because potential clients would suddenly become disinterested, after having problems with inspections and audits, after struggling to get any paperwork for anything, one day near the end of 2020, my mother called me, asking me to come to see her at once. I didn't know what was so urgent, but I left work and rushed to her apartment.

Upon entering, I was met by my mother and my sister, Anna Maria. They stared at me, after which my sister finally spoke.

"You were right!"

"Of course! I'm always right!" I laughed.

"Stop joking; this is serious. Mom, tell him what happened!"

"George," my mother began, "thirty minutes ago, I got a call from a high-ranking police officer. He introduced himself as F.M. Son, you were right!"

"In what was I right?" I wanted to know. "Please, say it quickly, Mom. They are waiting for me back at work."

"He asked if you still live here, with me and your father."

"That's a good one!" I said sarcastically. "As if they don't know where I live!"

"Son, they know everything. The man told me that in the last two years since you returned from prison, your phone was bugged, as well as your emails and every mode of communication you have. He told me that you were monitored very closely, and now they are finalizing some documents, which they will send to you for your signature."

"Did they tell you why I was being observed? Why did they need to listen to my phone communication and read my emails?"

"He told me to not worry about it, that they did it because there were a number of burglaries in the area, and you were one of the suspects."

"I was suspected of burglary? Don't make me laugh! Can you see me, a man weighing 140 kilograms, sneaking through houses to steal a TV set? I own a company with fifty employees, and I still have to steal to stay alive? That is just a pretext in order to get the documents they need to have access to my private life. Maybe they've even planted microphones in my office at work or even at home in the bedroom."

"Oh, no!" my mother exclaimed. "They can't do that! We don't live under communism anymore!"

"We don't call it communism, but... Oh well, at the end of the day, what does it matter? I knew what was happening, even if I didn't have an official confirmation. The problem is that I don't think it will stop now. Those people still want to find out what I say, what I eat, and with whom I meet. Don't you remember when your sister was all worked up because her neighbor, a police officer, said that I was to be arrested shortly? They'll come up with some reason to track me."

My mother put her head down, tears in her eyes.

"I'm sorry that I doubted you when you told me what was happening," my sister now put in, coming to give me a hug. "I thought it was all in your head, but I was beside Mom and heard the entire conversation with my own ears. What do these people want with you?"

"I don't know," I replied, "but I'll tell you again: the living and true God, the One I worship, will bring justice."

More than a year had passed since I had that conversation, and I had received nothing in the mail, no notifications or communications afterward.

But then another unusual situation occurred in the spring of 2021, just before I finished writing this book, which only confirmed, once again, that everything I have been living for a few years is true and that the enemy of my soul has no plans to stop.

One afternoon, I was called by a former employee who asked me to visit him. I was tired after almost twelve hours of work, and I had just gotten home. But, I went, hearing in his voice that it was something serious.

When I got to the former employee's home, he and his wife were visibly agitated. He invited me to sit in a chair, staring at me, and began.

"Mr. George, I have to tell you something; it's immediate."

I nodded. I had no idea what he was going to tell me.

"Do you know when I had a car accident in January, I was still working for the company you manage?"

"Yes, I know."

"From that moment until today, when my license was returned, I was in constant contact with the police.

"I think that's normal," I replied

"Somewhat normal; not all things happened in a normal and natural way."

"What do you mean?"

"Mr. George, I called you because both my wife and the rest of the family urged me to talk to you and tell you what we went through during this whole period from January until now."

"I'm all ears."

"During all this time, there was a fantastic pressure on me. I was harassed in a way that I did not know how to answer or what to do."

"By whom?"

"By the police."

"How so?"

"In the days following the accident, I was called to the police station, and I was told that they had opened a criminal case for the accident. I know that this is what the law requires, and I understood that this would be the case. But what seemed strange to me was that the officer who called me seemed more interested in you than in me or in the accident. But that moment was just the beginning."

"Only the beginning?"

"Yes, from that moment, I was called several times to the police, where my personal identification was taken from me, and I was made to wait a very long time. After that, I would be taken to different offices or to the investigation room for interrogation."

"Questions about the accident?"

"No, all the questions were related in one way or another to you. I was almost obsessively told that I was a man too good and kind to work with a bad person like you. They asked me things I had no idea about, for example, who do you meet? Who visits you at the office? What else do you do outside of work? It always occurred to me that if I knew something that was out of place and you were involved and I told them, I would immediately get my license back and not be called again. In an unusual way, they played very smartly with me. I was told that I would benefit if I told them compromising things about you. I don't know what you did or who you upset for this to have happened."

"How many times have they called you?"

"Many times. The problem was that they put a fantastic pressure on my psyche. Every time I was called, I panicked. When I got to them, the officer who was questioning me would take out my driver's license, show it to me, and ask me if I really wanted it. Then began the same questions, the same approaches. I was called only in the late hours, only after eight o'clock in the evening, and I stayed up late. This created suspicion with my wife, who at one point thought that the accident was much worse than I had told her."

My colleague's wife, who was next to us, told me that at one point, she thought that someone had died in that accident and that her husband was trying to hide this from her. This made her go through particularly difficult times, thinking of the worst. Why would a man be called to the police station so many times, at such late hours, for an accident without victims?

"Why didn't you tell me anything all this time?" I asked. "Good man, such a thing is not okay. We are in 2021 in Romania, not in Iran or North Korea. You had to tell me."

"I didn't know what to do. At first, I was afraid to tell someone what was going on; then I thought you noticed that I couldn't work anymore. I couldn't concentrate anymore. Customers started to get dissatisfied with my performance. I finally resigned from your company as you well know. They put too much pressure on me. I'm not used to that."

"Yes, I understand, but still, you should talk to me, man."

"I wanted to come and tell you a few times, but my driver's license was with the police; I was threatened that I would be without this document forever. I was afraid of losing it; for me and my family, this document is vital. If I don't have it, I can't go to work, so I can't put bread on the table for the children and my wife. I think they also knew this because, from the beginning, this document was withheld from them, and every time I was interrogated before starting with the questions, the officer took out my driver's license, showed it to me, and asked me if I really wanted it. I was suggested that if I say something compromising about you, they will return my license, and I will be able to continue working."

"One thing bothers me: I don't know how to proceed; beyond all this pressure, they committed an abuse; how can I react?"

"What do you mean? From my point of view, this whole incident is a gross abuse."

"Two months after the accident, I received a letter at home from the case prosecutor informing me that there would be no trial against me and that all the charges had been dropped because there were no victims in the accident. I understood from a friend who was a lawyer by profession that once I received that paper, I could go to the police and get my driver's license immediately."

"Yes, that's right, I also had an accident a few years ago, and the same thing happened."

"That would have been normal, only it didn't happen to me at all. When I received the letter from the prosecutor, I was extremely happy; I couldn't wait to be called again for questioning to hand this document to the gentlemen there, believing that my driver's license would be returned to me immediately. Only one of the officers, when they saw that document, took it and put it in his pocket and told me it would stay with him and I would get my license back when I said something really compromising about you. He was frustrated; he told me it'd been many weeks since he wasted his time with me. What could I do?"

"I don't know what you could do; calm down for now; now you have your driver's license, we can drive and work again."

"Yes, I have it, as I said to you today, they gave me the documents back, that's why I had the courage to call you to tell you everything that happened to me; to be honest, I'm afraid for you, sir, you have to do something."

"Rest assured, God is in control of the situation; He will protect me."

I would never have thought that our company could have been left without the best man in the sales department just because this colleague was under psychological pressure that he could no longer bear. It was a loss for our company, but looking back on the last years of activity, I realize that it was not a unique loss.

"Mr. George, they asked me many times how I got to work with you, who recommended me. I told them every time how we met by chance and how there is only a working relationship between us. What intrigued me was the conclusion of one of the officers who said to me in a sharp tone, 'Don't tell me that you, Orthodox Christian, were so suddenly accepted there at work, with all those evangelicals?' However, Mr. George, there are so many Orthodox Christian colleagues who work there with the evangelical Christians together, and the issue of religion has never been raised among us. I don't know what they want, what their interest is, but they behaved very badly with us. I don't know what else I could have done; I'm sorry."

"You shouldn't be sorry," I answered. "Other people should be sorry when they do such things. Stay calm; you did the right thing, exactly what I would have done and if I had been in your place. Now you can return to work quietly; that will be very good news to all the team."

"You know, I decided that it is better for us to leave Romania, to work in another country; I have already found a job, I signed the contract."

"Did this situation make you choose to leave Romania?"

My colleague's answer was neither yes nor no. He avoided giving me a concrete answer, but for me, there was no need for an answer. They were looking for peace and quiet, even if it meant having to leave their home country.

We finished the discussion after about forty-five minutes, and my ex-colleague seemed much more relaxed and free. Both he and his wife told me that they weighed whether or not they should tell me about all this, but they'd been encouraged by the rest of their family to do so. Only during the era of the communists do we remember the police behaving like this.

It's been almost three years since I returned home; since then, such episodes have happened. I tried to categorize them as simple evils, to overlook them, to pretend I can't see and I can't hear. I always talked to God, and He was always the one who strengthened me. He has always calmed my heart and mind, so I could go on every time.

The major problem at the moment is that those around me are affected by these situations without having any involvement and without understanding what is happening.

I have written here a few from many situations that are very similar to those above, some of which were very dramatic for me and for people close to me. Still, I did not write about them because I didn't want to bring any harm to the good people who came to talk to me about it.

I know for a fact that after publishing this book, many will say that everything was only in my mind. It is true, the battle was in my mind, and it could have stayed there. But, the devil involved others and transformed what was supposed to be my personal fight into a cruel reality which affected many more. This is how he works. The devil is not happy affecting only one person; he will go after as many as possible, and there are thousands of victims of the enemy every day in the world. If people would only realize that there is no weapon in this world to defeat the enemy of our souls but getting down on our knees and asking for the protection of our Lord Jesus, then the numbers of victims will decrease. At this very moment, a question is still to be asked, will the devil ever stop? I don't think so; he is here to deceive people, to hunt people. He is here to stay, and it is up to us to realize that and fight back against him.

Prayer is the weapon; there is no doubt for us, God in His goodness intended to speak to us about this situation. A few weeks ago, my wife and I went to visit a dear sister of faith named Dana. There, after we had a beautiful fellowship, we knelt down and prayed; during the prayer, sister Dana, speaking through the Holy Spirit, is saying to me, "Listen to what God is saying to you, young man: I'm ready to destroy a plan of the devil with regards to your life; this plan is made in secret, and it is well done, the devil wants to throw you in a cage where you can stay for a long time and not be able to feel happiness for long time, but My plan for you is different: I want to strengthen you, lift you up, and use you to bring many souls to salvation. I will tell you step by step what you must do, I will equip you and carry you through many places, and I will use you and those in your house, for I am the Lord, amen."

At the sound of these words, tears began to flow, both on my cheek and on Adriana's face; nothing can stand against the thoughts and decisions of God, there is no man who can oppose Him, there is no entity on earth or in the universe that can stay against the Lord of lords and the King of kings. We are the children of the Creator of the universe, we are under His protection, and that gives us the peace and quiet we need.

Again Among Champions

I got busier and busier at Urspack. Working hard helped me to focus on important things and not on what the enemy and people were doing or saying. Puiu and I tried our best to continue contributing to the business, which was not just a business; we always considered it God's work. Our goal was not only to turn a profit but to help people. We tried to run our business in the fear of God, taking great care when an ex-inmate contacted us for a job.

One morning at work, I received a call that surprised me.

"Good morning, big guy! I am L from the Romanian Wrestling Federation."

"Good morning! What a pleasure to hear your voice! It's been a few years..."

"It has been," he agreed. "I've been watching your movements in the news the last few years. You've had some tough times, but I understand that you are at home now and that you continue exercising and training."

"I am at home and doing well, thank God," I responded. "About the exercise, I still do it, but I'm not in top shape."

"Well, listen: I would like to make a proposal. Six weeks from now, the European Wrestling Championships will be held in Bucharest. We decided to invite you to represent Romania in the sport named grappling."

"Hmm... you took me by surprise," I stammered. "I don't know what to say."

"You don't have to give me a response today," he responded affably. "But please let us know by the end of the week."

"Sure! I will call you and let you know what I decide."

I had been a member of the national wrestling team, and later, a member of the national team for sambo and mixed martial arts, but several years had passed since I had done anything of the sort. The last match in which I had participated as a professional had been in 2014, five years before. I was honored to be invited to participate, but before making a decision, I had to ask God.

I had promised God that I would never fight again, and now I would have to ask Him for permission to do it again, although it wasn't exactly fighting. This was not in the ring or the cage; grappling is not a violent sport. That knowledge gave me the courage to come before God with my request.

I prayed, I sought counsel from respected brothers and from my pastor, and all answers were positive, so I called the man back and told him that I accepted his offer. It was a strange feeling to sign the contract that they sent; I had never expected that I would be representing Romania in a sports competition at thirty-five years old.

I began doing serious training and working out. I lost several kilograms and, slowly, began to get back in the proper shape.

Ten days before the competition, the team met in Bucharest. I was happy to reunite with colleagues, trainers, and staff from the federation, many of whom I had not seen for years. I got to know all the members of the group, many of them my junior by ten years or more. Some of the younger ones seemed to want to know me better.

"Hey, how's it going? I was so happy when I heard you were coming! I've wanted to meet you for a long time!" It was a young man of whom I had heard but never met.

"Hi!" I replied. "I'm happy to meet you too! I've heard you're one of the best grapplers in the country."

"That's what some say. To be honest, I've had good results in international competitions the last few years."

"So it is true," I pressed.

"Yes, I suppose so," he replied, dropping his pretentiousness.

There was something beautiful in his attitude. He was different. Though he was one of the best athletes in the country, he was humble about it.

"What do you think?" I asked him. "I've been out of international competitions for a number of years. Who are the ones that I might have trouble with in the heavyweight category?"

"Well," he replied thoughtfully, "the Russians are really good, followed by the Georgians and Ukrainians. You'll have some tough matches."

"Good, we'll see how it goes. May God give us health and keep us from any accidents."

"Yes, indeed," he returned. "May God help us! In fact, I wanted to ask you about your relationship with God that you've spoken of in the past years. I would like to know what happened and why you chose this path."

"Where did you hear it?" I queried.

"I saw your testimony on the internet, and I was surprised. Some say it's a game that you're playing, that you're not real. But it seems to me that something must have happened to make you choose the way you did. I think that you're sincere, but my colleagues never agree."

"Yes, it's true. God changed my life, and I will tell people so, regardless of what some choose to believe about me. I chose the best course as far as I'm concerned. Why do you ask? Does the subject interest you?"

"Well, my mother, you know...she turned to God several years ago. She prays for me, but there's a real fight inside whenever I think of making such a decision."

"There is a fight because your soul is at stake," I told him seriously. "The devil, the merciless enemy of our souls, will always put up a fight. He will tell you that the road with God is not a good one, that you're still young, that you have lots of time. The truth is you have no more time at all! Tomorrow might be too late; you must make the decision today. Would you like to pray together?"

We bowed our heads and prayed. We were not unobserved by our colleagues, who thought it strange to see two athletes praying, but we just asked God for His protection over our bodies. I prayed for my friend, that God would soften his heart and that he would make a wise choice for his soul.

The day of the competition arrived! Athletes from over thirty countries in Europe were gathered. The feeling was wonderful. The flags flying, all the athletes, the TV cameras—I remembered it all from the years where all I wanted was to be the best and put an Olympic gold medal around my neck. My foolish decisions had stolen my dream. I knew that it was only by the grace of God that only a few months after I huddled in a British prison cell shaking with fear and believing that I would never get home again, I could represent Romania at an athletic competition. I had seen God's promises come true, one by one. The difference between what the devil told me, what men said about me, and what God planned were so vastly different! All the promises of God are yes and amen, while all the lies of the devil and the deceptions of men are of no significance.

On the first day of the competition, I got to the gym at eight o'clock. Everyone was prepared. I discovered my first match would be with an athlete from Croatia. Tension was in the air. I started warming up with the friend with whom I had spoken the day before when a thought came into my heart, causing me to stop.

"Hey! How would it be if we prayed for the day and the competition? Let's pray that God would protect us from any accidents."

"Good idea!" he said. "Let's do it!"

We knelt in the corner of the gym, surrounded by athletes from many different nations. I closed my eyes and asked my friend to do the same, and then we began to pray. After several minutes I opened my eyes and received two surprises. First of all, another colleague from our group was now kneeling and praying with us, and the second was the shocked faces of those around us. They had never seen athletes like us. Muslim athletes pray in public, even on the mat in front of everyone. They are not ashamed of their religion, and I appreciate that in them. But it is extremely rare to see a Christian athlete pray in public; they seem to be ashamed of it. We were willing to be the exception, for which I thank God.

I won my match with the Croatian by a score of 12–2; scoring that well gave me confidence that I could be among the top three. I thought that perhaps I could win a medal! That would be wonderful! The last medal I had won was at the European championships in 2014 in sambo.

My second match was against a Moldovan athlete. If I won the match, I would get into the finals; if the Moldovan won, he would be assured a medal. I could not win the match and, in the end, placed eighth. The years in prison and my absence from sports had taken their toll. On the other hand, C, the young man that I prayed with, won all his matches up to the final, in which he was injured and lost. Even so, he received a silver medal, a notable achievement. I was happy for him but somewhat disappointed with myself; I would have loved to have won a medal.

The competition ended on Saturday afternoon. As I was saying goodbye to my colleagues and trainers, I took C aside and invited him to a church in Bucharest where I was planning to preach the next day. He happily accepted. I also went and invited the one that had knelt with us at the gym, and he accepted as well, so the following day, the three of us went to church.

The next day I shared my testimony at the church, one of the largest in Bucharest. The Lord spoke powerfully through my testimony, and at the end of the service, the pastor gave an altar call. I was surprised to see a number of men come to the front of the church. I prayed with all my heart that God would save more souls that evening.

The pastor was preparing to close the service when I lifted my head. Great was my surprise to see C, with his hands lifted toward heaven, among those that had responded to the call to follow Christ.

I again closed my eyes and began to pray, with tears of joy, for my friend. The silver medallist from the European Championships was giving his life to Christ. At that moment, I heard a voice telling me clearly, "Look, George, your medal! A medal won for heaven!"

It is always an honor to be able to represent your country not only in sport but in any competition. But much more than that, I consider it an honor to represent the Almighty God who created the universe, to be His ambassador here on this earth. This is a totally unique feeling.

I thanked the Lord for that evening. The happiness brought by a medal of the world, however shiny it may be, could never have equaled the joy of that evening. The men that gave their hearts to the Lord, particularly C, made the medals of the day before look unimportant. This, indeed, was the *most important medal.*

May God help me and you, dear reader, to always work not for medals of the world but medals for heaven!

Afterword

I have written these lines in the hope that they will be of help to those going through difficulties. All those who feel alone, that no one understands, that no one else has gone through what you are going through, that the "valley of the shadow of death" is unconquered, this book is for you.

I did not write for sympathy or empathy. I have learned not to expect from man what comes from God. I received empathy, mercy, and love from the hand of God in whom I trust every time I needed it. I received warm embraces—the kind you feel deep in your soul—from brothers in Christ whom I did not know well, but I have also been very disappointed by some of those close to me.

There is no greater feeling than to be received at the feet of the Creator of the universe after having been rejected by someone close to you. I cannot describe in words the wonderful times I have spent with God. In order to understand it, you, too, must experience it.

Another purpose of this book is to clarify some of the things that happened to me. Many have asked me, "George, is what I heard about you true?" I believe that those close to me, those that care about George Ignat, have the right to know the truth about everything that happened to me.

Before I began writing, I asked God to free my heart so that I would have the right motives in writing. I did not want my open wounds to influence my writing but rather to write everything with love for my fellow man.

I tried to write with no ill will, and I certainly don't want revenge on anyone. I am not looking for apologies. I can live the rest of my life in peace without knowing exactly what went on behind the scenes, knowing that God works everything out for good. I did what I believed was good to do, and I never wanted to hurt anyone. More than anything, I want to help heal those in pain. I found my medicine in Christ, and pain can definitely be healed by Him. He not only transformed my life and healed my heart, but He also changed my way of seeing things.

I want to share with you here some of my core beliefs:

I believe in a person's right to be rehabilitated. Some believe that this is only a fantasy, but it is a reality in which I live and for which I fight for others.

I believe in real religious liberty rather than the one that is offered on a "friendly" but superficial pretext. For some today, religious liberty is only a story; the cruel reality is that, in the last number of years, things have been becoming more and more difficult, even more bloody, for Christians.

Furthermore, I believe in the right of the individual to not feel well, to not be okay. The quote from Prince Harry often comes to my mind: "It's okay not to be okay." Those words have often encouraged me. I am still surprised that a man like him, a young prince who was born to such a privileged position, would think and talk of such problems. May God bless him for it.

I believe that those who battle with depression and other inner struggles can overcome them. And I encourage them to share their experiences with others. Remember that by doing so, you can help or encourage those who are facing similar battles; you could even save someone's life. In my own life, it was a great encouragement to me when a singer as popular as Kanye West was not afraid to talk about his struggles and the difficult times that he faced. He is quoted as saying, "The more you struggle, the less people understand you." Regardless, I encourage you: take your courage in both hands and speak.

I also believe that the results of spending a lot of time "feeding on technology" such as TVs, computers, and smartphones may be much more harmful to a person's psychological health than we realize. The devil uses technology to fill our minds with all kinds of garbage. I know that because I have seen him use that method on me.

I believe in the right of the individual to disagree with the conclusions of the majority or the minority. I believe each person is free to walk the path he has chosen and to express his belief system.

I also believe in sincerity, in those who are willing to help others, in those that see the other person, above all else, as a *person*.

I believe in churches full of the Spirit of God, whose leaders care more about physical, emotional, spiritual, and the salvation of others. I believe in the ministers of God that are left, who do the work to which they are called, without being subjected to pressures or obligations of the State. I believe that some, even today in democratic countries, are pressured in ways that we associate with communism.

I believe that there are and will be people who will not like me. This is reality and likely applies to each one of us. But I believe that when we accept the fact that there are those that believe or see things differently than I do, then we can peacefully coexist.

I want people who will read this to know that I'm not perfect, and I'm not pretending to be. I'm just a man like any other, one who made mistakes, for which he paid and served his sentences. A man with four children. A businessman with many and quite significant responsibilities who works many hours a day managing a business that keeps more than sixty people employed and helps many ex-prisoners gain a chance at a new life as productive members of society.

A man who, by the unspeakable grace of God, leads an NGO that, in the last three years, did a lot of work with strong social impact. I take no credit. I put my life at God's disposal, and He does all these wonderful works.

A man in whose life the goodness and mercy of God have manifested in wonderful ways, which is why I am motivated to speak publicly about these things whenever I have the opportunity. To be clear: telling others about the goodness that God has for us humans is a core part of what I am. I exist only because God has been good to me.

I have always talked, and I will keep doing that about the second chance that society refuses to give to those who have been convicted and gone through the penitentiary. On the contrary,

I promote the idea that God is ready to give this chance, that He can change mentalities, He can change the way we think. In a word, He can change lives.

I consider myself one of those whose lives God has changed. Who not only talks about it but, through physical, mental, and material efforts, works hard to prove that it is possible for anyone who desires a new life to have it through the grace and power of God.

I asked forgiveness from my dear family for the difficult times that they have experienced because of me, and I thank them for the undying love that they showed me for all the years in which I was very nearly alone. Their love motivated me to go on. The thought of their support gave me the courage to rise from my depression and do everything I could to get back to them. But you, Adriana, my beautiful wife, I especially thank you! God bless you for your faithfulness and the care that you have shown both to me and to our children. I thank you for your good heart, transformed by God. You are an angel—no exaggeration.

I also thank Brother Puiu and the few others—so dear to me—who kept supporting me all those years that I spent behind bars.

God is the ultimate One who never gave up on the man George Ignat. God is the One who accepted him as he was, with the small amount of good and the large amount of bad. God is the One who, when I was locked in a tiny cell—three by four meters—for twenty-three hours a day, came to me, personally, to lift me up when the devil was gaining the upper hand.

Once I sat alone on the edge of the bed in my tiny cell, elbows on my knees and head in my hands. As the pressure built, I began to pray. Suddenly, I felt the mattress under me move, as if someone had sat down on my right. For a moment, I wanted to turn quickly and see who it was, but I didn't have the courage to take my hands from my face, knowing that I was alone in my cell. There was no need to look, however; I immediately felt a deep sense of peace in my heart. Again, I cannot explain the feeling. I knew with all my heart that Jesus was sitting beside me. He had come down to my cell, just as He said in Matthew 25:36b (NIV), "I was in prison and you visited me..." I cried for joy. I am no mystic, but I do believe in divine intervention. God does what He, in His sovereignty, knows is best and not necessarily what we think is "normal." God has His reasons for miraculously intervening in people's lives. He does not always do so when we want Him to, He does not always do so when we think we need it, but He does do it. And when He does it, it is an amazing experience. Praise His name!

I could say so much more. The God in whom I trusted and to whom I dedicated my life has done so much for me that I could write many books. In fact, when I finish this one, I would like to write another volume in which I will tell about my life before Jesus Christ became my personal Saviour. I would like to write about where I was when Jesus saved me so that no one will be deceived by the devil into believing that they are too deep in sin to be transformed into a child of God.

I wrote these lines from my home in Romania where, by God's grace, I am a father, husband, son, brother, missionary, and businessman. I am all of those because God, in His goodness, worked in my life in a wonderful way.

I will end this book happy in the knowledge that whatever might happen to me in the future, God is already there and will ensure that things work out well for His son, George Ignat. I am happy knowing that if He takes my soul tonight, I will go to meet my Lord and Saviour, Jesus Christ. I am happy to see my children growing up in the church, and I pray that they, too, will soon accept Jesus as Saviour in their lives. I am happy that the Freedom House was not just a foolish dream of mine, but it was the plan of God. Therefore, with each passing day, the moment is drawing nearer when we will open its doors to those coming from prison. I am happy that every day, my heart is open to God, to others, and to every good work. No one but Jesus Christ, my Friend and Lord, could have brought that about. I love Him and look forward to spending the rest of my life and eternity with Him.

An Open Letter to Those Who Are Suffering

I would like to write a few words to several different groups of people, but there is a special group with which I would like to begin. To you who are in suffering while reading this book, I hope that you will find the answers for which you seek. I write to you who are hoping with all your heart to find a solution for your fear, your panic, your depression, or the evil intentions of those around you. I cannot promise that this book will solve your problems, but I can give you this guarantee: everything in this book came from a heart that wants you to know one thing, and that is that you are not alone. You may be certain that you are not, you never were, and you never will be alone in your suffering!

I know you can't fully explain what is happening to you. You would like to but don't know how. You may not really know when it started, and you certainly don't know when it will end. You have never faced something like it before, and even if you had the courage to tell someone about your experience, you doubt you could make yourself understood. I, too, was there. You fear ridicule or that you may lose your job. You think a confession might affect your relationship with your family. You think that you must go through it alone and that you dare not tell anyone of the pain that you bear.

My dear, I write to you from the depths of my heart, wanting to do something to help. Perhaps you are facing the same condition that I did, or perhaps it is something similar. Perhaps your mind is bombarded by lies. Perhaps you think that the light of day does not exist beyond the blackness of the night through which you stumble. Perhaps you are in the hospital with a serious illness, and the devil is telling you that all hope is gone; perhaps you are dealing with evil people and believe that you will never find another that will understand. I plead with you to take the time to read what follows.

Please, don't give up! That may seem like the easiest option at the moment. I know you are in pain and want so desperately to find relief, but remember that it is possible that the one that brought you to this point is none other than the enemy of your soul, who would like nothing better than to see you give up. That was his plan all along. Please, do not yield to that temptation; remember that you are not alone. Though the devil has told you that there is no one who will understand, know that there are others who have passed through the valley of the shadow of death as you are doing now. Remember what I tell you: this is your battle! You must stand and fight; no one else can do it for you.

Though you may be surrounded by people who make fun of you or who don't understand or who don't want to understand you, do not yield, regardless of the problem that you have. Perhaps you have a physical or emotional difficulty; perhaps your skin is the "wrong" color. Perhaps you are "too tall," "too short," "too skinny," "too fat." Or perhaps you are fighting depression, and others look down on you for it. I will tell you a secret that can help you immensely: do not stop loving them. You cannot love them, you say? There is a solution for that. Ask God to put love into your heart so you can emerge victoriously. The love that God will put in your heart will help you to love those that you could never, ever love by yourself. I have gotten the peace that I so desperately needed when I said, "Lord, I want to love those people."

Always remember that, while those around you make fun of you and laugh at your misfortune, there are others who are trying to understand, eager to support, anxious to help. More importantly, there is a God who loves you and, if you accept Him as your Lord and personal Saviour, will give you hope and a future. Perhaps you did not believe in God, or at least doubted His existence, but now is the time to understand that He is real, that He is here, and that He wants to help. There is no other way; He is your only hope, as He was my only hope.

There will be times when you will not understand anything. Your mind may be foggy, and your brain may feel nebulous. You may not even understand yourself. In those times, muster your strength and throw yourself into the arms of God. Let Him guide your thinking; let Him do your talking.

In those times, do not answer those that accuse you, those that mock you, or those that gossip about you. Anything you say, regardless of how well-intentioned it may have been, may be twisted and used against you. I say it from personal experience: don't answer, but pray.

I found a verse in the Bible that helped me enormously. Remembering that verse, I was often quiet when I would otherwise have spoken. Whatever I would have said would have been used against me. The Word of God is alive and can tell us when to speak and when to be quiet. This is how I found the verse.

One afternoon at Huntercombe prison, I was dying of impatience waiting for the guard to open my cell door so I could go to the visiting room. I had my brother, Nicu, visiting me with a very good friend. I was at the point of expressing my frustration for all the injustices to which I was being subjected. Without considering the fact that my every word was recorded, I was about to open my mouth and vent my feelings when a verse from the book of Amos, chapter 5, verse 13, popped into my mind, "Therefore the prudent keep silent at that time, for it is an evil time" (Amos 5:13, NKJV). That message caused me to keep my mouth shut, and I later realized that it had been for my good. It was a clear intervention by God in order to keep me from making my own situation worse. It was also a reminder of the importance of reading and memorizing Scripture; when we have the Bible in our memory, the Holy Spirit can bring to mind the verse that is appropriate for the situation. Hebrews 4:12 tells us how powerful the Word is:

> For the Word of God is living and powerful, and sharper than any two-edged sword, piercing even to the division of soul and spirit, and of joints and mar-

> row, and is a discerner of the thoughts and intents of the heart.
>
> Hebrews 4:12 (NKJV)

It is an effective weapon in spiritual warfare!

If you do not have a Bible, get one as soon as possible. You need that book!

How long your trials will last, only God knows. They may last a month, or two, or five. The only One that knows will not tell you. I experienced it personally. Many times, I asked Him how long this battle would last, and His answer was always the same. He always said that I must do my duty, and my duty was to fight. Your duty is to believe that He can take you to the rock at which you cannot arrive on your own, that He will take you to your desired haven. Your duty is to stay faithful to the end, regardless of how long God allows your battle to continue. Remember that there were many who gave up only a day or several hours before their battle would have ended and accepted the position of loser. Do not be one that gives up right before the finish line!

Now at home, healthy and with my family, having refused to give up even when everything seemed black, I thank God that I can write to you. I write from the depths of my heart because I want to be of assistance. I want you to win.

Someone asked if I wished to commit suicide. My answer is no. I never wanted to commit suicide, but it did occur to me. Before I received Jesus Christ as my Saviour, the thought was there, but it didn't come from me. The devil put that thought in my mind. The thought was there, but I fought it without fully realizing where it came from.

When the devil plants a thought in your mind, you are not guilty of thinking it because it didn't come from you. You must fight, resist, and call on Jesus. You become guilty when you believe the thought and put it into action. As long as you fight, even when the pressure is unbelievably intense, you remain the winner.

The devil might make you feel guilty. He has the power to influence those around you and cause them to accuse you. But do not forget: he cannot make you guilty. Only you can do that.

When you begin to entertain the idea that the devil put in your mind, you begin losing ground. When you put it into practice, the tide of battle turns against you. Then you are guilty, and the devil, your enemy, has won. Resist him!

I do not know your name, where you come from, or what problems you face. I do not know what thoughts are troubling you or the battle you are fighting. I know nothing about you, but I plead with you: before making a decision, think a thousand times! Please, consider well. Remember that you are not alone. Remember that there are millions who have walked the same path. Please, recognize that God can be your support if you wish Him to be. Even if you are plagued with every negative thought, choose life! Remember the good things you have done; think about your achievements. They certainly exist.

Dear reader, I implore you, think about the one that is putting those thoughts in your mind. He is trying to get your soul! Fight! Pray! Be strong, even if you have nothing left in this world. Remember that life is still worth living because your soul, once lost, can never be regained.

Find someone to talk to. Do not be afraid to tell someone about your struggles. Do not believe the lie that no one will listen, that no one will help. You will, of course, find some that do not understand. Remember that for me, it was even more difficult because I was locked up for twenty-three hours a day, giving the devil a terrible advantage. I did not have access to friends, but only to a few people who were not inclined to help. If you are free, there is much more cause for optimism. Thank God that you are at liberty to talk to those around you.

If you are incarcerated, pray. God can intervene, just as He did for me. He will give you victory if you cry to Him with all your heart.

Take courage! Talk! Do not concern yourself with what everyone else might say. That is not your problem. Do not forget that you are the one facing the battle, not them. They called me a rapist, a violent criminal, and a terrorist. Please believe me; I know how you feel.

I do not know how difficult your situation is. Perhaps you a facing "a dragon with seven heads," or perhaps you are up against a wall that, humanly speaking, you cannot climb.

Whatever your situation, remember that your enemy does not know your thoughts. He does not have that ability; it has not been granted to him by God. Even so, he does have a diabolical method of trying to figure out what you are thinking. For an effective attack, he needs information, so he will put some of his thoughts into your mind and read your reaction. He will try to influence you emotionally then watch the results. If he sees that you are afraid, he will attack like a shark that senses blood in the water; nothing will be held back.

Therefore it is very important to not fear him. Your fear is his food; he loves to see your fear, your anxiety, your depression. He finds them delicious, and he will do whatever he can to make you fear, for he who fears is easily controlled.

If you are reading these lines, remember that advice. Your enemy does not care where you come from, what your skin color is, how skinny or muscular you are, what your job is, how much money you have, how well-known you are, or how many followers you have on Instagram, Facebook, or any other social media platform. He is impressed by none of that, and he is absolutely merciless. You are made in the image of his Enemy, God, and he will do anything in his power to destroy you.

But—and there is always a "but"—this enemy has already been defeated. Remember that truth! The devil has lost the battle that would have given him your soul. He lost that battle many years ago. Now he can only use his ability to deceive you. Do not believe him!

Man was not made to carry such pressure on his shoulders; no one in this world can do that. This is why you see people taking their own lives every day because death for them looks much more simple and easy than fighting the pressure the devil puts in their minds. But there is One who was prepared from eternity especially for this work, One who is ready right now to lift the burden off your shoulders. I wish I could give you more than one option, but there is no such thing. If you are battling right now, remember this: the only way out is through Jesus Christ. You can choose to believe in the sacrifice of Jesus Christ at Golgotha that two thousand years ago handed the devil an eternal defeat, or you can choose to ignore everything that's been written here and wait to see what is going to happen. Trust me on this one: go for the first option. Jesus died so that you and I no longer must fall before this enemy. Jesus won the victory for you and for me in battle where we alone stood no chance. He won so that we can be winners today. Perhaps that fact never interested you before, but the moment has come when you must recognize it in order to win the battle for your soul. In Ephesians, chapter 6, the Bible tells us about the armor that we must wear in order to remain standing when attacked by the devil and his fiery darts.

Courageously, look your enemy in the face and tell him, "Jesus died on the cross so that I can have victory today. I have the power in the name of Jesus to throw you to the ground and go on under the holy protection of my Lord and Saviour, Jesus Christ."

Fight with all your heart! Come before God as you would before a dear friend and say, "'Even though I walk through the valley of the shadow of death, I will fear no evil, for you are with me' (Psalm 23:4a, NIV) (emphasis added). I will not fear, for you are my God. You are my helper. You strengthen me and hold me by my right hand. You have not given me the spirit of fear, but of power, and of love, and of a sound mind (2 Timothy 1:7). You will give me strength and fill me with love."

Surely goodness and mercy shall follow me all the days of my life! Praise God! Fear, hate, depression, paranoia, and anxiety, in the name of Jesus Christ, have no place in my life!

An Open Letter to the Church

I write to you, the church, knowing that you prayed for me. You understood that we are one body and that each member has the responsibility to support the other. I thank you, in the name of our Lord Jesus, for sustaining my family in prayer.

While I do thank you, I also must tell you that we, as the church, need to be more united. We must learn more about supporting those engaged in spiritual warfare.

If you are a minister and have never experienced such a struggle, praise God. That, however, does not mean that such battles are not real. Among God's people, there are many who are suffering and fighting those battles, very often alone. It pains me to say that we, the church, have looked on with skepticism, indifference, or even an attitude of superiority as these battles raged, thinking that somehow we deserve some credit for the fact that we never faced such struggles.

How is it possible that the church many times rejects or marginalizes those members of the Body of Christ that face depression? How can you look askance at those struggling with depression rather than taking the armor that Scripture puts at your disposal (Ephesians, chapter 6) and rushing to your brother's aid?

I know of a case where the church leaders asked the parents of a girl who was struggling with depression to refrain from bringing her to church for a while in order to protect the church's good name. But, dear church, we do not cast out children of God but the devil. We, through the new identity that we received at the new birth, are heirs of the kingdom of God, and we all belong in God's house. Let us throw the devil and all his demons out of the House of God, but always welcome other people.

Being in a spiritual fight doesn't mean God does not love you, nor does it mean He does not care for you. I look to the example of Lazarus; he was loved by Jesus (John 11:3), but still, he got sick and eventually died. However, his sickness was not for the worst but for the glory of God. So, let our battles, our weaknesses, our worst situations be for the glory of God and not for the win of our enemy.

We dare not be ruled by fear! I have been told by some Christians that they are afraid to pray for those engaged in spiritual struggles for fear of bringing the devil's wrath on themselves. That itself is a lie from the devil; he already hates us with all his being. From the day that we confessed Jesus Christ as our personal Lord and Saviour, this enemy of our souls has continually followed us, trying to deceive and destroy us.

We have no reason to fear! We should be launching a counteroffensive, knowing that victory in the battle does not depend on our power but on the power that Jesus won over Satan on the hill of Golgotha.

The Bible's message, "Fear not" or its equivalent, is found in Scripture 365 times, one time for every day of the year. These verses were the daily encouragement that I needed to keep going when I was struggling. I "ate and drank" these passages. I would not be here today if it had not been for the encouragement found in these verses.

The world today is full of fear. We fear that our spouse is hiding something from us. We fear that the bank will repossess our house or other earthly goods, leaving us broke. We fear losing our job. We fear being left all alone. We fear disease, crisis, death, life, people, circumstances, everything. Whatever the fear, we must remember that the fear of the world is unfounded. In the end, we should fear no one, as God is indeed giving us a spirit of strength and power; may God help us all.

I don't wish to condemn you, church leaders, but I plead with you to care about those at your doorstep. Get more involved in their lives, serve them, and claim the victory because many of your members do not know that they are already victors through Jesus Christ and, therefore, face all manner of problems. I was one of them, but praise God I was victorious through Jesus' blood.

I fought alone, continuously crying out to God for answers. He was good and sent me those answers through the Bible and in some books written by Christians that had the wisdom and courage to tell others about the struggles that they had gone through. I got answers by studying the books of Brother Neil Anderson, which I highly recommend for anyone struggling with depression, anxiety, or fear. Those books helped me understand my identity in Christ and the power of His blood. For me, having been ignorant of that, the battle was difficult.

Dear church, we are more than conquerors through the blood of Him that loved us and loves us, He that bore our struggles and emerged victorious every time in order for us to be free.

I praise God that He is working powerfully in the church today. I thank Him that He defends and protects us. Though we truly are as sheep in the midst of wolves, our powerful Good Shepherd does not allow us to be destroyed. Praise His holy name!

An Open Letter to Law Enforcement

God has used some of you in a special way in my life; I say that with complete sincerity. On the one hand, there were some of you who were benevolent and predisposed to help, while on the other, there were some who were less so.

All the experiences recorded in this book are about God's power in my life, and that power, first of all, means love. One cannot speak of God's power personified in one's life and yet hate another person, for God is love. Therefore, I can honestly say that I love you with all my heart, and I pray God that He may bless each one of you with eternal life. I warmly remember some of you that extended a helping hand when I was in need; may God repay you one hundred-fold.

I know that your good hearts motivated you to do what you did, and I am certain that I was not and am not the only recipient of your kindness. I know that there are many more that have benefited from your patience and assistance on their own way to a changed and rehabilitated life.

I would also like to extend the following heartfelt petition to all those in positions of authority and that work with people—

especially lawbreakers: remember that the person before you is not just a suspect, a criminal, or an inmate, but above all, a human, just like yourselves. He is man with parents, siblings, and possibly a wife and children. He is a man with aspirations, dreams, and plans, a man with a soul of inestimable value that was created in the image of God. Every man, no matter how corrupted by sin, not only carries God's image but is a person for whom Jesus died; he was bought with the priceless blood of the Son of God.

I know that seeing the image of God in the sin-hardened faces of cold-hearted criminals is not easy, particularly if you work among them day after day. But I ask you to remember that each one, whether a seasoned veteran of crime or a first-time petty thief, is a man with needs and to respond accordingly. Some of you did just that in my case, and I thank you from the bottom of my heart.

I close this message by thanking God for you and the work that you do so that we, ordinary people, can have peace and safety. God bless you!

CPSIA information can be obtained
at www.ICGtesting.com
Printed in the USA
BVHW040846250422
635249BV00016B/357

9 781685 561963